Autodesk® Navisworks® 2018
Using Autodesk Navisworks in a BIM Workflow

Learning Guide
1st Edition
Software Version 15.0.1314.36

AUTODESK.
Authorized Publisher

ASCENT - Center for Technical Knowledge®
Autodesk® Navisworks® 2018
Using Autodesk Navisworks in a BIM Workflow
1st Edition

Prepared and produced by:

ASCENT Center for Technical Knowledge
630 Peter Jefferson Parkway, Suite 175
Charlottesville, VA 22911

866-527-2368
www.ASCENTed.com

ASCENT
CENTER FOR TECHNICAL KNOWLEDGE

Lead Contributors: Martha Hollowell & Michelle Rasmussen

ASCENT - Center for Technical Knowledge is a division of Rand Worldwide, Inc., providing custom developed knowledge products and services for leading engineering software applications. ASCENT is focused on specializing in the creation of education programs that incorporate the best of classroom learning and technology-based training offerings.

We welcome any comments you may have regarding this learning guide, or any of our products. To contact us please email: feedback@ASCENTed.com.

Contents

Preface

The *Autodesk® Navisworks® 2018: Using Autodesk Navisworks in a BIM Workflow* learning guide teaches you how to better predict project outcomes, reduce conflicts and changes, and achieve lower project risk using the Autodesk® Navisworks® Manage software in a BIM workflow.

Building Information Modeling (BIM) encompasses the entire building life cycle. BIM includes all phases of the design process, from model creation, to construction, and ending at operations and maintenance. Using a BIM workflow, you will learn how a design changes throughout the BIM process, and how the changes affect the BIM model.

Over the course of this learning guide, you will learn how to consolidate civil, architectural, structural, and MEP models into one BIM model. Starting with an AutoCAD® Civil 3D® drawing file, you will append various Autodesk® Revit® and Autodesk® Inventor® models and check for conflicts. Next, you will use review and markup tools for communicating issues across disciplines. Finally, you will use TimeLiner, Animator, and Clash Detective to simulate construction and find constructibility issues and on-site clashes.

This learning guide is designed for new and experienced users of the Autodesk Navisworks software in multiple disciplines. This learning guide has been developed using software version 15.0.1314.36.

Topics Covered

- Understanding the purpose of Building Information Modeling (BIM) and how it is applied in the Autodesk Navisworks software.
- Consolidate Models
    - Navigating the Autodesk Navisworks workspace and interface.
    - Creating a composite model.
    - Transforming models for proper alignment.
- Review and Analyze Models
    - Using basic viewing tools.
    - Saving and retrieving views.
    - Sectioning a model.

- Investigating properties.
- Searching for items.
- Hiding and unhiding items.
- Communication
  - Measuring a model.
  - Adding tags and comments to model components.
  - Marking up and redlining the model.
  - Animate a model.
- Collaboration
  - Reviewing a model for clashes.
  - Consolidating redlines from other team members.
- Construction
  - Creating a construction timeline.
  - Animating a construction timeline.

Note on Software Setup

This learning guide assumes a standard installation of the software using the default preferences during installation. Lectures and practices use the standard software templates and default options for the Content Libraries.

Students and Educators can Access Free Autodesk Software and Resources

Autodesk challenges you to get started with free educational licenses for professional software and creativity apps used by millions of architects, engineers, designers, and hobbyists today. Bring Autodesk software into your classroom, studio, or workshop to learn, teach, and explore real-world design challenges the way professionals do.

Get started today - register at the Autodesk Education Community and download one of the many Autodesk software applications available.

Visit www.autodesk.com/joinedu/

Note: Free products are subject to the terms and conditions of the end-user license and services agreement that accompanies the software. The software is for personal use for education purposes and is not intended for classroom or lab use.

Co-Lead Contributor: Michelle Rasmussen

Specializing in the civil engineering industry, Michelle authors training guides and provides instruction, support, and implementation on all Autodesk infrastructure solutions, in addition to general AutoCAD.

Michelle began her career in the Air Force working in the Civil Engineering unit as a surveyor, designer, and construction manager. She has also worked for municipalities and consulting engineering firms as an engineering/GIS technician. Michelle holds a Bachelor's of Science degree from the University of Utah along with a Master's of Business Administration from Kaplan University.

Michelle is an Autodesk Certified Instructor (ACI) as well as an Autodesk Certified Evaluator, teaching and evaluating other Autodesk Instructors for the ACI program. In addition, she holds the Autodesk Certified Professional certification for Civil 3D and is trained in Instructional Design.

As a skilled communicator, Michelle effectively leads classes, webcasts and consults with clients to achieve their business objectives.

Michelle Rasmussen has been the Lead Contributor for *Autodesk Navisworks: Using Autodesk Navisworks in a BIM Workflow* since its initial release in 2017.

Co-Lead Contributor: Martha Hollowell

Martha incorporates her passion for architecture and education into all her projects, including the training guides she creates on Autodesk Revit for Architecture, MEP, and Structure. She started working with AutoCAD in the early 1990's, adding AutoCAD Architecture and Autodesk Revit as they came along.

After receiving a B.Sc. in Architecture from the University of Virginia, she worked in the architectural department of the Colonial Williamsburg Foundation and later in private practice, consulting with firms setting up AutoCAD in their offices.

Martha has over 20 years' experience as a trainer and instructional designer. She is skilled in leading individuals and small groups to understand and build on their potential. Martha is trained in Instructional Design and has achieved the Autodesk Certified Instructor (ACI) and Autodesk Certified Professional designations for Revit Architecture.

Martha Hollowell has been the Lead Contributor for *Autodesk Navisworks: Using Autodesk Navisworks in a BIM Workflow* since its initial release in 2017.

In this Guide

The following images highlight some of the features that can be found in this Learning Guide.

Practice Files

To download the practice files for this student guide, use the following steps:

1. Type the URL shown below into the address bar of your Internet browser. The URL must be typed **exactly as shown**. If you are using an ASCENT ebook, you can click on the link to download the file.

2. Press <Enter> to download the ZIP file that contains the Practice Files.

3. Once the download is complete, unzip the file to a local folder. The unzipped file contains an EXE file.

4. Double-click on the EXE file and follow the instructions to automatically install the Practice Files on the C:\ drive of your computer.

   Do not change the location in which the Practice Files folder is installed. Doing so can cause errors when completing the practices in this student guide.

http://www.ASCENTed.com/getfile?id=xxxxxxxx

Stay Informed!
Interested in receiving information about upcoming promotional offers, educational events, invitations to complimentary webcasts, and discounts? If so, please visit www.ASCENTed.com/updates/

Help us improve our product by completing the following survey:
www.ASCENTed.com/feedback
You can also contact us at: feedback@ASCENTed.com

Practice Files

The Practice Files page tells you how to download and install the practice files that are provided with this guide.

Link to the practice files

Chapter 1

Getting Started

In this chapter you learn how to start the AutoCAD® software, become familiar with the basic layout of the AutoCAD screen, how to access commands, use your pointing device, and understand the AutoCAD Cartesian workspace. You also learn how to open an existing drawing, view a drawing by zooming and panning, and save your work in the AutoCAD software.

Learning Objectives in this Chapter

- Launch the AutoCAD software and complete a basic initial setup of the drawing environment.
- Identify the basic layout and features of AutoCAD interface including the Ribbon, Drawing Window, and Application Menu.
- Locate commands and launch them using the Ribbon, shortcut menus, Application Menu, and Quick Access Toolbar.
- Locate points in the AutoCAD Cartesian workspace.
- Open and close existing drawings and navigate to file locations.
- Move around a drawing using the mouse, the Zoom and Pan commands, and the Navigation Bar.
- Save drawings in various formats and set the automatic save options using the Save commands.

Chapters

Each chapter begins with a brief introduction and a list of the chapter's Learning Objectives.

Learning Objectives for the chapter

Side notes

Side notes are hints or additional information for the current topic.

Practice Objectives

Instructional Content

Each chapter is split into a series of sections of instructional content on specific topics. These lectures include the descriptions, step-by-step procedures, figures, hints, and information you need to achieve the chapter's Learning Objectives.

Practices

Practices enable you to use the software to perform a hands-on review of a topic.

Some practices require you to use prepared practice files, which can be downloaded from the link found on the Practice Files page.

Chapter Review Questions

Chapter review questions, located at the end of each chapter, enable you to review the key concepts and learning objectives of the chapter.

Command Summary

The Command Summary is located at the end of each chapter. It contains a list of the software commands that are used throughout the chapter, and provides information on where the command is found in the software.

Practice Files

To download the practice files for this learning guide, use the following steps:

1. Type the URL shown below into the address bar of your Internet browser. The URL must be typed **exactly as shown**. If you are using an ASCENT ebook, you can click on the link to download the file.

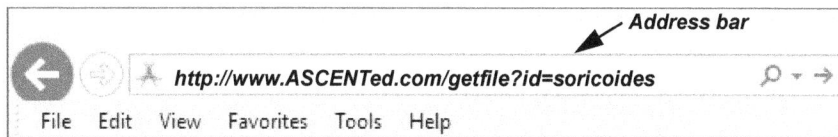

Address bar

http://www.ASCENTed.com/getfile?id=soricoides

File   Edit   View   Favorites   Tools   Help

2. Press <Enter> to download the .ZIP file that contains the Practice Files.

3. Once the download is complete, unzip the file to a local folder. The unzipped file contains an .EXE file.

4. Double-click on the .EXE file and follow the instructions to automatically install the Practice Files on the C:\ drive of your computer.

   Do not change the location in which the Practice Files folder is installed. Doing so can cause errors when completing the practices in this learning guide.

http://www.ASCENTed.com/getfile?id=soricoides

Introduction to Autodesk Navisworks

The Autodesk® Navisworks® software is used in the Building Information Modeling (BIM) workflow to review 3D designs. The software enables you to review and mark-up models from different disciplines. Navigating the model is a crucial part of efficiently reviewing a BIM model.

In this chapter you explore the user interface, and then uncover constructibility issues using the standard viewing tools, orbiting, and camera settings.

Learning Objectives in this Chapter

- Discover how to use Autodesk Navisworks to manage a project.
- Examine the user interface and understand how to use the parts most effectively.
- Identify constructibility issues in a model using the standard viewing tools.
- Improve your ability to walk and orbit around a model.

1.1 What is Navisworks?

The Autodesk Navisworks software is used in a Building Information Modeling (BIM) workflow for reviewing 3D designs. It enables you to consolidate 3D models from multiple sources and applications, which helps you to check for clashes between disciplines. As models are consolidated, the size of the model is drastically reduced to make it possible to review multiple large models at the same time. The Autodesk Navisworks software provides tools for reviewing and mark-up, construction simulation, and collaboration between multiple stakeholders.

BIM is a strategy for the entire building life cycle. It includes design, construction, and facilities management. The BIM process supports the ability to coordinate, update, and share design data with team members across disciplines. Using the Autodesk Navisworks software in a BIM workflow enables design teams to have a more holistic view of multiple, integrated models and data that make up the project, as shown in Figure 1–1. This enables them to:

- Better communicate design intent

- Ensure that everything fits together properly without clashes

- Set the construction time line and sequencing.

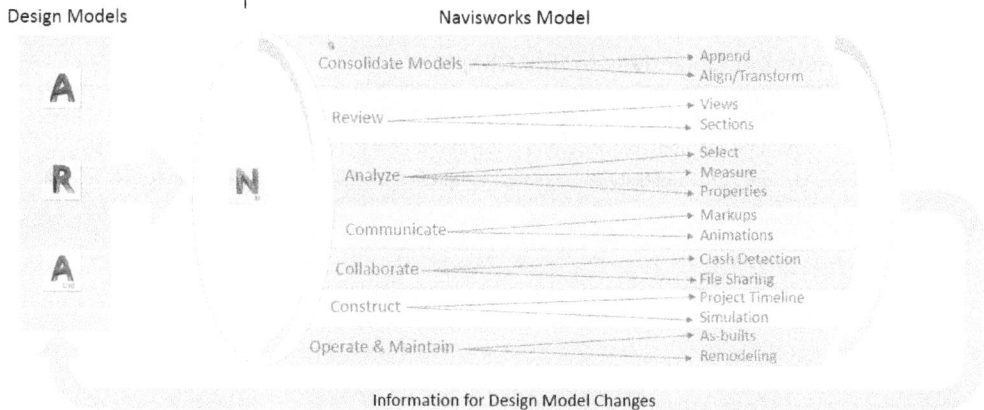

Figure 1–1

There are several components in the Autodesk Navisworks software:

5D analysis includes 3D modeling plus time and cost.

- Autodesk Navisworks Simulate provides review and communication tools for 5D analysis and coordination.

- Autodesk Navisworks Manage provides tools for 5D analysis, advanced coordination, and simulation.

- Autodesk Navisworks Freedom is a 3D viewer that enables stakeholders to review and explore a project model without needing the software that was used by the design team.

In this learning Guide, you will focus on the Autodesk Navisworks Manage software, with an emphasis on how to.

- Consolidate models from different disciplines into one complete model.

- Review a model with viewing tools, including the use of walkthroughs, sections, and basic animations.

- Analyze a model by selecting and investigating items using the Selection Tree, shown in Figure 1–2.

- Communicate with all members of a project team by redlining views, as shown in Figure 1–2.

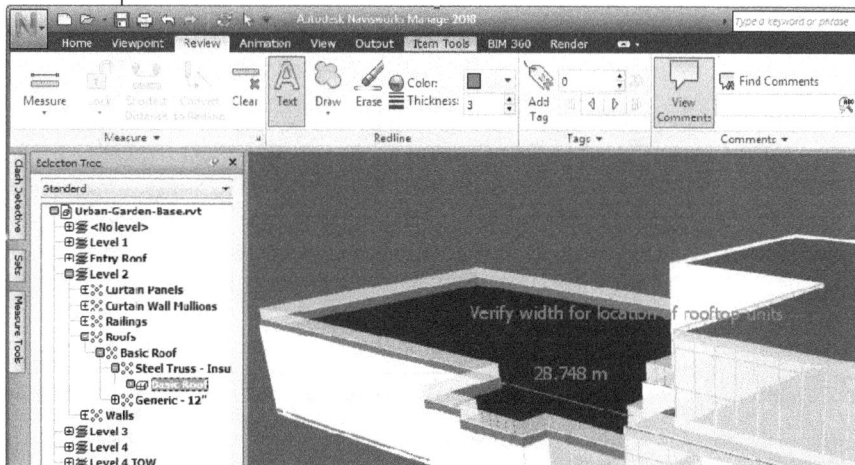

Figure 1–2

- Collaborate with all of the disciplines using clash detection tools that can be useful at all stages from early design development to construction.

- Construct the project virtually by visually reviewing the project schedule using TimeLiner.

- Operate and maintain the finished building by including links to as-builts and other information.

1.2 Overview of the Interface

The Autodesk Navisworks interface (shown in Figure 1–3) includes user interface tools that are common to most Autodesk® software, such as the Application Menu and Ribbon. Knowing where to find the tools that you use most and how to maximize screen space by positioning various dockable windows helps you more easily view and review the model.

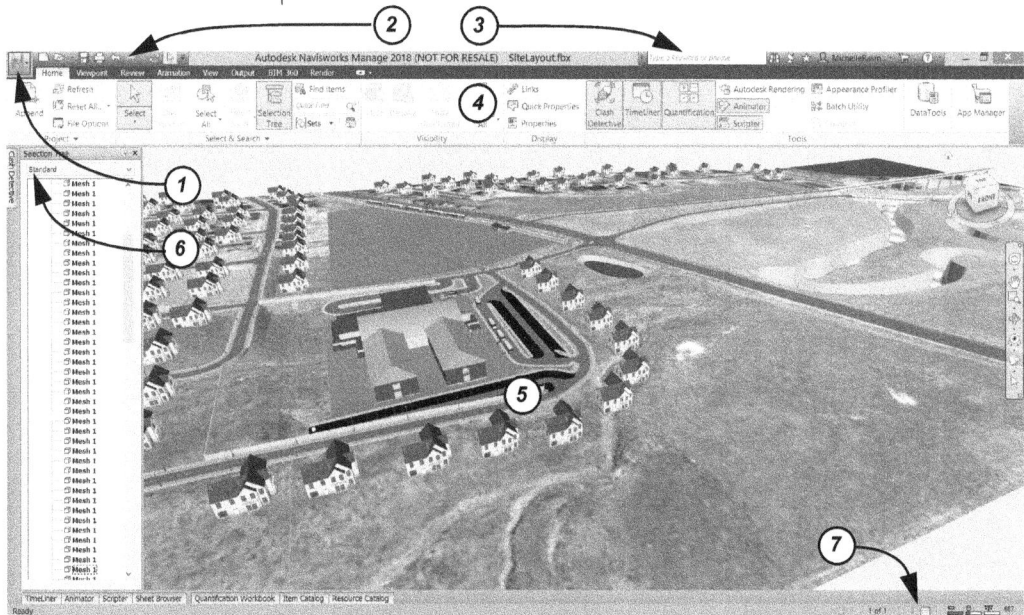

Figure 1–3

1. Application Menu	5. Scene View
2. Quick Access Toolbar	6. Dockable Windows
3. InfoCenter	7. Status Bar
4. Ribbon	

1. Application Menu

The Application Menu provides access to file commands, settings, and documents. You can hover the cursor over a command to display a list of additional tools, as shown in Figure 1–4.

If you click on the primary icon, rather than the arrow, it starts the default command.

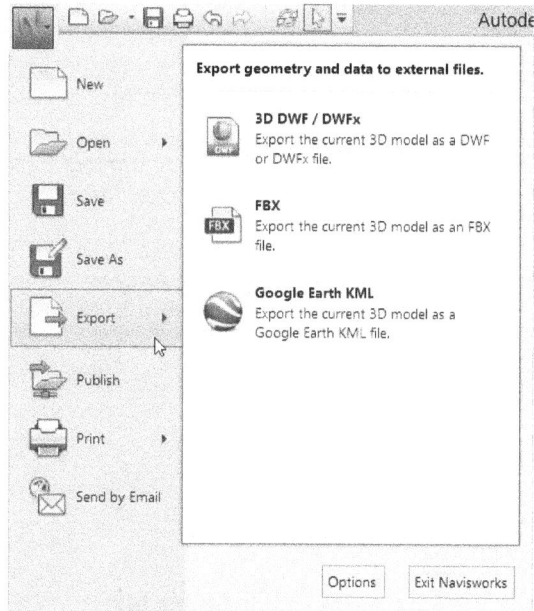

Figure 1–4

*Click **Options** to open the Options Editor where you can setup the user interface and other tools.*

- When no command is selected, a list of recently used documents displays. The documents can be reordered if required, as shown in Figure 1–5.

Click ⫟ (Pin) next to a document name to keep it available.

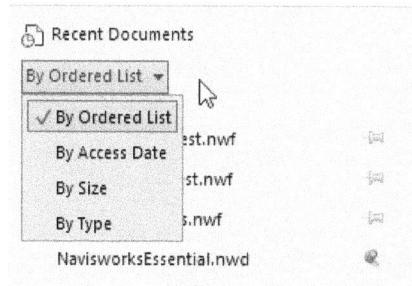

Figure 1–5

2. Quick Access Toolbar

The Quick Access Toolbar includes commonly used commands, such as **New**, **Open**, **Save**, **Print**, **Undo**, **Redo**, **Refresh**, and **Select**, as shown in Figure 1–6.

Figure 1–6

Hint: Customizing the Quick Access Toolbar

To change the docked location of the toolbar, or to add, relocate, or remove tools on the toolbar, right-click on the Quick Access Toolbar.

You can also right-click on a tool in the ribbon and select **Add to Quick Access Toolbar**, as shown in Figure 1–7.

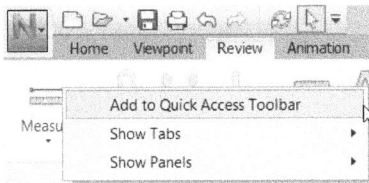

Figure 1–7

3. InfoCenter

The InfoCenter (shown in Figure 1–8) includes a search field to find help on the web, and also provides access to the Subscription Center, Communication Center, Autodesk A360 sign-in, and other help options.

Click here to collapse the search field to save screen space.

Figure 1–8

4. Ribbon

The ribbon contains tools in a series of tabs and panels, as shown in Figure 1–9. Selecting a tab displays a group of related panels. The panels contain a variety of tools, grouped by task.

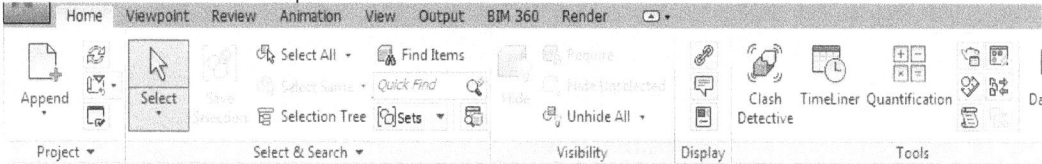

Figure 1–9

When you select an element in the scene view, the ribbon displays the *Item Tools* tab. This contains item specific tools, as shown in Figure 1–10.

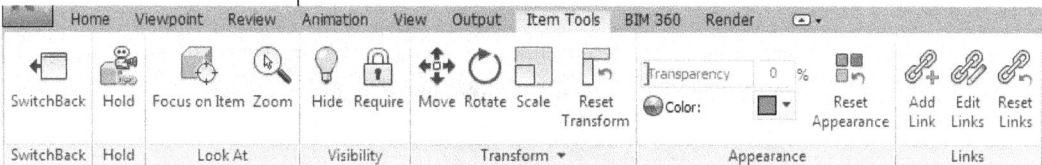

Figure 1–10

- When you hover the cursor over a tool on the Ribbon, tooltips display the tool's name and a short description, as shown in Figure 1–11.

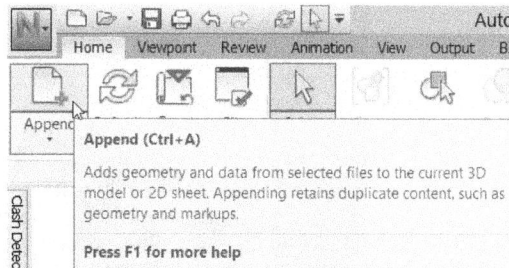

Figure 1–11

Do not press <Enter> when typing shortcuts.

- Many commands have keyboard shortcuts. For example, you can press <Ctrl>+<A> for **Append**, or <Ctrl>+<1> for **Select**. The keyboard shortcuts are listed next to the name of the command in the tooltips, as shown in Figure 1–11 (above).

- To rearrange the order in which the ribbon tabs are displayed, select the tab, hold <Ctrl>, and drag the tab to a new location. The location is remembered when you restart the software.

- Any panel can be dragged by its title into the scene view area to become a floating panel. Click **Return Panels to Ribbon** (as shown in Figure 1–12) to return a panel to the ribbon.

Figure 1–12

5. Scene View

The scene view is where you view the model, as shown in Figure 1–13. You can reorient the view using viewing tools such as the ViewCube and Navigation Bar. You can also select items in the scene view.

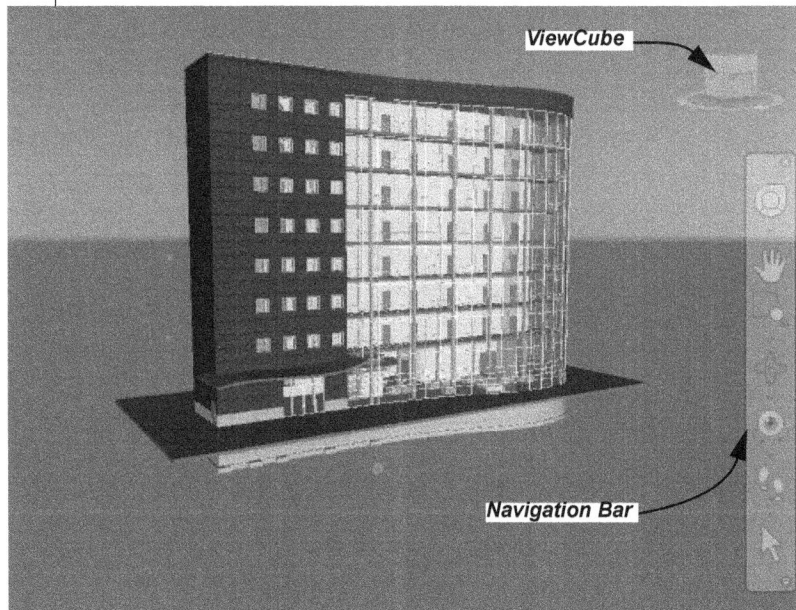

Figure 1–13

- The background of the scene view varies depending on the type of view you are in. Figure 1–13 displays a perspective view with a horizon line with the *Render Style* set to **Full Render.**

6. Docking Windows

Many of the tools in the Autodesk Navisworks software have windows that include information you can use while you are working. These windows can float in the scene view, or be docked to the top, bottom, or sides of the screen. They can be auto-hidden to display just a tab, as shown in Figure 1–14.

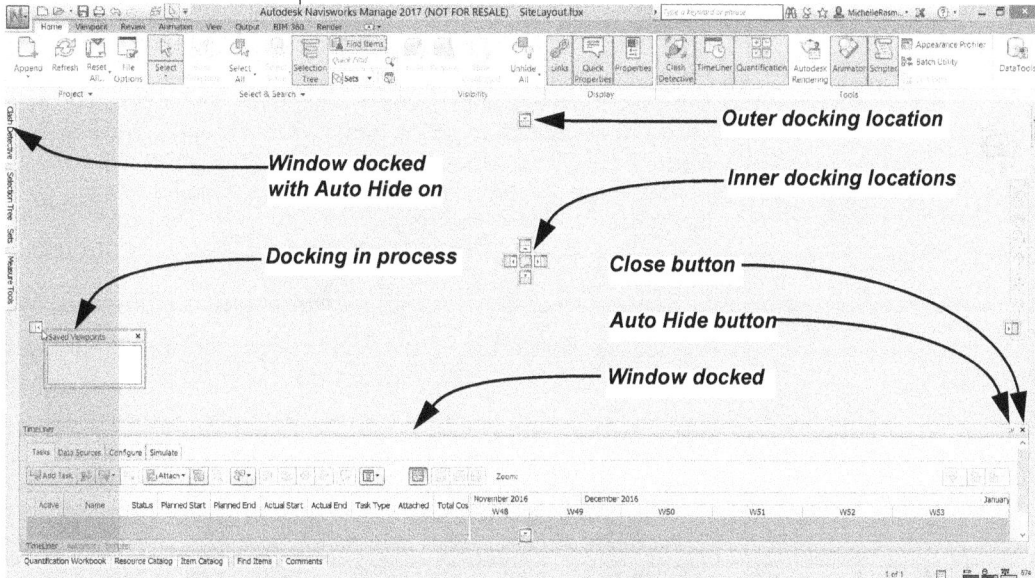

Figure 1–14

Holding <Ctrl> while moving a window prevents it from automatically docking.

- To dock a window, drag it by the title and hover over one of the location icons. A transparent blue box displays where the window can be docked. Release the cursor to place it.

- To undock a window, drag the title bar into the scene view.

- To hide a docked window, click ⬇ (Auto Hide).

- To display a hidden window, hover over the tab.

- To close a window, click **Close**.

- You can toggle on or off any of the twenty-five dockable windows through the *View* tab>Workspace panel>

  ▦ (Windows) drop-down list.

- Windows can be tiled in the interface

Hint: Inner Docking Locations

Only the docking locations on the outer edges of the application interface enable you to pin/unpin windows. Inner docking locations cause windows to float over the scene view or tile on top of each other.

7. Status Bar

The Status Bar includes the Sheet Browser and File Performance information, as shown in Figure 1–15. The Sheet Browser enables you to access multi-sheet DWF files (such as shop drawings) that might be attached to a project. The File Performance information displays information about the performance of the project file, such as the amount of memory being used by the software.

Sheet Browser   *File performance*

Figure 1–15

Hint: Right-Click Menus

Right-click menus enable you to quickly access required commands. These menus provide access to basic viewing commands, recently used commands, and all of the major Viewpoint commands, as shown in Figure 1–16. Additional options are available if you have an item selected.

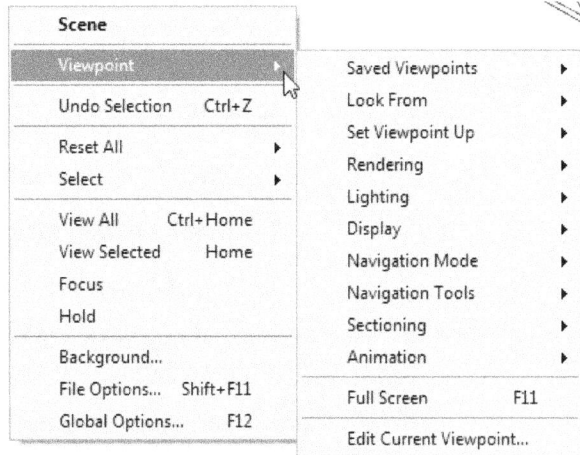

Figure 1–16

Customizing the Interface

You can customize and save the layout of the user interface for easy access to specific commands. This can help you switch between specific toolbars and windows that have the tools you require to perform certain jobs.

- When a workspace is saved, the location and size of each open window is captured.

- Changes to the ribbon or Quick Access Toolbar are not saved in the workspaces.

- Workspaces can then be shared with other users for more efficient access to corporate standards.

When the Autodesk Navisworks software is first loaded, four workspaces are available, as shown in Figure 1–17. The default workspace is the **Navisworks Standard** workspace.

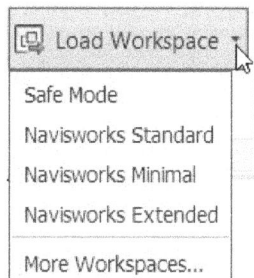

| Load Workspace |
| Safe Mode |
| Navisworks Standard |
| Navisworks Minimal |
| Navisworks Extended |
| More Workspaces... |

Figure 1–17

How To: Save a Workspace

1. Open, resize, and arrange windows as required.
2. In the *View* tab>Workspace panel, click 🖼 (Save Workspace).
3. In the Save Current Workspace dialog box, type a name for the workspace to create a new workspace, or select the name of an existing workspace to overwrite it.
4. Click **Save**.

How To: Load a Workspace

- In the *View* tab>Workspace panel, expand 🖼 (Load Workspace) and select a saved workspace from the drop-down list.

Practice 1a

Explore the User Interface

Practice Objectives

- Configure the user interface layout.

In this practice, you will start by loading the Navisworks Standard workspace. Then you will toggle windows on and off in the workspace to configure it to your needs.

Estimated time for completion: 5 minutes

Task 1 - Load a workspace.

1. In the *View* tab>Workspace panel, expand ▣ (Load Workspace) and select **Navisworks Standard**, as shown in Figure 1–18.

You do not need to have a model open for this practice.

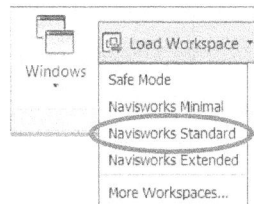

Figure 1–18

2. Review the user interface. Note the hidden, dockable windows to the left and right of the scene view.

3. In the *Home* tab>Select & Search panel, click ▤ (Selection Tree) or press <Ctrl>+<F12> to toggle off the Selection Tree window.

4. Click ▤ (Selection Tree) again to toggle the Selection Tree window back on.

5. In the Selection Tree window title bar, click ⇥ (Auto Hide) to force the window to always display.

6. Click and drag the Selection Tree window title bar and move the window to the middle of the scene view to undock it.

7. Double-click on the Selection Tree window title bar to re-dock it to the left side of the screen.

8. In the Selection Tree window title bar, click ⇥ (Auto Hide) to hide it.

1.3 Using Basic Viewing Tools

One of the most basic and powerful uses of the Autodesk Navisworks software is to navigate around and through a model. This enables you to present the model to others and locate any constructibility issues.

Because navigating is such a useful tool in the Autodesk Navisworks software, there are many different methods to navigate a model, including the mouse wheel, the ViewCube, the Navigation Bar, and the *Viewpoints* tab>Navigate panel, as shown in Figure 1–19.

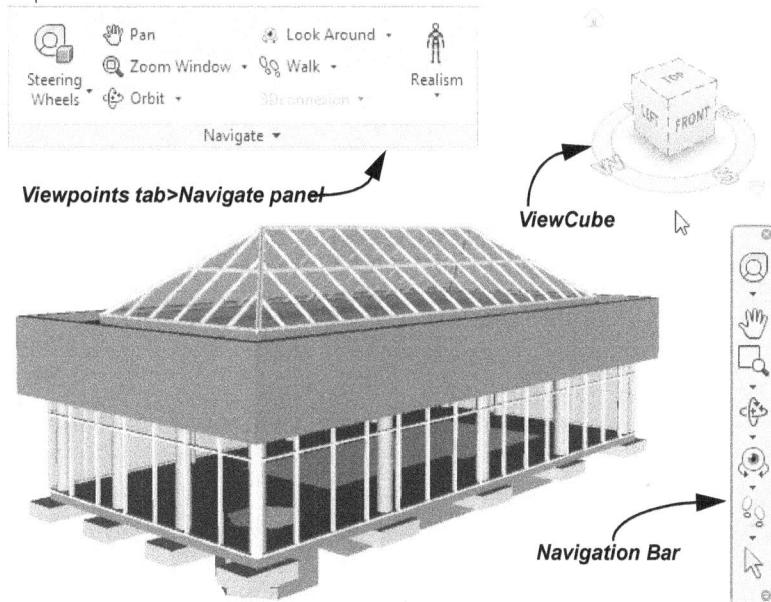

Figure 1–19

*   Some of the navigation tools move the model within the view, while others are more like holding a camera.

*   In the Autodesk Navisworks software, you can walk through walls.

*   The camera position (x,y,z) is displayed at the bottom left of the main view to provide positional feedback, as shown in Figure 1–20.

Figure 1–20

Using the Mouse Wheel

You can use the mouse wheel to move around the scene. The movement is based on a pivot point, as shown in Figure 1–21.

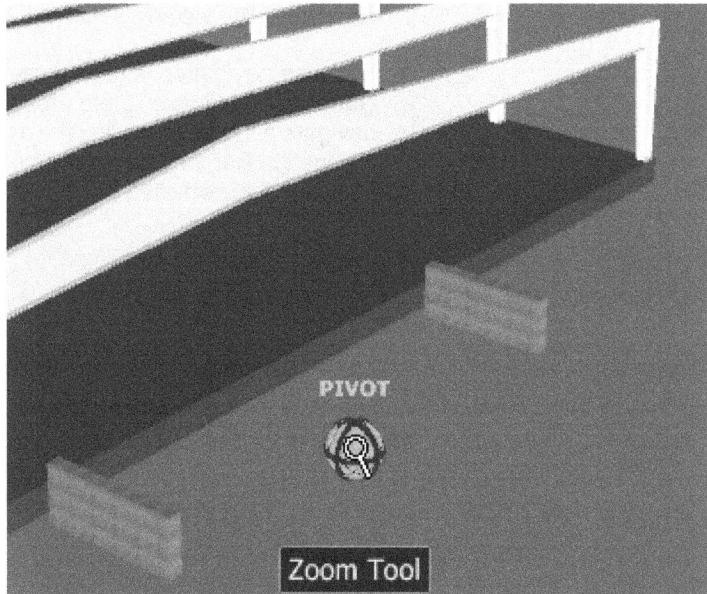

Figure 1–21

- Note that the mouse wheel functionality changes depending on the command you are currently using. To **Zoom**, **Pan**, or **Orbit** a model, in the Quick Access Toolbar or Navigation Bar, click (Select), and then use the mouse wheel as follows:
  - **Zoom** - Scroll the mouse wheel up to zoom in and down to zoom out.
  - **Pan** - Hold the mouse wheel and then move the mouse to pan.
  - **Orbit** - Hold <Shift> and the mouse wheel, and then move the mouse to orbit around the scene.

- When you zoom, the current location of the cursor is the pivot point.

- Pan and Orbit use the pivot point defined by the most recent zoom.

Orbiting Around a Model

Viewing a model from all angles is an important part of using the Autodesk Navisworks software. While you can orbit a model using the mouse wheel, there are also several orbiting tools on the Navigation bar and the *Viewpoint*>Navigate panel, as shown in Figure 1–22.

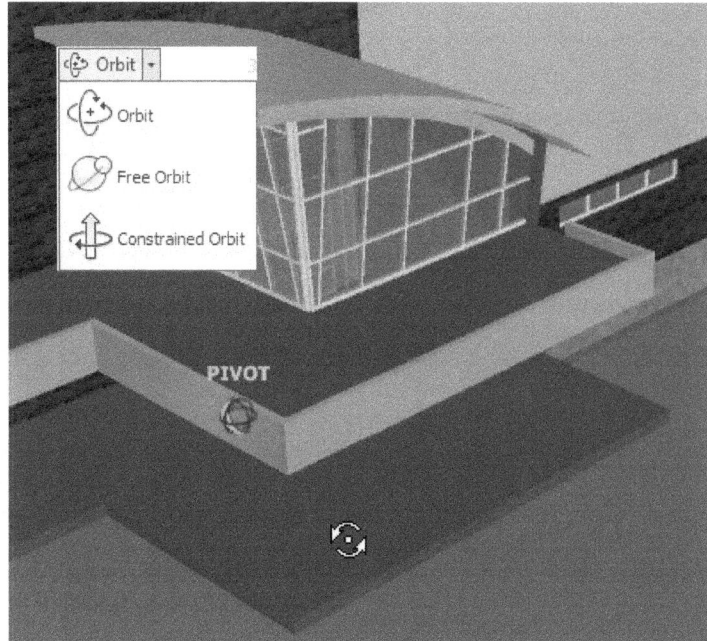

Figure 1–22

- The orbit commands all revolve around a pivot point. To specify the pivot point, hold <Ctrl> and click in the scene before orbiting.

- To use the orbit commands, select the command, click and hold the left mouse button, and then move the mouse:

  - (Orbit) - Rotates in all directions while maintaining the "up" orientation.

  - (Constrained Orbit) - Rotates with the model remaining on the original plane.

  - (Free Orbit) - Rotates freely in any direction.

Using the ViewCube

The ViewCube provides visual clues as to where you are in a 3D view. It helps you move around the model with quick access to specific views (such as **Top**, **Front**, and **Right**), corner views, and directional views, as shown in Figure 1–23.

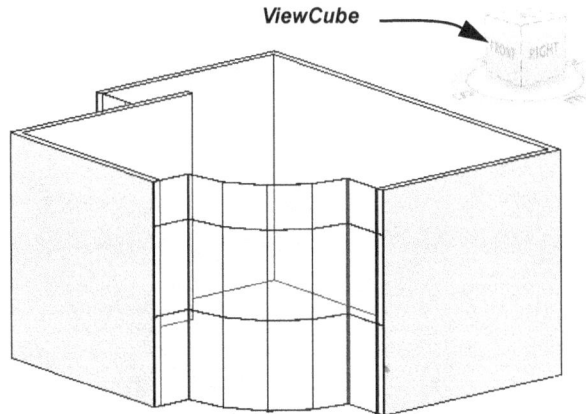

Figure 1–23

Hover the cursor over any face of the ViewCube to highlight it and then click to reorient the model. You can also click and drag the ViewCube to rotate it, which also rotates the model.

If you get lost in a model, use ⌂ (Home) to return to a familiar view.

- ⌂ (Home) displays when you hover the cursor over the ViewCube. Click to return to the view defined as **Home**.

- The right-click menu connected to the ViewCube includes options to:
  - Switch between **Perspective** and **Orthographic** mode.
  - Set the current view as the **Home** or **Front** view.
  - Open the Options Editor to access the ViewCube Options, including how the ViewCube looks and what happens when you switch views.

- In the *View* tab>Navigation Aids panel, click ▢ (ViewCube) to toggle the ViewCube on or off.

Hint: Perspective Views and Camera Options

You can switch between ⬡ (Perspective) and

⬜ (Orthographic) mode in the *Viewpoint* tab>Camera panel.

When in a perspective view, you can modify the F.O.V. (Field of View) using the slider bar. Alternatively, expand the *Camera* panel and specify the exact position and target of the camera, as shown in Figure 1–24.

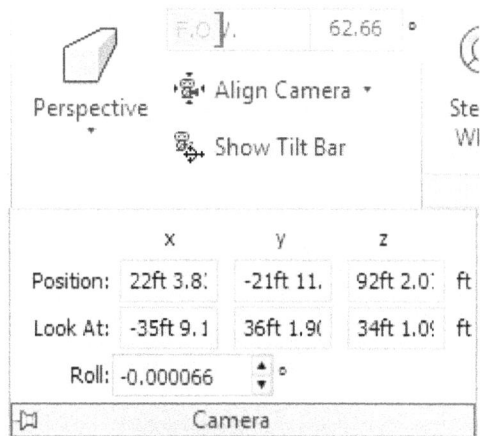

	x	y	z
Position:	22ft 3.8:	-21ft 11.	92ft 2.0:	ft
Look At:	-35ft 9.1	36ft 1.9(	34ft 1.0(	ft
Roll:	-0.000066		

Figure 1–24

- ⬡ (Align Camera) provides options to straighten the camera or focus on the X-, Y-, or Z-axes. These are similar to the faces of the ViewCube.

- ⬡ (Show Tilt Bar) toggles a window with a slider bar where you can move the model up and down. This is similar to scrolling the mouse wheel up and down.

Zoom and Pan Commands

The Navigation Bar includes several standard viewing commands that are similar to those used in other Autodesk software, as shown in Figure 1–25. These options are also available in the *Viewpoint* tab>Navigate panel.

- In the *View* tab>Navigation Aids panel, click ▣ (Navigation Bar) to toggle it on and off.

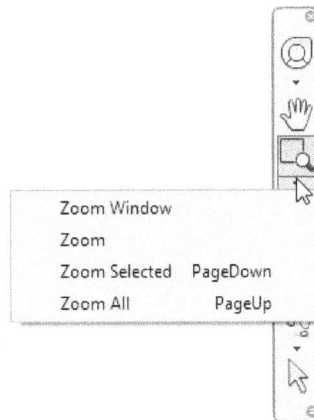

Figure 1–25

- (2D Wheel): Provides cursor-specific access to **Zoom** and **Pan**.

- (Pan): Move across a scene using the left mouse button.

- (Zoom Window): Zooms into a region that you define. To define the rectangular area you want to zoom in to, drag the cursor or select two points. This is the default command.

- (Zoom): Zoom in and out of a scene using the left mouse button.

- (Zoom Selected): Zooms in on any selected item in the scene.

- (Zoom All): Zooms in or out to fit the full model on the screen.

Walk

The ᔆᔆ (Walk) command works as if you are walking along with a camera. Drag the left mouse button to move forward or back as you walk around and through the model.

- To help you know where you are going, you can toggle on an avatar, such as the construction worker shown in Figure 1–26. In the Navigation Bar, expand the Walk drop-down list and select **Third Person** (or press <Ctrl>+<T>).

*To change the avatar, in the Options Editor> Viewpoint Defaults> Collision pane, click **Settings**.*

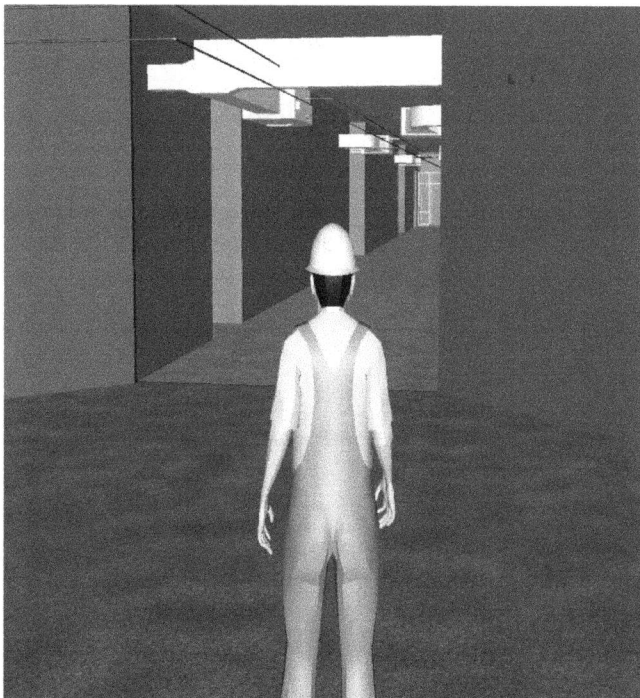

Figure 1–26

- Hold <Shift> as you drag to double the movement speed.

- Scroll the mouse wheel to move up and down, or press the wheel to move side to side. This changes the position of the camera.

- You can set the *F.O.V.* and camera *Position* (including the **Z**, which controls the height of the camera) in the *Viewpoint* tab>Camera panel.

Look Around

The ⊛ (Look Around) command is a stationary camera that enables you to look right and left, up and down by dragging with the left mouse button.

Fly

The ▷ (Fly) command is similar to game navigation tools. The camera follows the direction of the mouse. Click the mouse and move it forward to start moving. Ascend or descend by moving the mouse up or down. Move left and right by moving the mouse in that direction.

Realism

The ⚶ (Realism) command enables you to change how the camera interacts with the model. There are four settings you can turn on or off, as shown in Figure 1–27:

- **Collision:** Causes the camera to stop when it runs into a solid object in the model.

- **Gravity:** Causes the camera to remain a set distance from the top of objects to simulate walking on top of them.

- **Crouch:** Permits the camera to dip below objects in the model to get around them if there is enough room.

- **Third Person:** Toggles on an avatar to simulate a person being in the model.

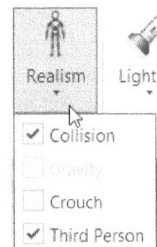

Figure 1–27

Hint: Controlling the Speed of Navigation Commands

In the *Viewpoint* tab, expand the Navigate panel to modify the *Linear Speed* and *Angular Speed*, as shown in Figure 1–28.

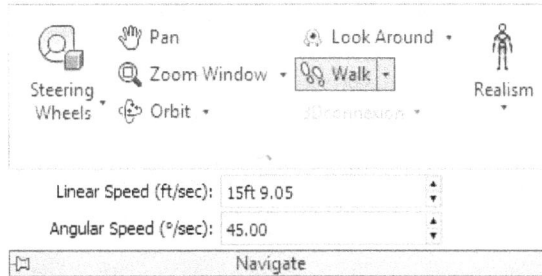

| Linear Speed (ft/sec): | 15ft 9.05 |
| Angular Speed (°/sec): | 45.00 |

Navigate

Figure 1–28

Practice 1b

Use Basic Viewing Tools

Practice Objectives

- Navigate the scene using the mouse.
- Navigate the scene using the ViewCube.
- Navigate the scene using the Navigation Bar.

Estimated time for completion: 5 minutes

In this practice you will look around the model outside of the building and inside the building (shown in Figure 1–29) using various navigation tools.

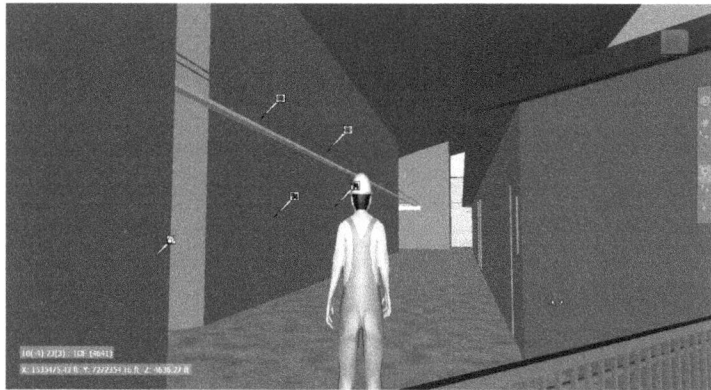

Figure 1–29

- The exact views you see might vary from the ones shown in this practice.

Task 1 - Navigate the model with the mouse and keyboard.

1. In the Quick Access toolbar, click 📂 (Open).

2. In the Open dialog box, navigate to the *C:\Navisworks BIM Practice Files* folder and review the list of subfolders used in these practices.

3. Open the *Intro* folder.

4. In the Files of type drop-down list, select **Navisworks (*.nwd)**.

5. Select **NewElementarySchool-Intro.nwd** and click **Open**.

6. In the Navigation Bar, expand the zoom options and select **Zoom**, as shown in Figure 1–30.

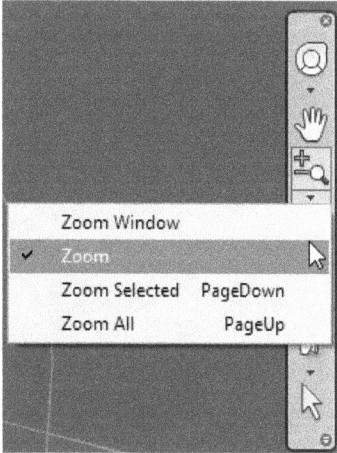

Figure 1–30

7. In the model, center the cursor over the building (as shown in Figure 1–31) and scroll with the mouse wheel to zoom in and out.

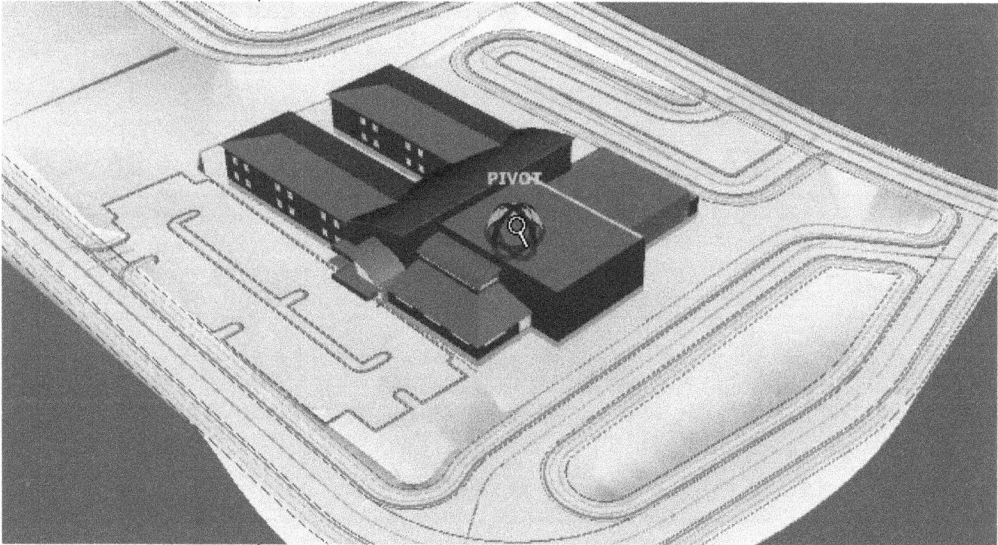

Figure 1–31

8. Hold <Shift> and the mouse wheel to orbit around the scene until the view of the model is similar to that shown in Figure 1–32.

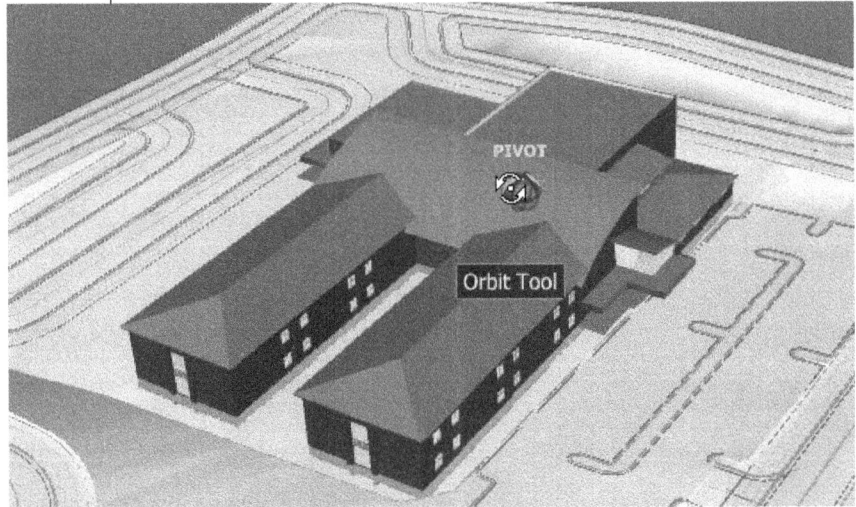

Figure 1–32

9. Hold the mouse wheel and move the mouse to the right to pan the scene and display the East side of the building, as shown in Figure 1–33.

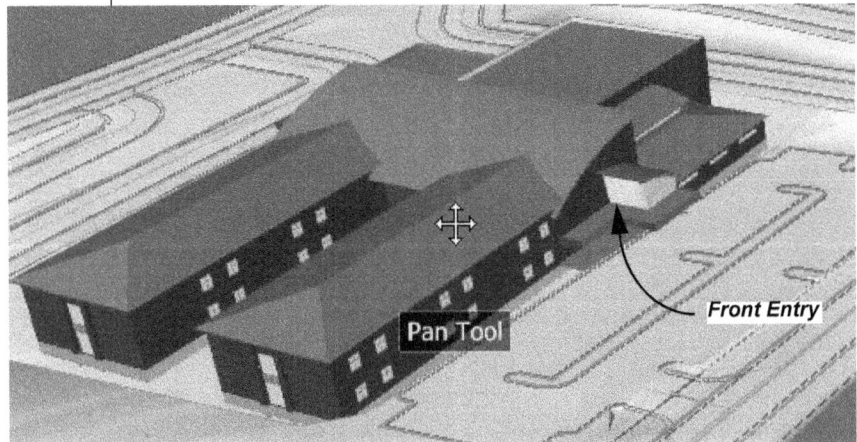

Figure 1–33

10. Place the pivot point near the front entry, shown in Figure 1–33.

11. Use the mouse to zoom and pan the scene until you can see inside the building, such as the view shown in Figure 1–34.

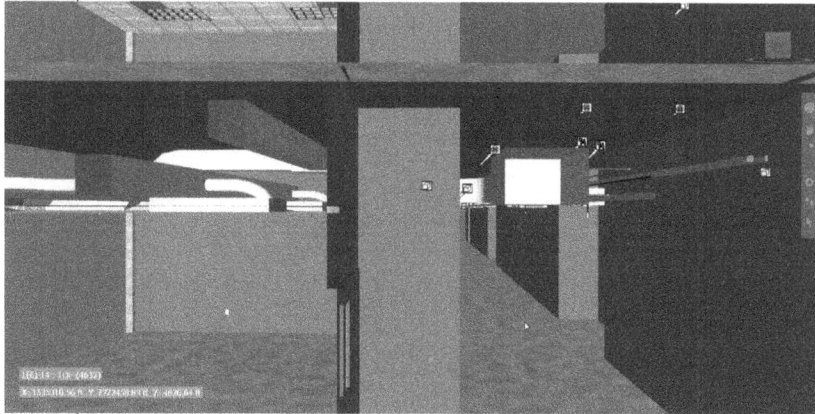

Figure 1–34

Task 2 - Navigate the model using the Navigation Bar and Navigation panel.

1. Continue working in the same model.

2. In the selection tree, expand
   **NewElementarySchool-Intro.nwd>
   Elementary-School-Architectural.rvt>Second Floor>
   Railings>Railing>Guardrail - Rectangular** and then select
   the second **Railing**, as shown in Figure 1–35.

3. In the Navigation bar, click ⚲ (Zoom Selected), as shown in
   Figure 1–36.

Figure 1–35

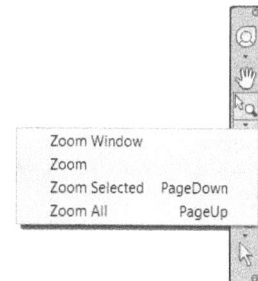

Figure 1–36

4. In the Navigation Bar, click ⊕ (Look Around). Hold the left mouse button and move the cursor until you are looking the other way down the hall, as shown in Figure 1–37.

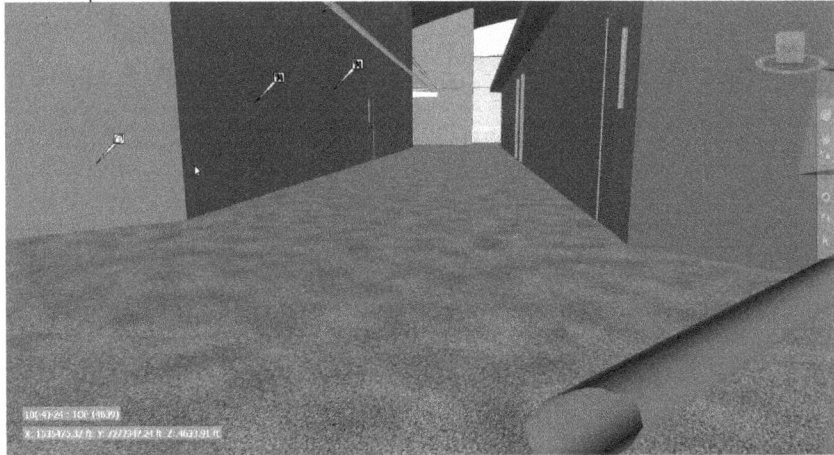

Figure 1–37

5. In the Navigation Bar, click ⚲ (Walk).

6. Hold the left mouse button as you move the mouse slowly forward to simulate walking forward.

7. In the Navigation Bar, expand the Walk drop-down list and select **Third Person** to display the construction worker avatar, as shown in Figure 1–38

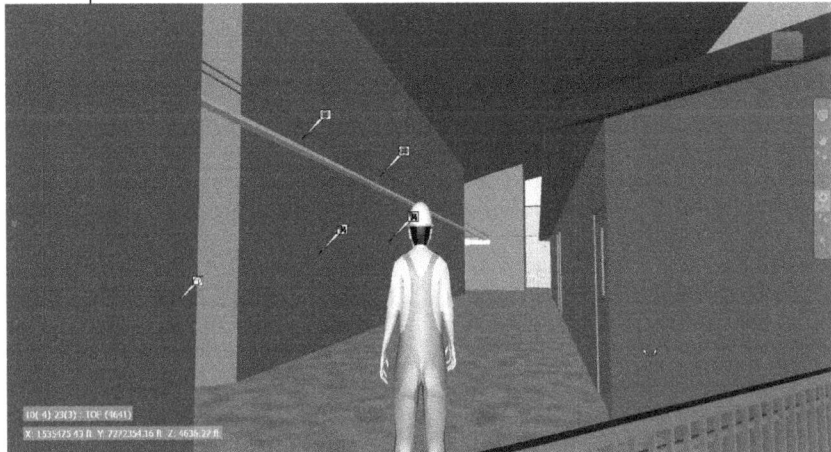

Figure 1–38

8. Continue dragging the mouse forward until you are half way down the hall. Then, pull the mouse backward slightly to simulate walking backward. Finally, move the cursor forward and to the right and watch as you walk through the wall into the bathroom.

9. Once in the bathroom, in the Navigation Bar, click ⊕ (Look Around).

10. Hold the left mouse button as you move the mouse slowly forward to simulate looking up, then pull it back to look down. Next, move the mouse to the right to look around the room. Move it left to return to the original focus.

11. Hover the cursor over the ViewCube, and then click

    ⌂ (Home).

12. In the ViewCube, click on the top south-east corner (as shown in Figure 1–39) to view the model in a perspective view.

Figure 1–39

13. In the Navigation Bar, click ▷ (Fly)

14. Click the left mouse button and then move the mouse forward to start moving. Ascend or descend by moving the mouse up or down. Move left and right by moving the mouse in that direction.

15. In the *Viewpoint* tab>Navigate panel, expand 👤 (Realism) and toggle on **Collision**.

16. Purposely move directly into the building and note how the camera stops as it collides.

17. Click **Home** on the ViewCube.

18. In the Navigation Bar, expand **Fly**, toggle off **Collision** and **Third Person**, and then select **Walk**.

19. In the Quick Access Toolbar, click ▢ (New). This closes the file you were working in and opens a blank file.

Chapter Review Questions

1. If you have lost all of your dockable windows and tools, what is the fastest way to get them back?

   a. Reinstall the software.

   b. Close and restart the software.

   c. Select the required workspace.

2. In the following parts of the User Interface, where are you most likely to find viewing tools?

   a. Quick Access Toolbar

   b. Dockable Window

   c. Scene View

   d. Status Bar

3. What do you do if you want a window available, but not taking space from the scene view?

   a. Dock it to the side.

   b. Set it to Auto Hide.

   c. Move it off the screen.

   d. Open and close it.

4. How do you pan sideways in a model?

   a. Hold the mouse wheel and drag the mouse sideways.

   b. Hold the left mouse button and drag the mouse sideways.

   c. Hold the right mouse button and drag the mouse sideways.

5. How do you ensure that the camera cannot go through walls?

   a. Toggle on the **Collision** option.

   b. There is no way to prevent the camera from going through walls.

   c. Toggle on the **Background** option.

   d. Toggle on the **Gravity** option

6. How do you quickly return to a default preset view of a model?

   a. Use the mouse wheel to zoom out.

   b. Hover the cursor over the ViewCube and then click

      (Home).

   c. In the Navigation Bar, click (Zoom All).

   d. Click on the top, south-east corner of the ViewCube.

Command Summary

Button	Command	Location
	Constrained Orbit	• Navigation Bar • **Ribbon:** *Viewpoint* tab>Navigate panel> expand Orbit
	Fly	• Navigation Bar> expand Walk • **Ribbon:** *Viewpoint* tab>Navigate panel> expand Walk
	Free Orbit	• Navigation Bar • **Ribbon:** *Viewpoint* tab>Navigate panel> expand Orbit
	Load Workspace	• **Ribbon:** *View* tab>Workspace panel
	Look Around	• Navigation Bar • > expand Zoom
	Navigation Bar	• **Ribbon:** *View* tab>Navigation Aids panel
	Open	• Application Menu • Quick Access Toolbar
	Orbit	• Navigation Bar • **Ribbon:** *Viewpoint* tab>Navigate panel
	Orthographic	• Navigation Bar • **Ribbon:** *Viewpoint* tab>Camera panel
	Pan	• Navigation Bar • **Ribbon:** *Viewpoint* tab>Navigate panel
	Perspective	• Navigation Bar • **Ribbon:** *Viewpoint* tab>Camera panel
	Save Workspace	• **Ribbon:** *View* tab>Workspace panel
	Steering Wheels	• Navigation Bar • **Ribbon:** *Viewpoint* tab>Navigate panel
	ViewCube	• **Ribbon:** *View* tab>Navigation Aids panel
	Walk	• Navigation Bar • **Ribbon:** *Viewpoint* tab>Navigate panel
	Windows	• **Ribbon:** *View* tab>Workspace panel

	Zoom	• Navigation Bar> expand Zoom • **Ribbon:** *Viewpoint* tab>Navigate panel> expand Zoom
	Zoom All	• Navigation Bar> expand Zoom • **Ribbon:** *Viewpoint* tab>Navigate panel> expand Zoom
	Zoom Selected	• Navigation Bar> expand Zoom • **Ribbon:** *Viewpoint* tab>Navigate panel> expand Zoom
	Zoom Window	• Navigation Bar> expand Zoom • **Ribbon:** *Viewpoint* tab>Navigate panel> expand Zoom

Consolidate Trade Models

The Autodesk® Navisworks® software is a complex Building Information Modeling (BIM) application that enables design teams to view project information independent of the software used to create the original design. Multiple models can be opened and stitched together inside the Autodesk Navisworks software to ensure all parts of the project work together. In this chapter, you learn how to open a model and append additional models to it for the Consolidate Models step of the BIM Workflow.

Learning Objectives in this Chapter

- Open and save Autodesk Navisworks software-specific files.
- Consolidate a model using files from different types of software.
- Set the units for an appended model.
- Align models from different design team members.

BIM Workflow: Consolidate Models

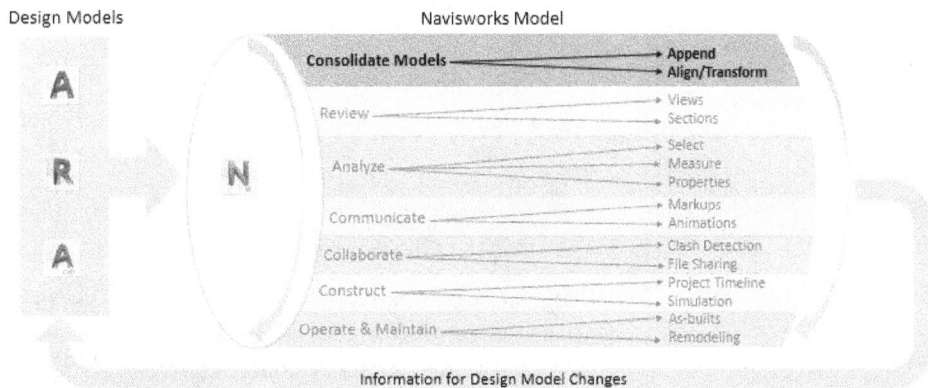

2.1 Consolidating the Model

The Autodesk Navisworks software is primarily used to combine CAD and BIM files from different disciplines into one composite model. These files can be 2D or 3D, and can be created in Autodesk® software (e.g., AutoCAD®, AutoCAD® Civil 3D®, Autodesk® Revit®, etc.) or in software provided by other vendors. The advantage of using the Autodesk Navisworks software to combine models is the reduction in file sizes. For instance, if you have a 30 MB Autodesk Revit file, when you bring it into the Autodesk Navisworks software, it is reduced to 4 MB. The software simplifies the model to speed up visualization without losing details.

Many different file formats can be opened directly in the Autodesk Navisworks software or can be appended together into a single consolidated model. Figure 2–1 shows two appended models with the structural model selected.

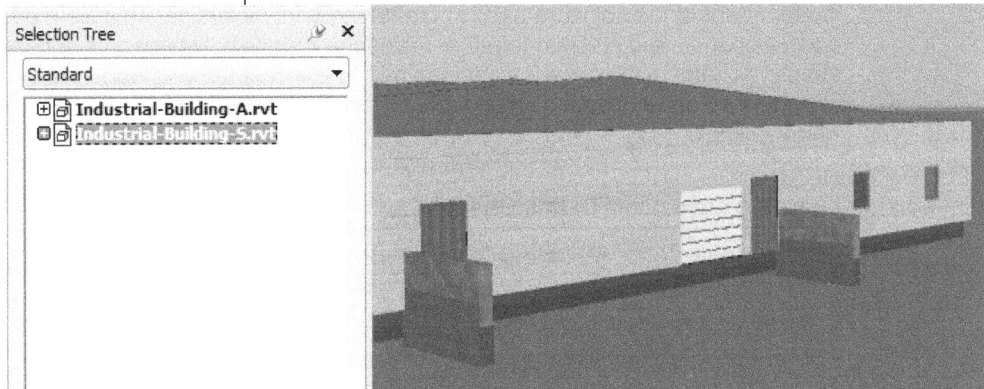

Figure 2–1

There are three main file types created by the Autodesk Navisworks software:

- **Navisworks (.NWD):** The current state (or "snapshot") of a project, with all of the model geometry and redlines included.
  - These files do not update if a change is made to the original linked files.
  - A .NWD file is typically sent out for others to review at set stages of the project.

- **Navisworks File Set (.NWF):** Includes links to the original files that form an Autodesk Navisworks model and redlines.
  - The model updates in these files when changes are made to the linked files.

To refresh an updated models inside the .NWF file, you might need to delete the .NWC file.

- The .NWF file is typically the file that you work in the most.

- **Navisworks Cache (.NWC):** Snapshots of each original file that are created automatically when you open or append files from other software.
  - As long as the original file is not updated, the Autodesk Navisworks software uses these cache files as the data source when a file set is opened.
  - You typically do not work in cache files.

How To: Start a Navisworks Project

1. In the Quick Access Toolbar or Application Menu, click

   ▢ (New). Alternatively, open a compatible file type.

2. In the *Home* Tab>Project panel, click ▢ (Append). Alternatively, in the Quick Access Toolbar, expand

   ▷ (Open) and click **Append**, or press <Ctrl>+<A>.

3. In the Append dialog box, expand the Files of type drop-down list and select the file format you want to use, as shown in Figure 2–2.
   - You can open or append many types of files, including Autodesk Navisworks, Autodesk Revit, AutoCAD, .DWG, and .DWF formats, as shown in Figure 2–2.

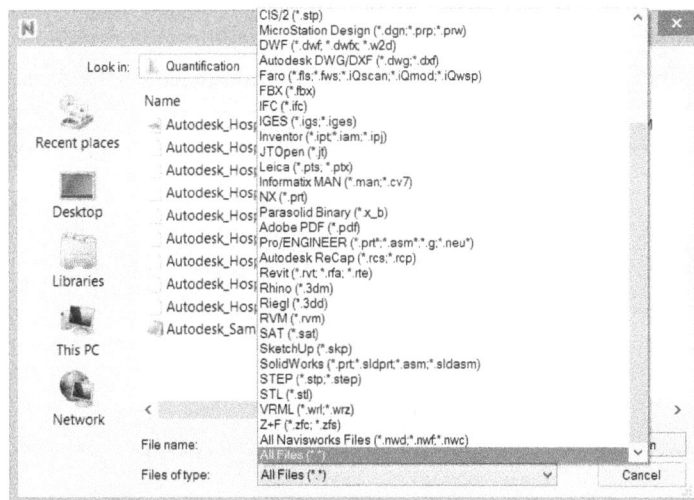

Figure 2–2

You can select multiple files to open or append by holding either <Shift> or <Ctrl>.

4. Navigate to the appropriate folder and select a file.
5. Click **Open**.
6. Continue appending other models as required.
7. In the Quick Access Toolbar or Application Menu, click

   🖫 (Save). The first time you save a file, the Save As dialog box opens. Select the type of Autodesk Navisworks file you want to save.

   - Files can be saved as Navisworks File Set (.NWF) or Navisworks (.NWD). You can also save files so that they are compatible with previous versions of the Autodesk Navisworks software, as shown in Figure 2–3.

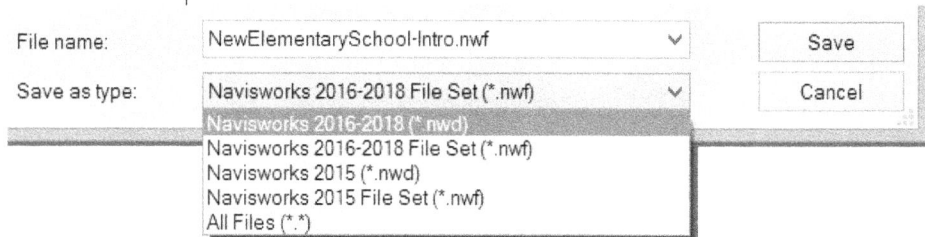

File name:	NewElementarySchool-Intro.nwf	∨	Save
Save as type:	Navisworks 2016-2018 File Set (*.nwf)	∨	Cancel
	Navisworks 2016-2018 (*.nwd)		
	Navisworks 2016-2018 File Set (*.nwf)		
	Navisworks 2015 (*.nwd)		
	Navisworks 2015 File Set (*.nwf)		
	All Files (*.*)		

Figure 2–3

2.2 Aligning Models

When appending multiple models together, it is important to ensure that they are scaled properly and line up with each other correctly. By doing this, you can ensure that you get the correct measurements when you measure the model, and that clash detections are as accurate as possible.

Note that you are not asked for an insertion point or a scale factor during the Append process. These are set after the model is appended using the Units and Transform dialog box.

File Units

Each file has its own units. When you append files, they inherit the units of the base file and are scaled to match. If the units do not match as expected, you can modify each model's units, as shown in Figure 2–4.

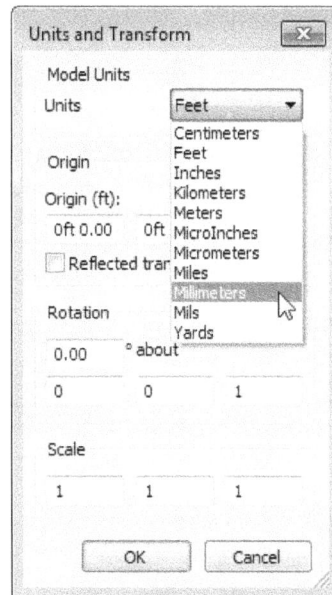

Figure 2–4

How To: Set the File Units

1. Confirm with the owner of the model which coordinate system they used to create their model.

2. Expand ![icon] (Application Menu) and select **Options**.

3. In the Options Editor dialog box, set the units for the base Autodesk Navisworks model as follows, as shown in Figure 2–5:

- In the left panel, expand **Interface** and select **Display Units**.
- In the right panel, select the required units for *Linear Units* and *Angular Units*.
- Set the *Decimal Places* precision for the units.
- Click **OK**.

Select the units you want to use for your measurements in the Autodesk Navisworks model.

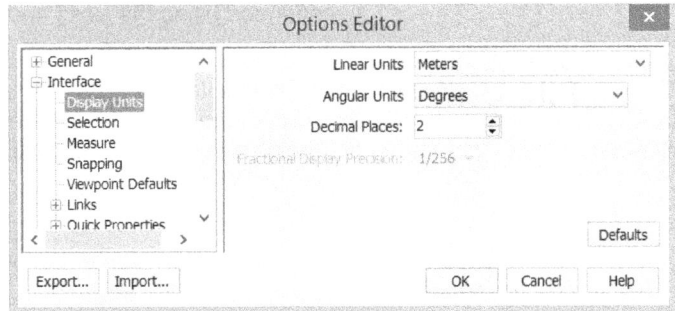

Figure 2–5

4. In the Selection Tree, select an appended model, right-click on it, and select **Units and Transform...** to set only that model's units.
5. In the Units and Transform dialog box, select the units that the file was created in, as shown in Figure 2–6. Click **OK**.

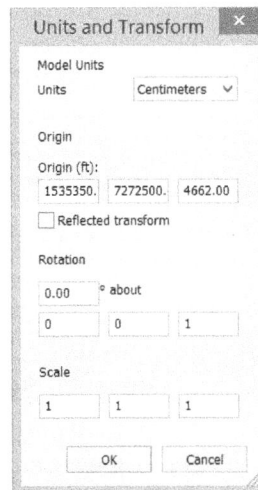

Figure 2–6

The appended model is scaled to match the base model's units.

File Transformation

Civil engineers typically work in real world coordinates, like state plane coordinate systems. Each of their models often have a different base point according to where their projects are located in the world. On the other hand, architects often have a model base point of 0,0,0, unless they input the project point manually inside of the Autodesk Revit software.

You must perform a file transformation when the models from different design team members do not line up correctly. There are two ways to transform a file:

- **Using real world coordinates:** This setting uses the real world coordinates (as shown in Figure 2–7) located at the centroid of the appended model. Note that each model must be transformed individually when using this method.

- **Using a difference in coordinates:** This enables you to enter the distance you need the models to move in the X-,Y-, and Z-directions, as shown in Figure 2–8. This method can be used on multiple models simultaneously if they all need to move the same distance.

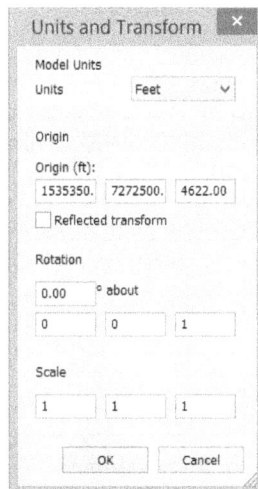

Figure 2–7

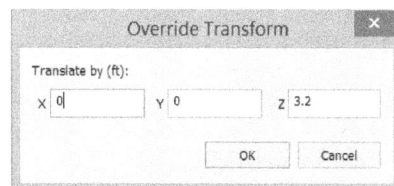

Figure 2–8

How To: Transform a File Using Real-World Coordinates

1. Confirm with the owner of the model which coordinate system they used to create their model.
2. In the Selection Tree, select an appended model, right-click on it, and select **Units and Transform** to set the model's units.

3. In the Units and Transform dialog box, enter the origin X-, Y-, and Z-coordinates, as shown in Figure 2–9.

Figure 2–9

4. Click **OK**.

How To: Transform Models Using a Difference in Coordinates

1. In the Selection Tree window, select all of the files that need to be transformed.
2. Right-click on any one of the selected files and select **Override Item>Override Transform**, as shown in Figure 2–10.
3. In the Override Transform dialog box, type the required X-, Y-, and Z-distances to move the models (as shown in Figure 2–11), and then click **OK**.

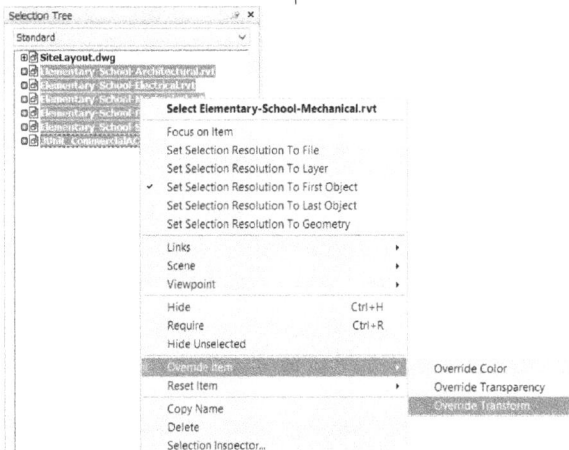

Figure 2–10

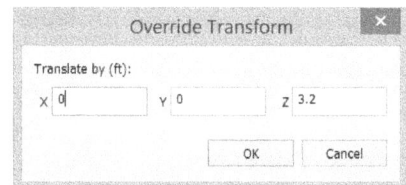

Figure 2–11

Hint: Heads Up Display (HUD)

You might need to determine where you are in a model before you can calculate the transformation coordinates to use. The Heads Up Display (HUD) information displays in the lower-left corner of the scene view, as shown in Figure 2–12.

- The location information that is displayed is the current camera location.

- Panning and zooming in the scene causes the coordinates in the HUD to change without moving the cursor.

- To toggle the display the various HUD elements, in the

  View tab>Navigation Aids panel, expand ▢ (HUD) and select **XYZ Axes**, **Position Readout**, or **Grid Location**.

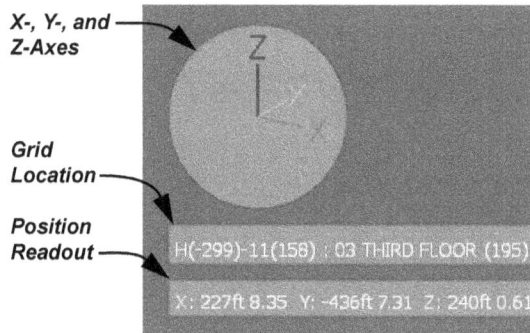

X-, Y-, and Z-Axes

Grid Location

Position Readout

H(-299)-11(158) : 03 THIRD FLOOR (195)

X: 227ft 8.35 Y: -436ft 7.31 Z: 240ft 0.61

Figure 2–12

Practice 2a

Consolidate Models

Practice Objectives

- Consolidate models from multiple software sources.
- Align models with each other.

Estimated time for completion: 15 minutes

In this practice you will open the preliminary planning phase to review the initial project layout, as shown in Figure 2–13. Then you will consolidate many of the design models into one Autodesk Navisworks file as the first step in the BIM Process.

Figure 2–13

Task 1 - Open the preliminary design and review the project.

In this task you will open an .FBX file that was created from an Autodesk InfraWorks model during the preliminary planning phase of the project. This enables you to review the early design of the project.

1. In the Quick Access toolbar, click 📂 (Open).

2. In the Open dialog box, set the *Files of type* to **FBX (*.fbx)**.

3. Navigate to the practice files *Project Files>InfraWorks Files* folder and select **SiteLayout.fbx**.

4. Click **Open**.

5. In the ViewCube, click on the SW corner to view the model in a South-West isometric view.

6. Zoom and pan the model to become familiar with it.

If the Selection Tree is not displayed, go to the View tab>Workspace panel, expand **Windows** *and select* **Selection Tree**.

7. In the Selection Tree, expand **SiteLayout.fbx>ID 0>ID -1** and select the first 7 **Mesh 1** items one at a time to view the items that are highlighted in the scene, as shown in Figure 2–14.

Figure 2–14

8. Press <Esc> to release the selection.

Task 2 - Consolidate multiple models into one file.

In this task you will open a .DWG file that was created in the AutoCAD Civil 3D software. Then you will append Autodesk Revit and Inventor models into it.

To view files created in AutoCAD Civil 3D you need to have the Civil 3D object enabler installed on your system. See the Appendix to learn more.

1. In the Quick Access toolbar, click 🖗 (Open).

   • Opening a file automatically closes any other open file.

2. In the Open dialog box, change the *Files of type* to **All Files (*.*)**.

3. Navigate to the practice files *Project Files>Civil Files> Source Drawings>Surfaces* folder and open **SiteLayout.dwg**.

4. In the *Home* Tab>Project panel, click 🗋 (Append).

5. In the Append dialog box, expand the *Files of type* drop-down list and set the file format to **Revit (*.rvt; *.rfa; *.rte)**, as shown in Figure 2–15.

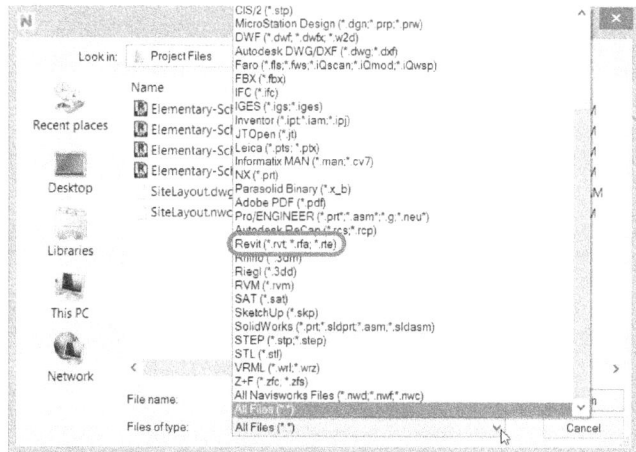

Figure 2–15

Hold <Ctrl> to select more than one.

6. Navigate to the practice files *Project Files>Revit Files* folder and select the following files:

   - **Elementary-School-Architectural.rvt**
   - **Elementary-School-Electrical.rvt**
   - **Elementary-School-Mechanical.rvt**
   - **Elementary-School-Plumbing.rvt**
   - **Elementary-School-Structure.rvt**

7. Click **Open**.

8. Use the ViewCube and other viewing tools to zoom in closer to the building on the site, as shown in Figure 2–16. Note that the AutoCAD Civil 3D file includes both 2D and 3D elements. Ensure that you zoom in on the 3D elements.

Figure 2–16

9. Note that all of the Revit files line up with the AutoCAD Civil 3D drawing file. This is because a project point was set in the Autodesk Revit files.

10. In the Quick Access Toolbar or Application Menu click,

   (Save).

11. Save the model in the *Consolidate* practice files folder as **NewElementarySchool-<*your initials*>.nwf**.

Task 3 - Set units and transform the model.

In this task, you will finish appending models and set any units and transformations, as required.

1. Expand (Application Menu) and select **Options**.

2. In the Options Editor dialog box, set the units for the base Autodesk Navisworks model as follows, as shown in Figure 2–17:

   • In the left pane, select **Interface>Display Units**.
   • In the right pane, set *Linear Units* to **Feet**.
   • Set *Angular Units* to **Degrees**.
   • Set *Decimal Places* to **2**.
   • Click **OK**.

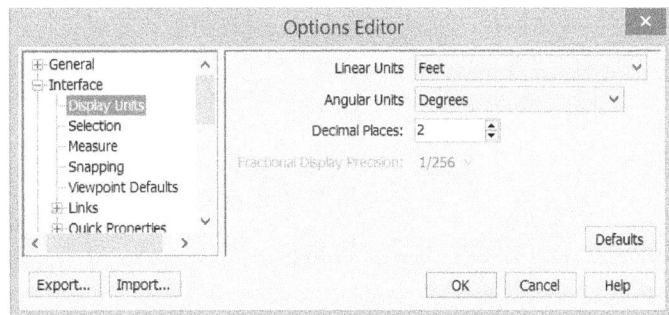

Figure 2–17

3. In the *Home* Tab>Project panel, click (Append).

4. In the Append dialog box, expand the *Files of type* drop-down list and set the file type to **Inventor (*.ipt, *.iam, *.ipj)**.

5. Navigate to the practice files *Project Files\HVAC Files* folder and select **1Unit_CommercialAC.iam**. Click **Open**.

The A/C unit might not display because it came in at the wrong location.

6. In the Selection Tree window, right-click on the newly appended Autodesk Inventor file and select **Units and Transform**.

7. In the Units and Transform dialog box, set the following, as shown in Figure 2–18:

   - *Units:* **Centimeters**
   - *Origin (ft): X:* **1535375**, *Y:* **7272450**, *Z:* **4658**
   - *Rotation:* **0**

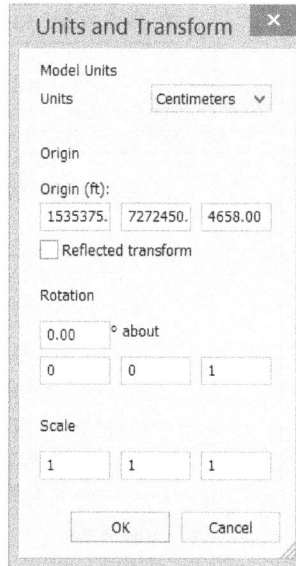

Figure 2–18

8. Click **OK**.

9. Note that the A/C unit is still not in a useful spot. In the Selection Tree, right-click on **1Unit_Commercial AC.iam** and select **Override Item>Override Transform**, as shown in Figure 2–19.

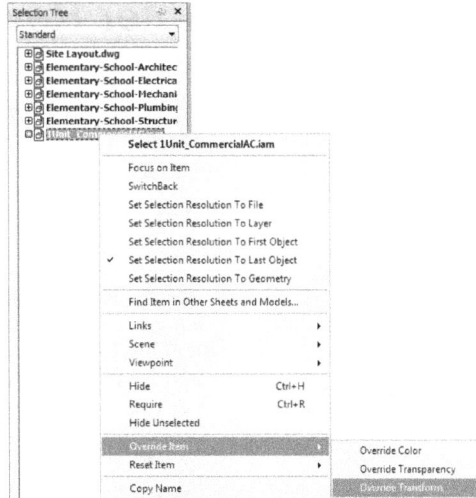

Figure 2–19

10. In the Override Transform dialog box, set *Translate by (ft)* to
X: **150**, Y: **-50** (as shown in Figure 2–20), and then click **OK**.

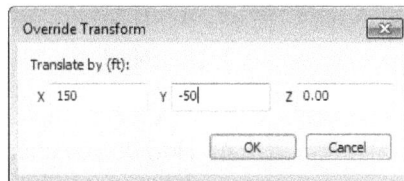

Figure 2–20

11. Note that the unit moves to the top of the flat roof, as shown
in Figure 2–21. Save the file.

Figure 2–21

Chapter Review Questions

1. In Autodesk Navisworks, if you open a file that was created in a different software program, can you append other types of files to it?

   a. Yes

   b. No

   c. It depends on the file type

2. Which file format is automatically created when you open or append a file into an Autodesk Navisworks project?

   a. .NWD

   b. .NWF

   c. .NWC

3. Which file format should you use if you want an Autodesk Navisworks project to stay linked to the original models and update as the original models update?

   a. .NWD

   b. .NWF

   c. .NWC

4. How do you change the measurement units for an Autodesk Navisworks model?

   a. You cannot change the units.

   b. In the Options dialog box, change the *Display Units*.

   c. You must start the project using the correct template at the beginning.

   d. The units must be changed in the original model.

5. How would you change the units for just one appended model?

   a. In the Options dialog box, change the *Display Units*.

   b. You cannot change one appended model independently, you must change them all at the same time.

   c. In the Selection Tree window, right-click on the model name and select **Override Item>Override Transform**.

   d. In the Selection Tree window, right-click on the model name and select **Units & Transform...**.

Command Summary

Button	Command	Location
	Append	• **Ribbon:** Home tab>Project Panel • **Quick Access Toolbar:** Expand Open
N/A	**File Units**	• **Right-click:** (with an item selected) **Units and Transform...**
	HUD	• **Ribbon:** *Views* tab>Navigation Aids panel
	New	• Application Menu • Quick Access Toolbar
	Open	• Application Menu • Quick Access Toolbar
N/A	**Options**	• Application Menu
	Save	• Application Menu • Quick Access Toolbar
	Save As	• Application Menu • Quick Access Toolbar

Review Models

In a BIM workflow, once you have consolidated the models, you need to review the models. Model review enables stakeholders to preview the project with all of the components included. In doing so, sight-lines, lighting, security, and many other criteria can be reviewed and verified. In this chapter, you learn how to section the model and save views for easy reuse. You also set up appearances and view options.

Learning Objectives in this Chapter

- Save scenes for later reuse.
- Section a model.
- Set up view options.

BIM Workflow: Review

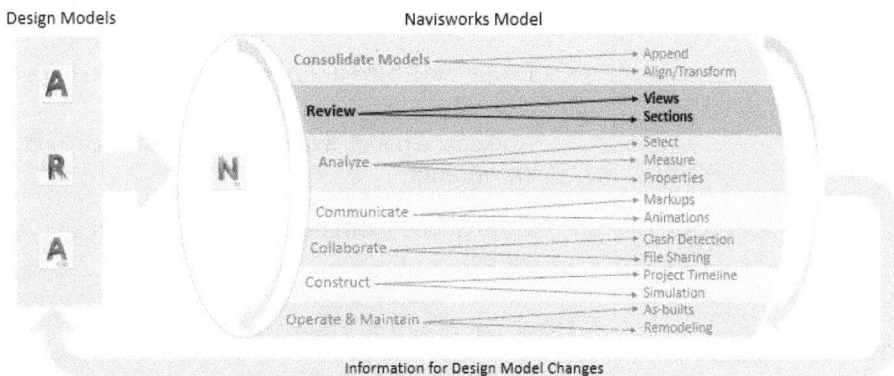

Design Models   Navisworks Model

Consolidate Models — Append / Align/Transform

Review — Views / Sections

Analyze — Select / Measure / Properties

Communicate — Markups / Animations

Collaborate — Clash Detection / File Sharing

Construct — Project Timeline / Simulation

Operate & Maintain — As-builts / Remodeling

Information for Design Model Changes

3.1 Saving and Retrieving Views

In the Autodesk® Navisworks® software, saved views are called Viewpoints, which can be accessed through the Saved Viewpoints window, as shown in Figure 3–1. Viewpoints help you focus on specific conditions in a scene so that you can share information quickly with others. Viewpoints save the scene conditions, such as varying materials, lighting, or what is displayed or hidden. They can also include comments and redline tags.

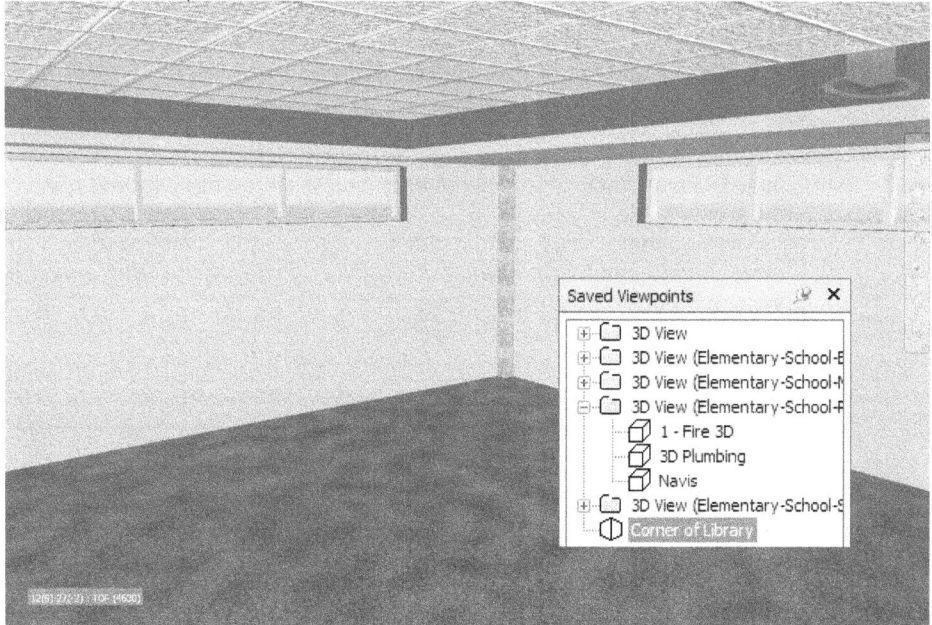

Figure 3–1

- To open the Saved Viewpoints window, in the *View* tab> Workspace panel, expand (Windows) and select **Saved Viewpoints**.

- In the Saved Viewpoints window, click on any view to make it current.

How To: Save a Viewpoint

1. Set up the view as required.
2. In the Saved Viewpoints window, right-click on a blank space and select **Save Viewpoint**, as shown in Figure 3–2.

- Alternatively on the *Viewpoint* tab>Save, Load & Playback panel, click ⬚ (Save Viewpoint) .

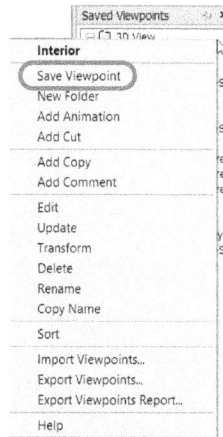

Figure 3–2

3. Type a name for the viewpoint and then press <Enter>.

Hint: Autodesk Revit Views

If a 3D view exists inside the Autodesk Revit software, it will be imported with the model. To ensure the view is recognized, you must ensure that you set the options shown in Figure 3–3 before appending the Revit model.

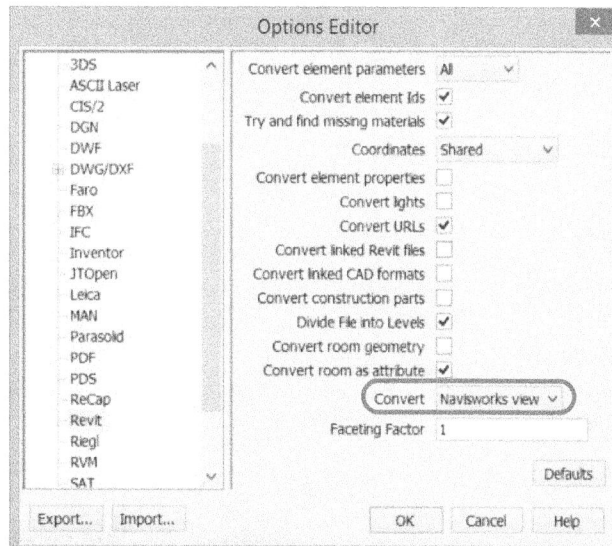

Figure 3–3

Editing Viewpoints

*You might want to make a copy of a viewpoint before you start editing it. To do this, select **Add Copy**.*

You can edit and update viewpoints. In the Saved Viewpoints window, select a view and right-click on it to display the menu shown in Figure 3–4.

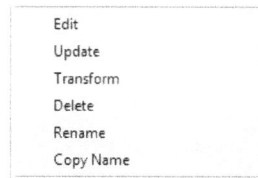

Edit
Update
Transform
Delete
Rename
Copy Name

Figure 3–4

The viewport editing options are as follows:

- **Edit:** Opens the Edit Viewpoint dialog box, shown in Figure 3–5. The available options include changes to the camera, animation, saved attributes, and collision settings for the view.

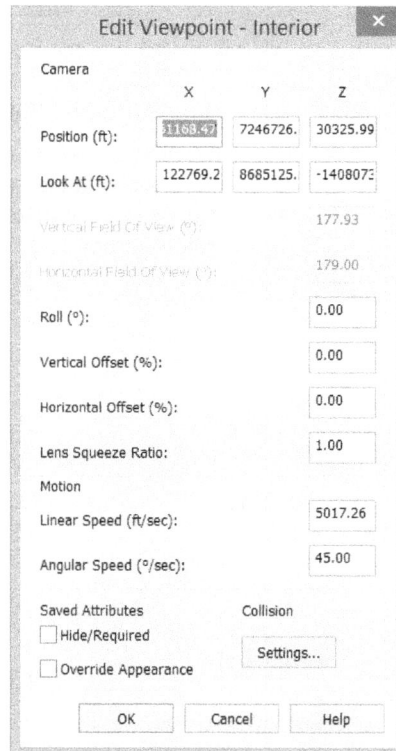

Figure 3–5

- **Update:** If you have made changes of any kind to the view, this option updates the saved viewpoint with those changes.

- **Transform:** Opens the Transform dialog box (shown in Figure 3–6), which enables you to specify X, Y, and Z values to move the entire view these distances.

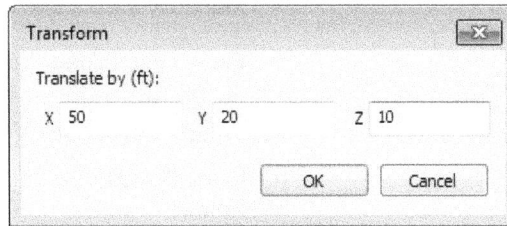

Figure 3–6

- **Delete:** Removes the view from the project.

- **Rename:** Enables you to type in a new name. You can also double-click on the name to do this.

Hint: Viewpoint Defaults

The viewpoint defaults impact all new viewpoints. To change the viewpoint defaults, proceed as follows:

1. Expand ![icon] (Application Menu) and select **Options**.
2. In the Options Editor dialog box, do the following, as shown in Figure 3–7:
   - In the left pane, select **Interface>Viewpoint Defaults**.
   - In the right pane, select the Viewpoint settings required.
   - Click **OK**.

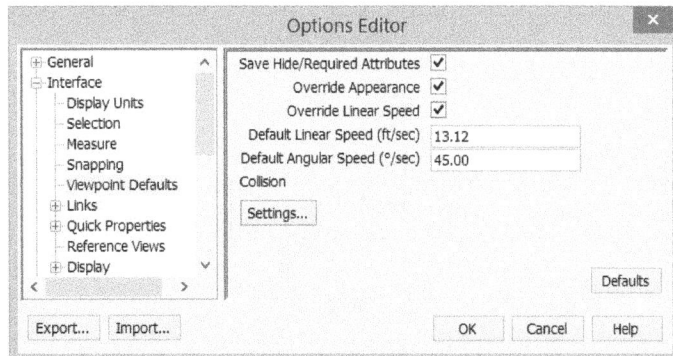

Figure 3–7

Organizing Viewpoints

You can sort viewpoints in the following ways:

- Alphanumerically

- Manually sorted into custom order

- Moved into folders which can also be sorted alphanumerically

How To: Organize Viewpoints into Folders

1. In the Saved Viewpoints window, right-click and select **New Folder**.
2. Type a name for the new folder and press <Enter>.
3. Drag and drop any saved views into the new folder.
4. In the Saved Viewpoints window, right-click and select **Sort** to sort the folders and views alphanumerically.

Practice 3a

Save and Retrieve Viewpoints

Practice Objectives

- Restore existing saved viewpoints.
- Create new viewpoints.
- Modify a saved viewpoint.
- Organize saved viewpoints into folders.

Estimated time for completion: 10 minutes

In this practice you will review several existing viewpoints, as shown in Figure 3–8. You will then create interior and exterior viewpoints and separate them into folders.

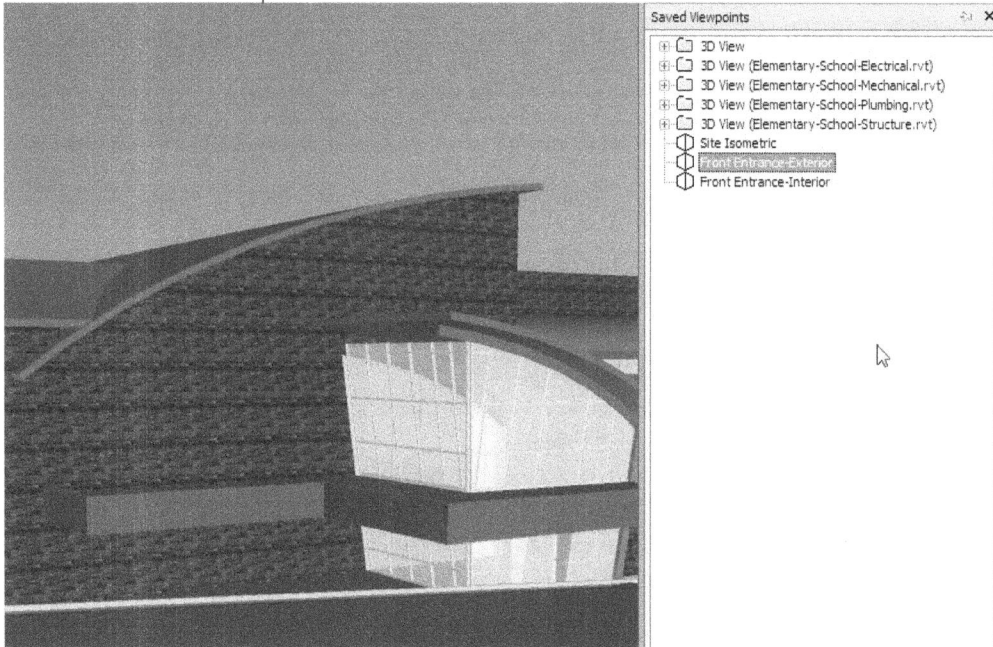

Figure 3–8

Task 1 - Restore Viewpoints.

*If a Resolve dialog box opens that says that .PNG file cannot be found, click **Ignore**.*

1. In the *Review* practice files folder, open **NewElementarySchool-Viewpoints.nwf.**

2. In the *View* tab>Workspace panel, expand (Windows) and select **Saved Viewpoints** to open the window (if not already visible).

In the Saved Viewpoints window, review several of the existing saved viewpoints. Some of the viewpoints were originally imported with the associated Autodesk Revit file, but might not display what you are expecting.

3. Select the saved viewpoint **Front Entrance-Interior.**

4. Save the file.

Task 2 - Save new viewpoints.

1. From the front entrance area, use the viewing tools to look around the interior of the building.

2. When you see the angled front office, in the *Viewpoint* tab> Save, Load & Playback panel, click ⬜ (Save Viewpoint).

3. In the Saved Viewports window, enter the name **Office-Interior**, as shown in Figure 3–9.

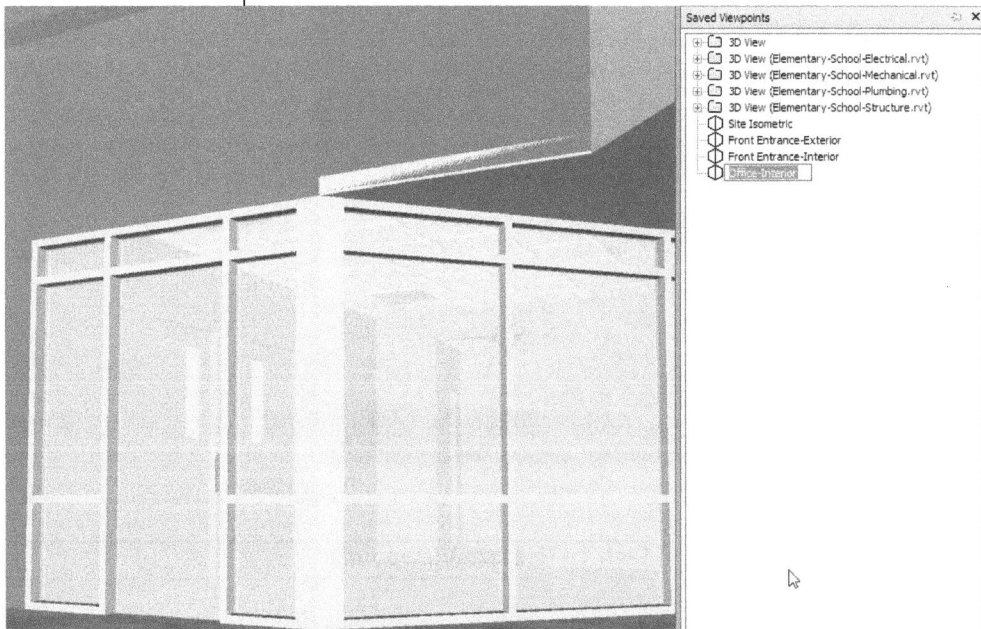

Figure 3–9

4. Continue viewing the interior of the building and make several additional viewpoints.

5. Save the file.

Task 3 - Edit a viewpoint.

1. In the Saved Viewpoints window, right-click on **Overall Site** and select **Add Copy**.

2. Click on the copy and rename it **Site Isometric Close-up**.

3. Zoom in on the building.

4. In the *Viewpoint* tab>Camera panel, expand

   ⬭ (Perspective) and select ⬛ (Orthographic).

5. In the Saved Viewpoints window, right-click on **Site Isometric Close-up** and select **Update**.

6. Switch between the two viewpoints and note the differences.

7. Save the file.

Task 4 - Organize the new viewpoints.

1. Open and pin the Saved Viewpoints window.

2. Right-click in the window and select **New Folder**. Do this again to add a second new folder.

3. Rename the new folders **Interior** and **Exterior**.

4. Drag and drop the viewpoints into the appropriate folder, as shown in Figure 3–10.

The exact names of your views might vary.

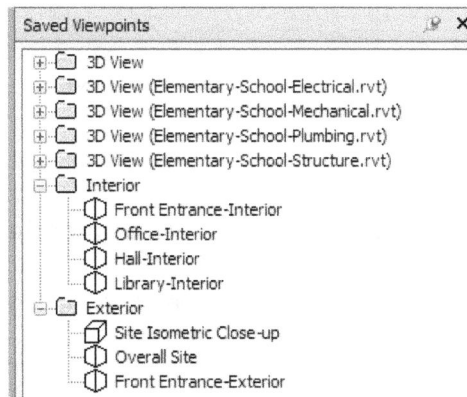

Saved Viewpoints

- 3D View
- 3D View (Elementary-School-Electrical.rvt)
- 3D View (Elementary-School-Mechanical.rvt)
- 3D View (Elementary-School-Plumbing.rvt)
- 3D View (Elementary-School-Structure.rvt)
- Interior
  - Front Entrance-Interior
  - Office-Interior
  - Hall-Interior
  - Library-Interior
- Exterior
  - Site Isometric Close-up
  - Overall Site
  - Front Entrance-Exterior

Figure 3–10

5. Save the project.

3.2 Sectioning the Model

A powerful way to view the model in the Autodesk Navisworks software is to create sections. When you enable sectioning, you can create and modify cut planes to customize the views you need. There are six, preset cut planes that correspond to the sides of a box that you can modify, as shown in Figure 3–11.

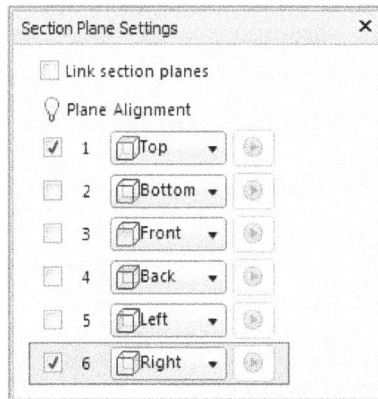

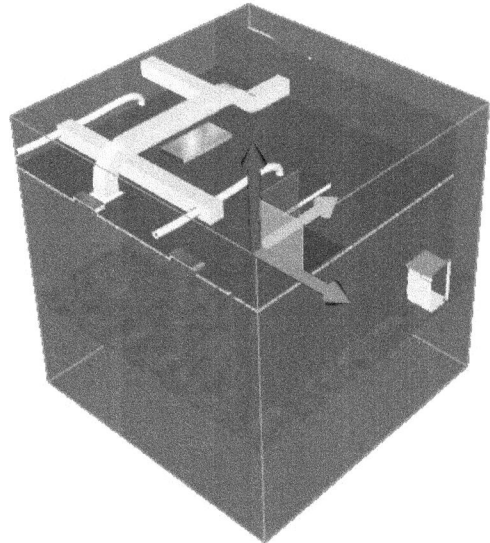

Figure 3–11

There are two modes used in sectioning:

- ⬜ **(Planes):** Enables you to toggle and modify any of the six preset planes.

- ⬜ **(Box):** Automatically cuts all six planes of the box.

How To: Modify Sections in Plane Mode

1. In the *Viewpoint* tab>Section panel, click ⬜ (Enable Sectioning).
2. The first cut is made on the model and the *Sectioning Tools* tab displays, as shown in Figure 3–12.

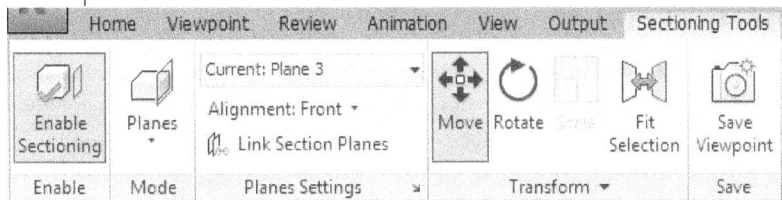

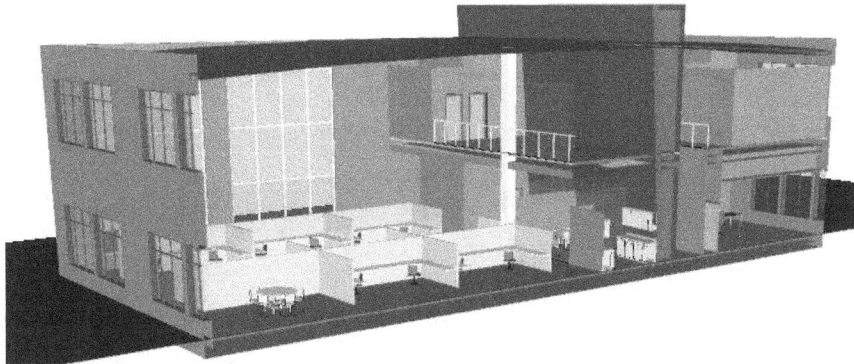

Figure 3–12

3. In the Planes Settings panel, expand the drop-down list shown in Figure 3–13 and click on a light bulb icon to toggle a plane on or off. Multiple planes can be displayed.
4. Click on the plane number to set the *Current Plane*.

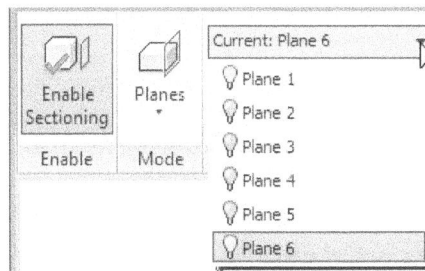

Figure 3–13

5. Use the tools on the *Sectioning Tools* tab>Transform panel to set the location of the current plane.

• When using Box mode, you modify all of the planes at the same time.

• Use the ⬡ (Save Viewpoint) command to save the location of the section planes.

Transforming Sections

The transform tools enable you to modify the location of the plane or box to create the exact section you need, such as the rotated plane shown in Figure 3–14. Each of the primary transform tools use the gizmo to modify the locations of the planes or box.

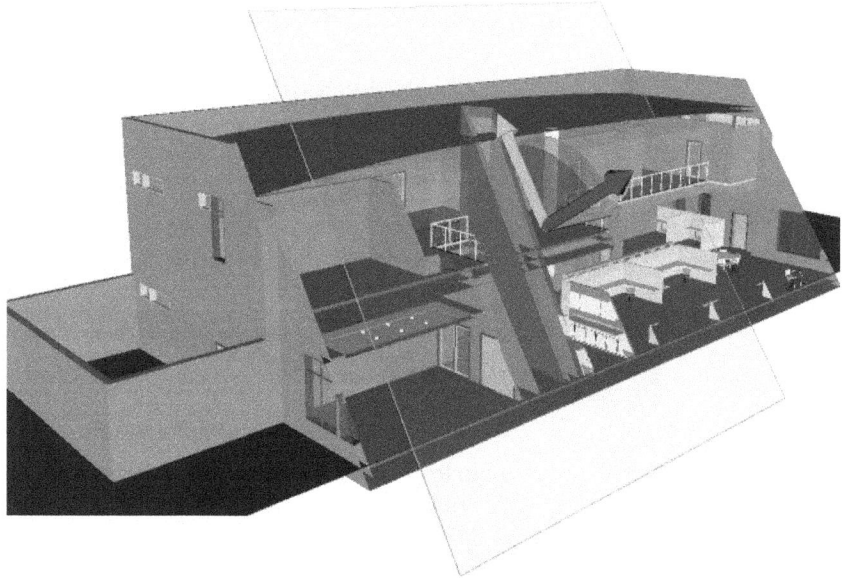

Figure 3–14

Each gizmo is based on the Cartesian coordinate system and has three directions and three planes that can be modified, as shown in Figure 3–15.

Red is the x-axis
Green is the y-axis
Blue is the z-axis

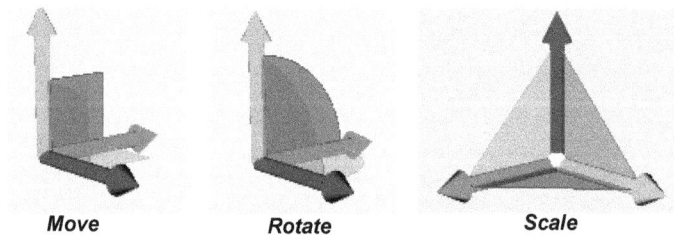

Move   **Rotate**   **Scale**

Figure 3–15

- In Planes mode, the gizmo is fixed on the current plane.

- In Box mode, the gizmo is fixed at the center of the box.

Transform Tools

- ✛ **(Move):** Moves the current plane or the entire box based on the arrow or plane you select.

- ○ **(Rotate):** In plane mode, enables you to rotate the current plane. In Box mode, the tool rotates the entire box. You can only use the planes of the gizmo, not the arrows.

- ▢ **(Scale):** Available only in box mode, the tool enables you to move the opposing sides of the box to create a rectangle. In the example shown in Figure 3–16, the y-axis arrow was used to create a cut on both the front and back of the building.

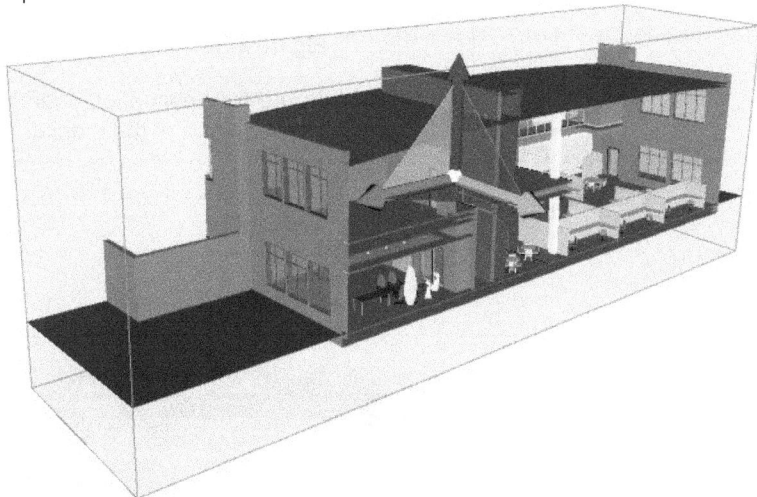

Figure 3–16

- ⋈ **(Fit Selection):** In Plane mode, the tool moves the current plane so that the selected items are in the displayed area of the section. In box mode, the tool fits the box tightly around the selected items. This tool does not use a gizmo.

Additional Sectioning Tools

Alignment: In the Planes Settings panel, you can use the drop-down list shown in Figure 3–17 to specify the alignment of the current plane. This changes the Section Plane Settings. For example, when the alignment for *Plane 1* is changed to **Front**, it displaces the original Top Alignment, as shown in Figure 3–18.

To display the Section Planes Setting dialog box click the Planes Settings panel title.

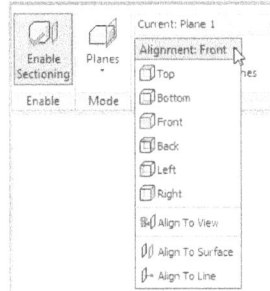

Figure 3–17

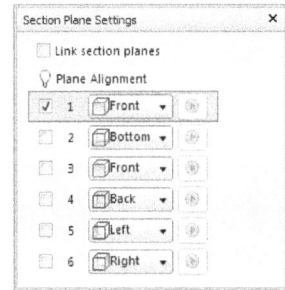

Figure 3–18

- The **Aligned to View** option orients the plane so that it is parallel to the plane of the monitor, as shown in Figure 3–19.

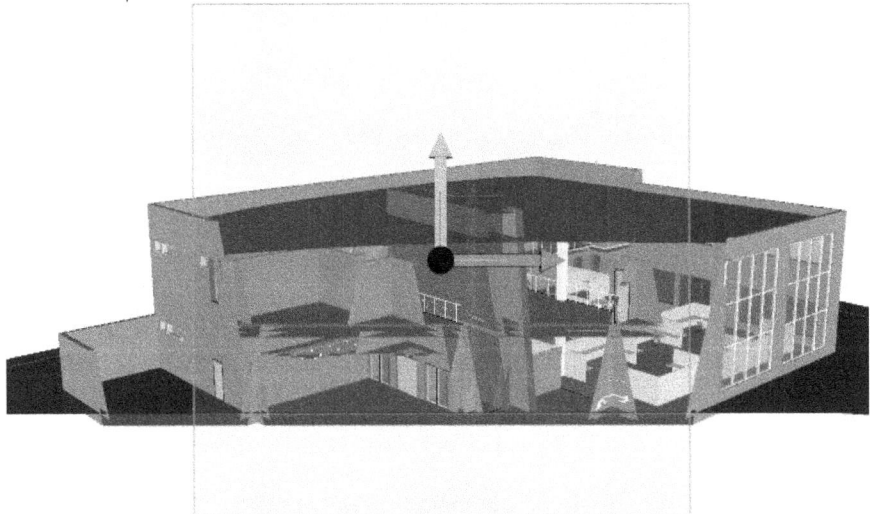

Figure 3–19

- The **Align to Surface** option orients the plane to a selected surface in a 3D model. To change the location, you can repeat the command or, in the Section Planes Settings dialog box, click ⊙ **Re-select** (as shown in Figure 3–20) and select a different surface.

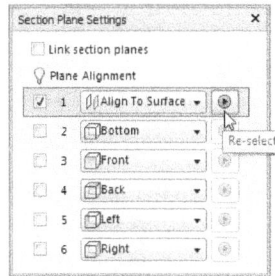
Figure 3–20

- The **Align to Line** option orients the plane to a selected line in a 2D drawing.

- The **Link Section Planes** option enables you to select several planes to move together. In the Section Plane Settings dialog box, select **Link section planes** and then place a checkmark in front of the planes that you want to link.

Hint: Reference Views

Reference Views are like map keys in that they indicate where you are in the model. A triangular marker in the reference view enables you to navigate the scene by dragging the triangle to a new location.

In the *View* tab>Navigation Aids panel, expand (Reference Views) and select **Plan View** or **Section View**.

- Plan View displays the entire model from the top, as shown in Figure 3–21.

- Section View displays the entire model from the front.

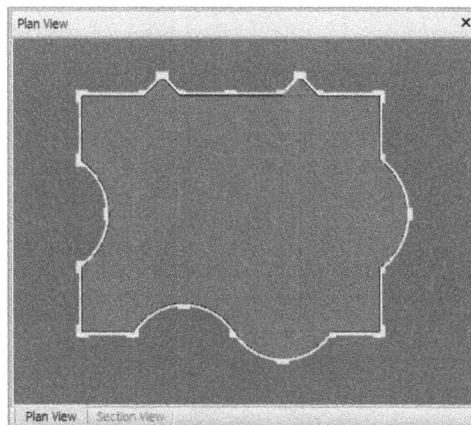
Figure 3–21

Practice 3b

Section the Model

Estimated time for completion: 10 minutes

Practice Objective

- Create sections of a model.

In this practice you will cut sections using individual planes and a box section, as shown in Figure 3–22. Then you will modify the sections using the Transform tools.

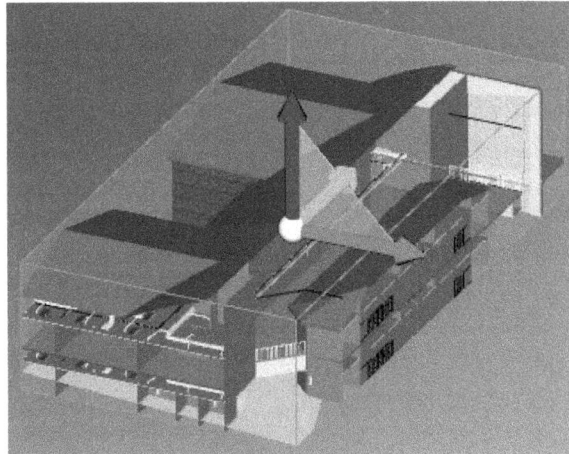

Figure 3–22

Task 1 - Create Plane Sections.

1. In the *Review* practice files folder, open **NewElementarySchool-Sections.nwf**.

2. Open the Saved Viewpoint **Exterior for Sectioning**.

3. In the *Viewpoint* tab>Section panel, click 🖾 (Enable Sectioning).

4. In the *Sectioning Tools* tab>Mode panel, select 🗗 (Planes) from the drop-down list.

5. In the Planes Settings panel, expand the *Current Plane* drop-down list and click on the light bulb icon next to **Plane 3** to toggle the plane on. Select **Plane 3** to make it current, as shown in Figure 3–23.

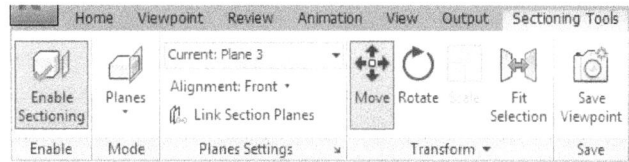

Figure 3–23

*If the gizmo does not display, toggle **Move** off and then on again.*

6. In the *Sectioning Tools* tab>Transform panel, click

   ✛ (Move). Click and drag the blue arrow of the gizmo forward to position the section as shown in Figure 3–24. The section should cut through the A/C unit on the roof.

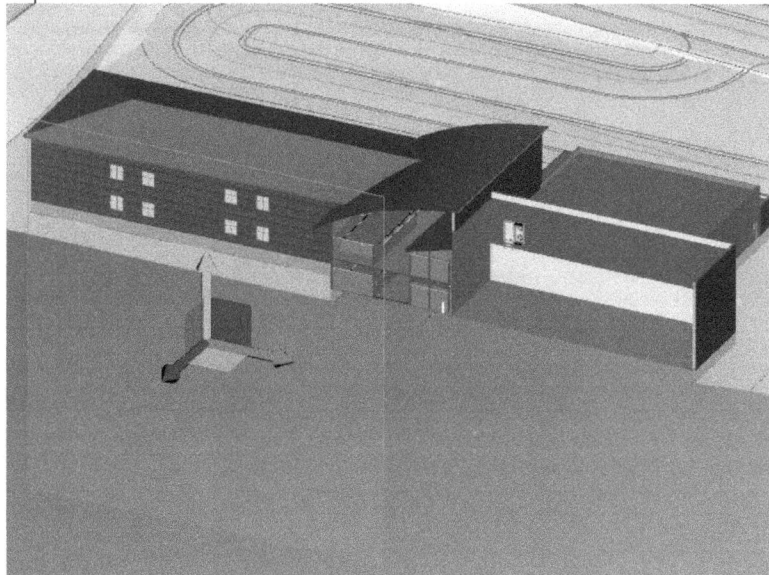

Figure 3–24

7. In the *Sectioning* Tools tab>Save panel, click 📷 (Save Viewpoint) to save the section position. Type **Section-North Wing** for the viewpoint name.

8. In the Current Plane drop-down list, click the Plane 4 light bulb icon to toggle the plane on. Then click the Plane 3 light bulb icon to toggle the plane off.

9. In the Planes Settings panel, make **Plane 4** current and set the *Alignment* to **Right**, as shown in Figure 3–25.

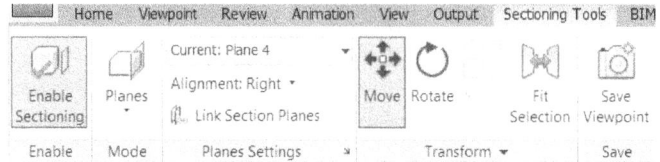

Figure 3–25

10. In the *Sectioning Tools* tab>Transform panel, click

    ✛ (Move). Click and drag the gizmo to position the section as shown in Figure 3–26 so that it cuts through the building entrance.

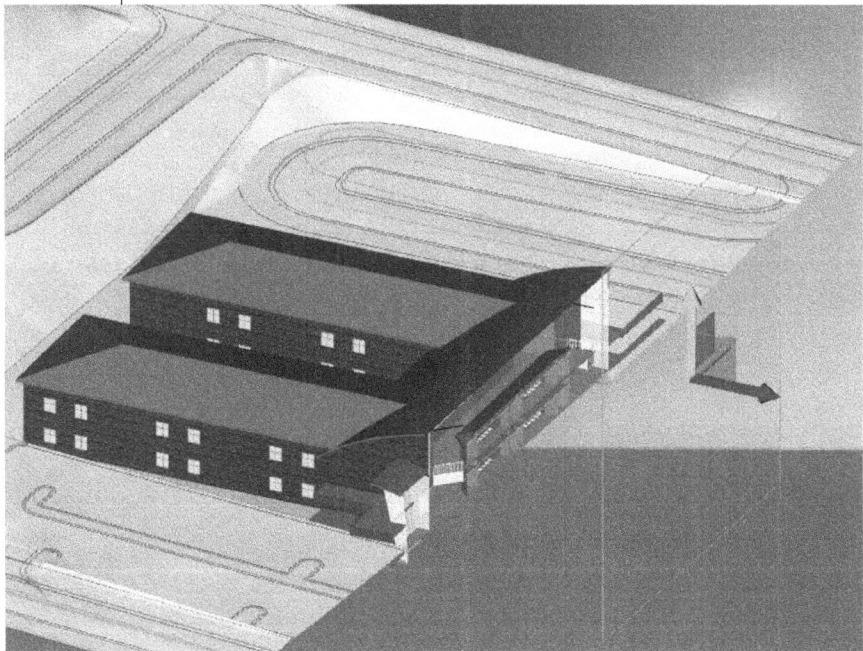

Figure 3–26

11. In the *Sectioning* Tools tab>Save panel, click 📷 (Save Viewpoint) to save the section position. For the viewpoint name, enter **Section-Entrance**.

Task 2 - Edit and save a viewpoint.

1. In the Saved Viewpoints window, click **Section-North Wing**.

2. Pan, zoom, and orbit to adjust the view for a closer look at the rooftop A/C unit, as shown in Figure 3–27

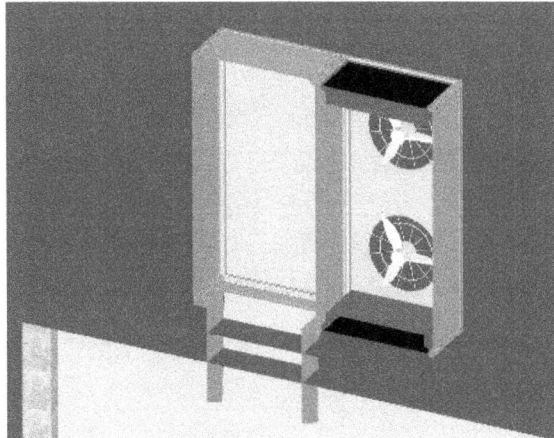

Figure 3–27

3. In the Saved Viewpoints window, right-click on a blank space and select **Save Viewpoint**.

4. Type **AC Unit** for the name and press <Enter>.

Task 3 - Create a box section.

1. Open the saved viewpoint **Exterior for Sectioning**.

2. In the *Viewpoint* tab>Section panel, click (Enable Sectioning).

3. In the *Sectioning Tools* tab>Mode panel, select (Box).

4. In the Selection Tree window, select **Elementary-School-Architectural.rvt**.

5. In the *Sectioning Tools* tab>Transform panel, click ⋈ (Fit Selection). The section box is created up close to the building, as shown in Figure 3–28.

Figure 3–28

6. Press <Esc> to release the selection.

7. In the *Sectioning Tools* tab>Transform panel, click ☐ (Scale).

8. Click and drag the z-axis (blue arrow) on the gizmo to position the section so that the building roof and slab below are cut off, as shown in Figure 3–29.

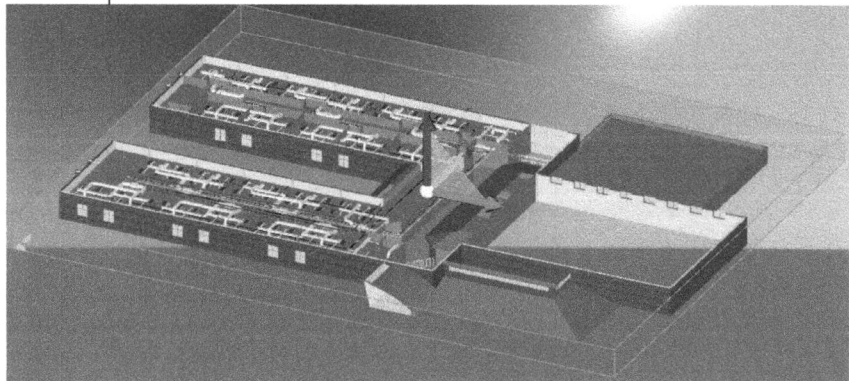

Figure 3–29

9. Save the viewpoint as **Section-Ductwork**.

10. Save the model.

3.3 Setting View Options

Controlling how a scene displays can helps you see more clearly how things work together. You can change the way the view is rendered, and toggle the display of structural grids.

Render Style Modes

Each scene view has a render style which specifies the shading of the building model, such as the example shown in Figure 3–30 for a hot tub in a pool house in Full Render mode.

Figure 3–30

The **Render Style** options are found in the *Viewpoint* tab>Render Style panel. These options apply to all types of views. For example, when the Render style is set to Full Render, you can see shadows, texture, reflections, and more. The list below describes each type of render style mode available.

- (Full Render): Displays the materials and textures of items, including lights, reflections, and shadows. This is the default view type.

- (Hidden Line): Displays the lines, edges, and surfaces of the elements, but it does not display any colors.

- (Wireframe): Displays the lines and edges of elements, but hides the surfaces. This can be useful when you are dealing with complex intersections.

- ⬜ **(Shaded):** Displays the surface color but not the textures of materials, as shown for the same hot tub and pool house scene in Figure 3–31.

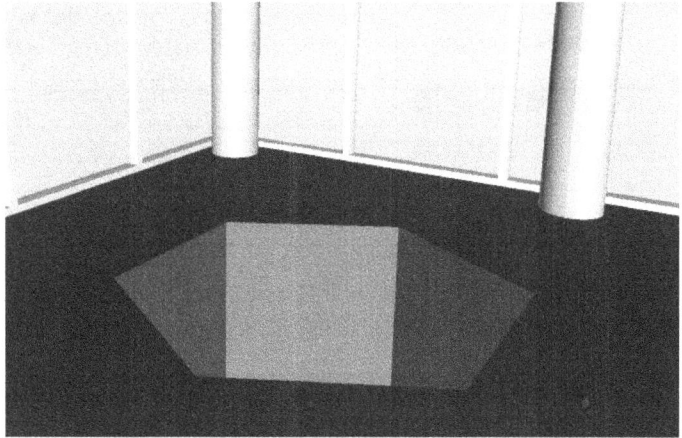

Figure 3–31

Photo-realistic scenes can be created using the Autodesk Rendering system.

Hint: Lighting Modes

You can control how a 3D scene is lit using one of the following lighting modes:

- **Full Lights:** Lights defined by the Autodesk Rendering tool.

- **Scene Lights:** Lights defined by the native CAD file. If the original file did not include lights, the light is defined by two default opposing lights.

- **Head Light:** Single directional light positioned at the same location as the camera and pointing in the same direction as the camera.

- **No Lights:** All lights are switched off, leaving the scene shaded with flat rendering.

Displaying Grids

Autodesk Revit grids are available for display in the Autodesk Navisworks software, as shown in Figure 3–32. When working in a large project or when identifying a specific area, toggling on grids can help you describe feature locations in the model.

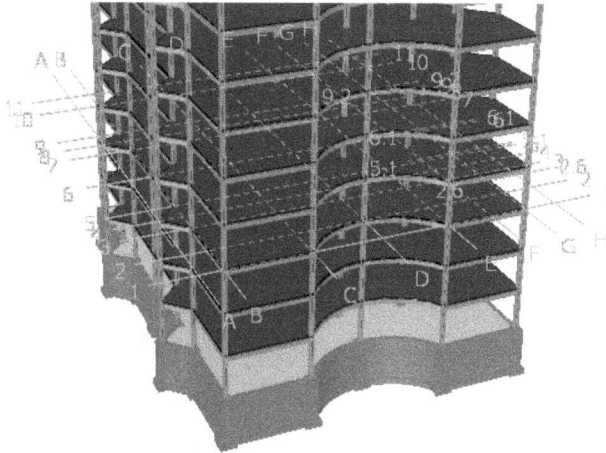

Figure 3–32

If a grid was not included in one of the Autodesk Revit models, the Show Grid tool is grayed out because it is unavailable.

- In the *View* tab>Grids & Levels panel, click ⊞ (Show Grid).

- If you have multiple files, the ▭ (Active Grid) drop-down list enables you to specify the model whose grid you want to use.

- Grid Modes control the display of the grids in relation to the current camera position:

  - ▧ **(Above and Below):** Displays red grids above and green grids below.

  - ▽ **(Above):** Displays only red grids.

  - ◿ **(Below):** Displays only green grids.

  - ▤ **(All):** Displays red and green grids, as well as halftone images of all of the other grid locations.

  - ▣ **(Fixed):** Displays grids at the level specified in the drop-down list for the ◑ (Display Level). It does not change the location of the grid as you orbit around the model.

3.4 Setting up Appearances

From time to time, an object might display in its wireframe color. This is because the material or texture for the object that was imported from the original model is unsupported. When this happens, you might have to override an object's appearance. You can do this in two ways:

- Individually

- Globally

How To: Override Appearances Individually

1. In the model, click on the objects that need to be changed to select them.
2. In the *Item Tools* contextual tab>Appearance panel, expand

    ☐ ▾ (Color) and select a color square, as shown in Figure 3–33.

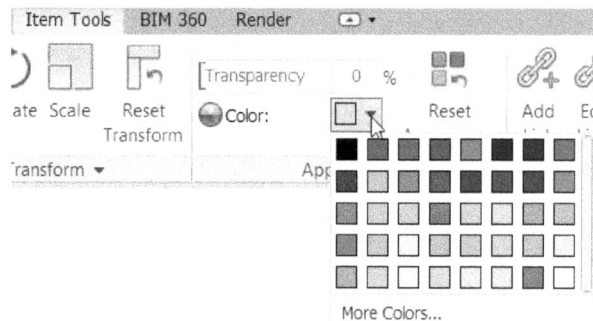

Figure 3–33

3. In the *Item Tools* contextual tab>Appearance panel, click and drag the *Transparency slider* to make the object more or less opaque, as required.
4. If the changes did not have the required results, or if you need to revert back to the original color or transparency, in

    the *Item Tools* contextual tab>Appearance panel, click ▨↩ (Reset Appearance).
5. Press <Esc> to clear the selection and view the changes.

Modify Appearances Globally

Materials can be edited in all new viewpoints globally. You can do this in the Options Editor dialog box.

How To: Override Appearances Globally

1. Expand ▣▼ (Application Menu) and select **Options**.
2. In the Options Editor dialog box, do the following, as shown in Figure 3–34:
   - In the left pane, expand *Interface* and select **Viewpoint Defaults**.
   - In the right pane, select **Override Appearance**.
   - Click **OK**.

Defaults affect all new Viewpoints.

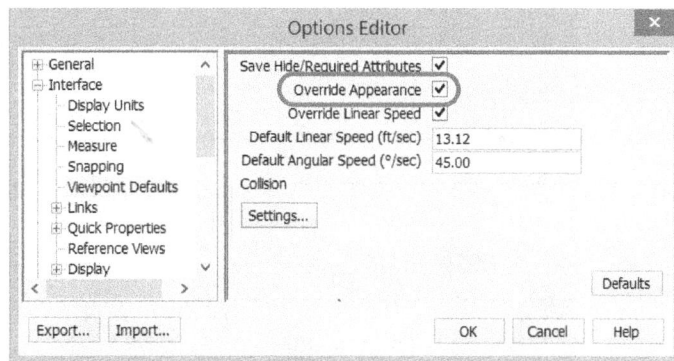

Figure 3–34

3. In the Scene View, select the objects that need a material override.
4. In the *Item Tools* contextual tab>Appearance panel, expand

   ▢▼ (Color) and select a color square.
5. In the *Item Tools* contextual tab>Appearance panel, click and drag the *Transparency slider* to make the object more or less opaque.
6. Press <Esc> to clear the selection and view the changes.
7. In the Saved Viewpoints window, right-click on the viewpoint that you want to set to appearance override and select **Update**.

Practice 3c

Set Up the Display

Practice Objectives

- Display a grid to help communicate where something is in the model.
- Set up appearances.

Estimated time for completion: 10 minutes

In this practice you will turn on the grid that was imported with the Autodesk Revit model and change the display appearances for the site and the AC unit, as shown in Figure 3–35.

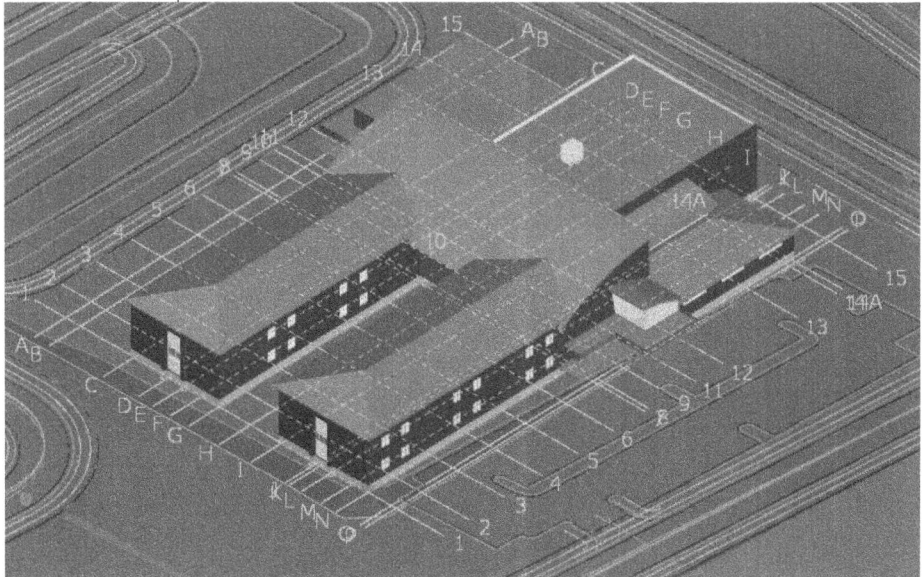

Figure 3–35

Task 1 - Display a grid.

1. In the *Review* practice files folder, open the file **NewElementarySchool-Appearances.nwf**. In the Saved Viewpoints window, expand the *Exterior* folder and click **Site Isometric Close-up**.

2. In the *View* tab>Grids & Levels panel, click (Show Grid) to toggle it on and off a couple times. Note how the grid displays in the model. With the grid toggled on, continue to the next step.

3. Open another exterior viewpoint. Note that the grid displays in this view as well. Displaying the grid is a toggle and is not impacted by the saved viewpoints.

4. In the Selection Tree, select the **Site Layout.dwg** model. Note that the grids are easier to see against the dark blue of the selection color.

5. Orbit around the model and zoom in on the intersection of Grid A and Grid 14. Your display should be similar to that shown in Figure 3–36.

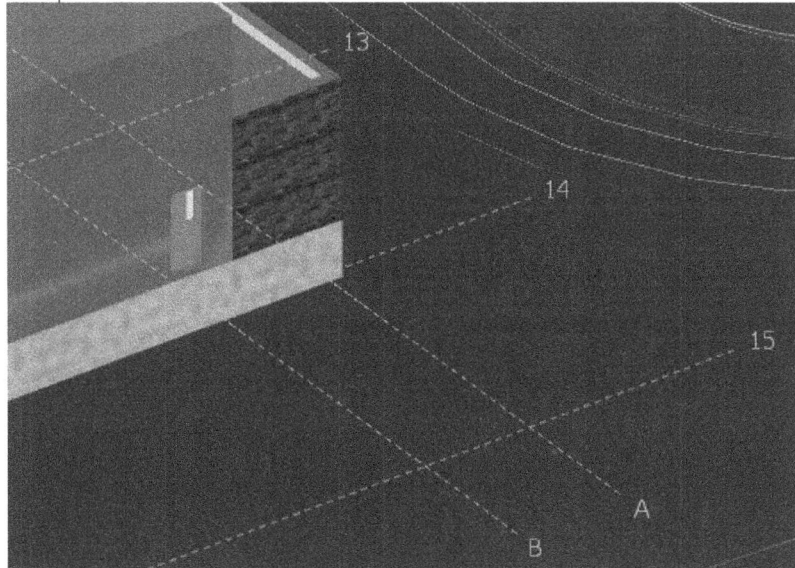

Figure 3–36

Task 2 - Change appearances.

1. With the site model still selected, in the *Item Tools* contextual tab>Appearance panel, expand □ ▼ (Color) and select the dark green color shown in Figure 3–37.

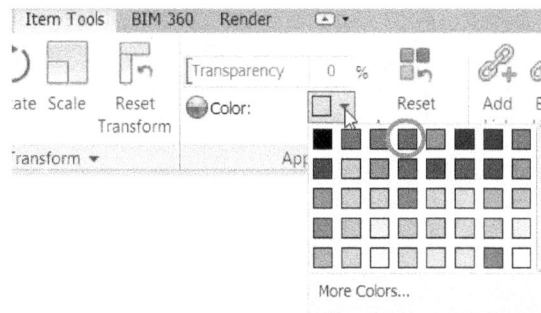

Figure 3–37

2. Press <Esc> to clear the selection and view the changes. Note that the site now displays in dark green.

3. Select the site again.

4. In the *Item Tools* contextual tab>Appearance panel, click and drag the *Transparency slider* to **80%** to make the surface more transparent

5. Press <Esc> to clear the selection and view the changes.

6. Open the saved viewpoint **Section-AC Unit** .

7. In the *Home* tab>Select & Search panel, expand ⌖ (Select) and click ⌗ (Select Box).

8. Drag a selection window around the AC Unit on top of the roof to select it, as shown in Figure 3–38.

Figure 3–38

9. In the *Item Tools* contextual tab>Appearance panel, expand ▢▾ (Color) and select the Cyan square shown in Figure 3–39.

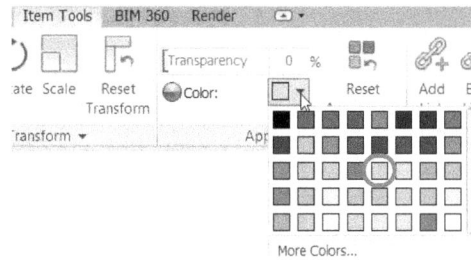

Figure 3–39

10. Press <Esc> to clear the selection of the AC unit. Note that it now displays in the cyan color.

11. Open the saved viewpoint **Exterior>Site Isometric Close-up**.

12. Zoom in on the AC unit.

13. Note that some of the unit is still gray, as shown in Figure 3–40. Use the Select Box tool and draw a window around the entire unit.

14. In the *Item Tools* tab>Appearance panel, select a different color. Press <Esc> and the full AC unit displays in the new color, as shown in Figure 3–41.

Figure 3–40

Figure 3–41

15. In the *View* tab>Grids & Levels panel, toggle off ⊞ (Show Grid).

16. Save the file.

Chapter Review Questions

1. Which of the following can be edited for a saved Viewpoint? (Select all that apply)

   a. Position of the camera

   b. Focus point of the camera

   c. Sun settings

   d. Section planes

2. Viewpoints can be automatically arranged alphanumerically.

   a. True

   b. False

3. When creating a section with the Box option, how many section planes are cut at one time?

   a. 1

   b. 2

   c. 4

   d. 6

4. Which render style mode includes the materials and textures of items, including lights, reflections, and shadows?

   a. Full Render

   b. Hidden Line

   c. Wireframe

   d. Shaded

5. How do you create a grid in a scene to help you to describe where something is in the model?

   a. *Home* tab>Visibility panel.

   b. *Viewpoint* tab>Navigate panel.

   c. You cannot create a grid in the Autodesk Navisworks software. It must be included in the original Autodesk Revit model.

   d. *View* tab>Grids & Levels panel.

6. Why would an object display in its wireframe color?

   a. The Render Style Mode is set wrong for the scene.

   b. The material or texture for the object that was imported from the original model is unsupported.

   c. The lighting mode is set wrong for the scene.

   d. Objects do not display in wireframe in the Autodesk Navisworks software.

Command Summary

Button	Command	Location
Viewpoints		
N/A	**Add Animation**	• **Right-Click:** in the Saved Viewpoints Window>**Save Viewpoint**
▷	**Animation Tools**	• **Ribbon:** *Viewpoint* tab>Save, Load & Playback panel
🖉	**Edit Current Viewpoint**	• **Ribbon:** *Viewpoint* tab>Save, Load & Playback panel
📷	**Save Viewpoint**	• **Ribbon:** *Viewpoint* tab>Save, Load & Playback panel • **Right-Click:** in the Saved Viewpoints Window>**Save Viewpoint**
↘	**Saved Viewpoints Dialog Launcher**	• **Ribbon:** *Viewpoint* tab>Save, Load & Playback panel title
Sectioning		
⬚	**Box**	• **Ribbon:** *Sectioning Tools* tab>Mode panel
⬚	**Enable Sectioning**	• **Ribbon:** *Viewpoint* tab>Sectioning panel
⋈	**Fit Selection**	• **Ribbon:** *Sectioning Tools* tab>Transform panel
✥	**Move**	• **Ribbon:** *Sectioning Tools* tab>Transform panel
⬚	**Planes**	• **Ribbon:** *Sectioning Tools* tab>Mode panel
↻	**Rotate**	• **Ribbon:** *Sectioning Tools* tab>Transform panel
⬚	**Scale**	• **Ribbon:** *Sectioning Tools* tab>Transform panel
Other Viewing Tools		
⬚	**Full Render**	• **Ribbon:** *Views* tab>Render Style panel> expand Mode
⬚	**Hidden Line**	• **Ribbon:** *Views* tab>Render Style panel> expand Mode
⬚	**Reference View**	• **Ribbon:** *Views* tab>Navigation Aids panel

	Shaded	• **Ribbon:** *Views* tab>Render Style panel> expand Mode
	Show Grid	• **Ribbon:** *Views* tab>Grids & Levels panel
	Wireframe	• **Ribbon:** *Views* tab>Render Style panel> expand Mode

Analyze Models

When you review a BIM model, you should also analyze the model at the same time. Performing a model analysis helps stakeholders predict the project outcome and reduce the number of RFIs (Requests for Information) and changes that are required during construction. In this chapter, you will learn how to select features to investigate their properties and save selection sets. Then you will learn how to hide features to gain a clearer view of specific parts of the model.

Learning Objectives in this Chapter

- Select items in a model to evaluate their properties.
- Drill down into the content of a model using the Selection Tree.
- Save selections so that they can be retrieved later.
- Find items by using the selection filtering options.
- Hide items so that they are not obstructing your view.
- Unhide items when they need to be viewed again.

BIM Workflow: Analyze

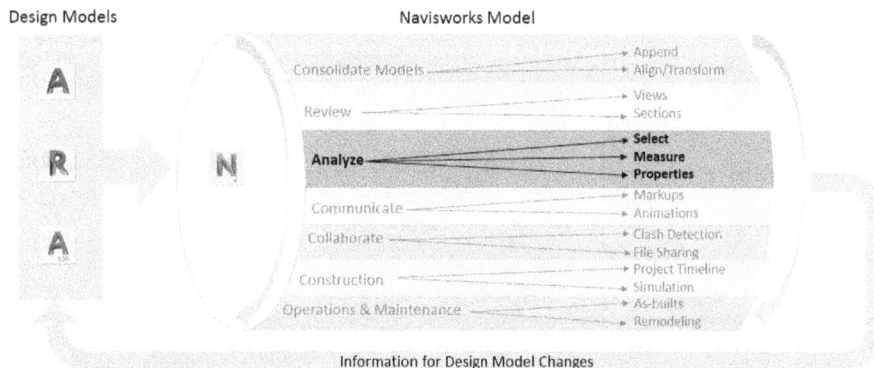

Design Models   Navisworks Model

Consolidate Models — Append, Align/Transform

Views, Sections

Review —

Analyze — **Select, Measure, Properties**

Markups, Animations

Communicate —

Collaborate — Clash Detection, File Sharing, Project Timeline

Construction — Simulation, As-builts

Operations & Maintenance — Remodeling

Information for Design Model Changes

4.1 Selecting Items

A powerful part of using the Autodesk® Navisworks® software is selecting items and then discovering more about them, as shown in Figure 4–1. Selections can be grouped into sets that enable you to modify their visibility and reselect them when they are needed again.

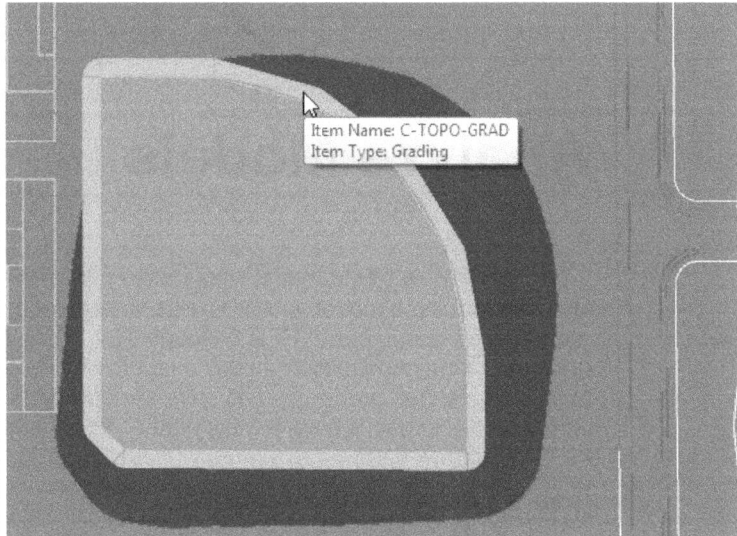

Figure 4–1

The ⬈ (Select) tool is available in multiple locations, including the Quick Access Toolbar, the Navigation Bar, and the ribbon in the *Home* tab>Select & Search panel, as shown in Figure 4–2.

Figure 4–2

Additional options to select features are as follows:

- Press <Ctrl>+<1> to toggle on the ⬈ (Select) tool.

- Hold <Ctrl> while selecting to add items to a selection.

- ⬚ (Select Box) enables you to draw a window around groups of items. Only items that are totally inside the box are selected. Expand the **Select** tool for access.

- ⬚ (Select All) selects everything in a project.

- ⬚ (Select None) clears the selection. You can also press <Esc> to do this. Expand the **Select All** tool for access.

- ⬚ (Invert Selection) switches the selection to everything that was not previously selected. Expand the **Select All** tool for access.

- With at least one items selected, the ⬚ (Select Same) tool adds other similar items to the selection set. You can chose from a list of categories that match the selected item, as shown in Figure 4–3.

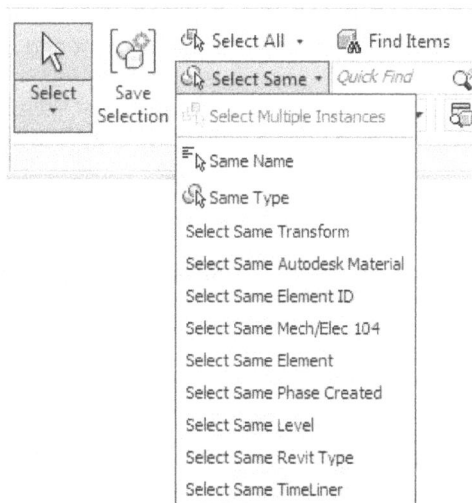

Figure 4–3

- When multiple items are selected, the list displays only the overlapping properties, such as **Same Name** and **Same Type**.

Selection Sets

If you need to select the same group of features frequently, you can save them as a selection set.

How To: Save Selections

1. Select the items you want to save in a selection set.
2. In the *Home* tab>Select & Search panel, click ⌗ (Save Selection).
3. The Sets window displays with the new selection set, as shown in Figure 4–4. Type in a name for the selection set.

Figure 4–4

Using Saved Selections

- In the *Home* tab>Select & Search panel, expand the **Sets** drop-down list and select a set.

- To display the Sets window, expand the Sets drop-down list and select **Manage Sets**.

- The Sets window can be docked and set to auto-hide, similar to other windows.

- Several options are available in the Sets window:

  - ⌗ **(Save Selection):** Saves the current selection.

  - 🔍 **(Save Search):** Saves a search selection you made.

  - 📁 **(New Folder):** Adds a folder that you can name and use to organize sets.

  - **(Duplicate):** Duplicates an existing set

  - 💬 **(Add Comment):** Opens the Add Comment dialog box, where you can type in information about the set.

  - ⬇ **(Sort):** Organizes the sets into alphabetical order.

  - **(Import/Export):** Enables you to import and export selection sets.

4.2 Investigating Properties

Selecting items enables you to review and add information to item properties. These properties include basic information, such as the *Item Name* and *Item Type,* as shown using the Quick Properties in Figure 4–5. The full list of properties is displayed in the Properties window.

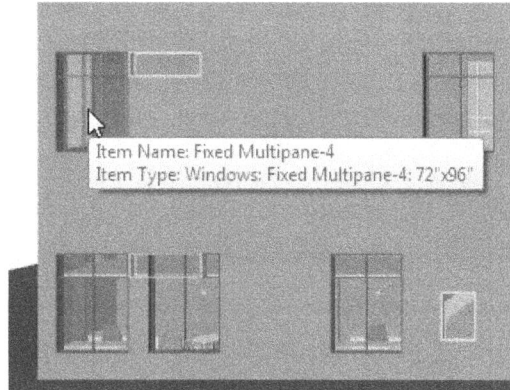

Item Name: Fixed Multipane-4
Item Type: Windows: Fixed Multipane-4: 72"x96"

Figure 4–5

* To toggle the display tools on or off, in the *Home* tab>Display

    panel, click ⬚ (Quick Properties) or ⬚ (Properties) .

Viewing Properties

In the Properties window, you can investigate the full range of properties for a selected item. They are divided by categories accessed through a series of tabs, as shown in Figure 4–6.

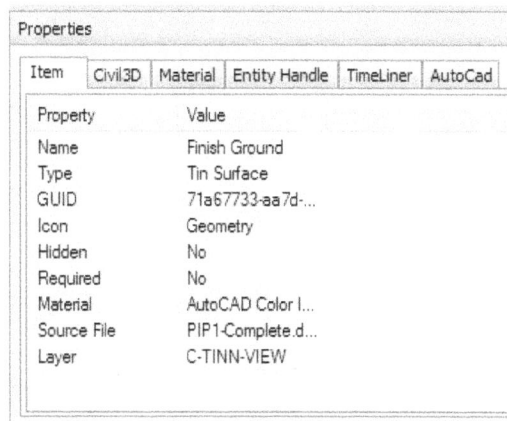

Properties

| Item | Civil3D | Material | Entity Handle | TimeLiner | AutoCad |

Property	Value
Name	Finish Ground
Type	Tin Surface
GUID	71a67733-aa7d-...
Icon	Geometry
Hidden	No
Required	No
Material	AutoCAD Color I...
Source File	PIP1-Complete.d...
Layer	C-TINN-VIEW

Figure 4–6

Depending on the authoring software of the original file, there could potentially be many properties. For example, an item from the AutoCAD® Civil 3D® software might only have a few categories (as shown in Figure 4–6), while an Autodesk® Revit® model might have more, as shown in Figure 4–7.

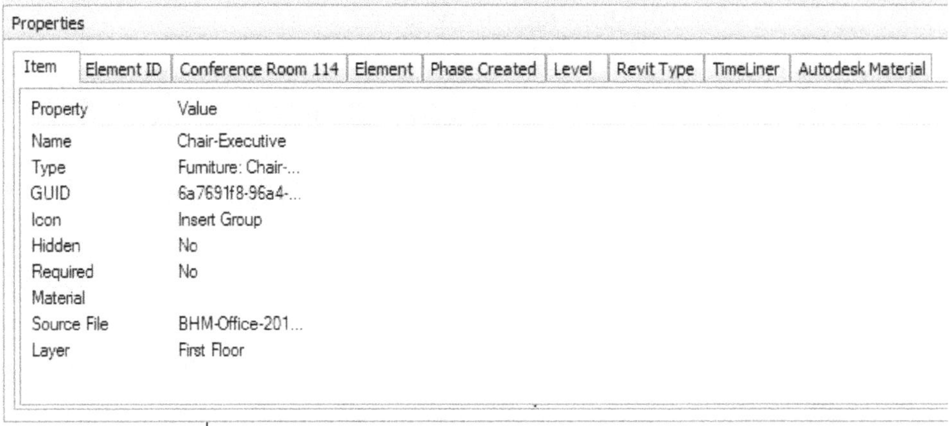

Properties								
Item	Element ID	Conference Room 114	Element	Phase Created	Level	Revit Type	TimeLiner	Autodesk Material

Property	Value
Name	Chair-Executive
Type	Furniture: Chair-...
GUID	6a7691f8-96a4-...
Icon	Insert Group
Hidden	No
Required	No
Material	
Source File	BHM-Office-201...
Layer	First Floor

Figure 4–7

- Autodesk Revit items, such as walls, might have many more tabs, especially if rooms or spaces are assigned to the model.

Hint: How to Create User Data

1. Right-click in the Properties dialog box and select **Add New User Data Tab**.
2. Select the new tab, right-click and select **Rename Tab** to type in a new name.
3. Right-click on the tab again, expand **Insert New Property**, and then select the type of data you want to add, as shown in Figure 4–8. The data types are as follows:
   - **String:** Alphanumeric characters
   - **Boolean:** Either Yes or No
   - **Float:** Decimal-based numbers
   - **Integer:** Numbers without any decimal

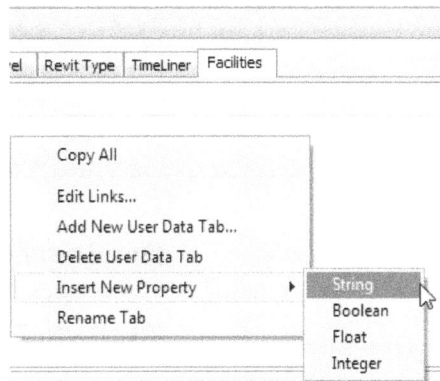

Figure 4–8

4. Once you have the new property in place, you can add a value. Select the property you want to modify and select **Edit Property Value**.
5. In the Edit Property Value dialog box, add the required information and then click **OK**.

- If you set up a Boolean option, you are prompted to select either Yes or No, as shown in Figure 4–9

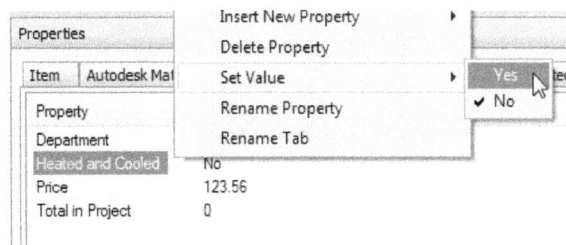

Figure 4–9

Selection Inspector

To view the properties of more than one element you need to use the Selection Inspector. In the *Home* tab>Select & Search panel, click ⧉ (Selection Inspector). By default, Selection Inspector displays the same information as Quick Properties, as shown in Figure 4–10

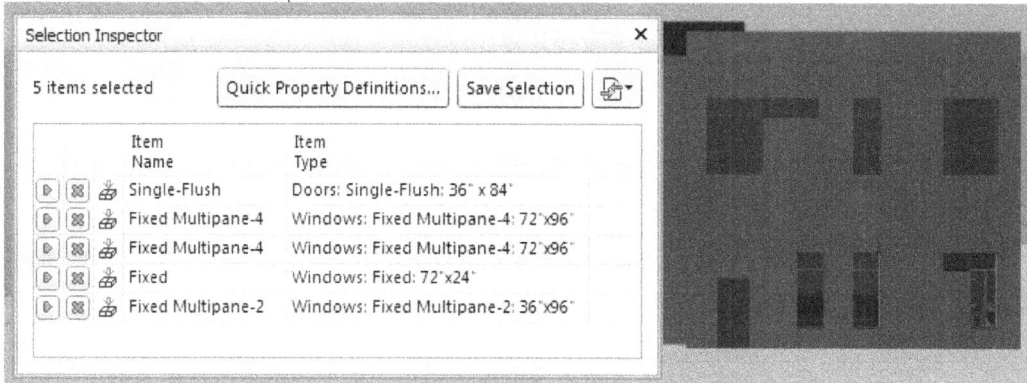

Figure 4–10

- ▷ **(Show Item):** Zooms in on the selected item in the view.

- ⊠ **(Deselect):** Removes the item from the selection set.

- The next icon varies according to the item type, such as group, composite object, or surface:
  - **Quick Property Definitions:** Enables you to add other properties to the list.
  - **Save Selection:** Adds a list to a set.

- ⧉▾ **(Export):** sends the information from the window to a .CSV file.

Practice 4a

Select and Investigate Items

Practice Objectives

- Select objects in the model.
- Save selection sets.
- Review object properties.

Estimated time for completion: 5 minutes

In this practice you will select objects in the model and create selection sets, as shown in Figure 4–11. You will then review the properties of selected items.

Figure 4–11

Task 1 - Use selection tools to select model features.

1. In the *Analyze* practice files folder, open **NewElementarySchool-Select.nwf**.

2. In the Saved Viewpoints window, click **NE-View**.

3. In the *Home* tab>Select & Search panel, click (Select).

Hold <Ctrl> to be able to select more than one rooftop.

4. In the Scene view, select the rooftops shown in Figure 4–12.

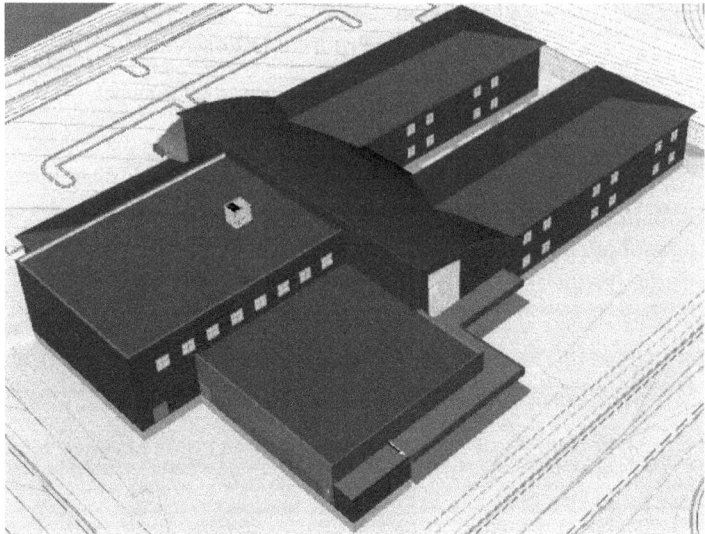

Figure 4–12

5. In the *Home* tab>Select & Search panel, click [⬚] (Save Selection). Type **Roofs** for the name.

6. In the *Home* tab>Select & Search panel, expand ⬚ (Select All) and click ⬚ (Select None) to clear the selection of the roof tops.

7. Use the **Select Box** tool to select the AC unit.

8. Save the selection as **AC Unit**.

Task 2 - Investigate model feature properties.

---

1. In the *Home* tab>Select & Search panel, expand the Sets drop-down list and select **Roofs**.

2. In the *Home* tab>Display panel, click ⬚ (Quick Properties) and ⬚ (Properties) to toggle the tools on, if required.

3. Hover the cursor over one of the roofs to display the Quick Properties for the entire selection set, as shown in Figure 4–13.

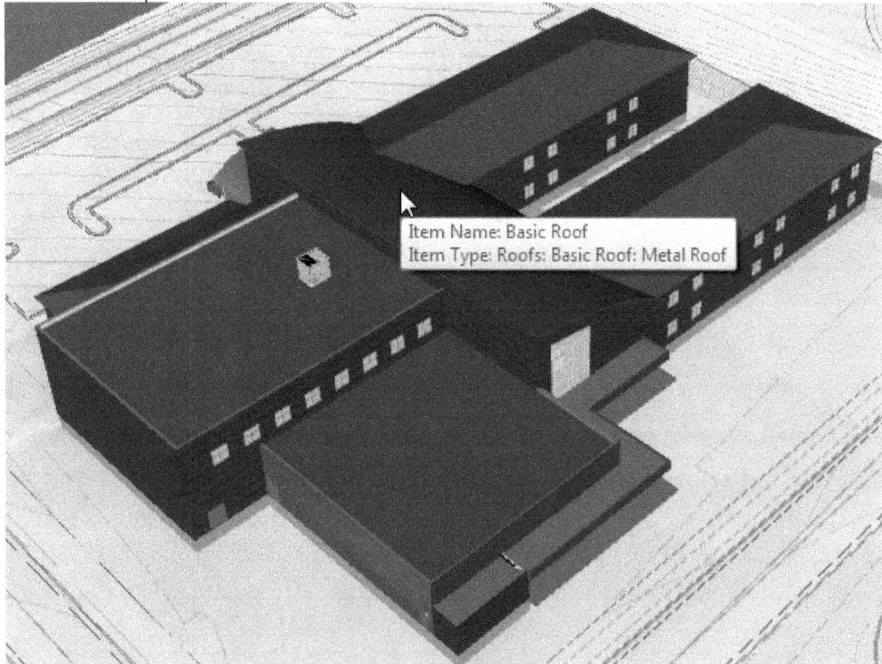

Figure 4–13

4. Expand the Properties window (which might be docked on the right-side of the window) and note that no properties are displayed. This is because more than one item is selected.

5. In the *Home* tab>Select & Search panel, click 🔲 (Selection Inspector).

6. In the Selection Inspector window, click ▷ (Show Item) next to each of the items in the list to zoom in on the selected item in the view.

7. In the Selection Inspector window, beside each of the

Generic - 12" roofs, click ⊠ (Deselect) to remove the items from the selection set, as shown in Figure 4–14.

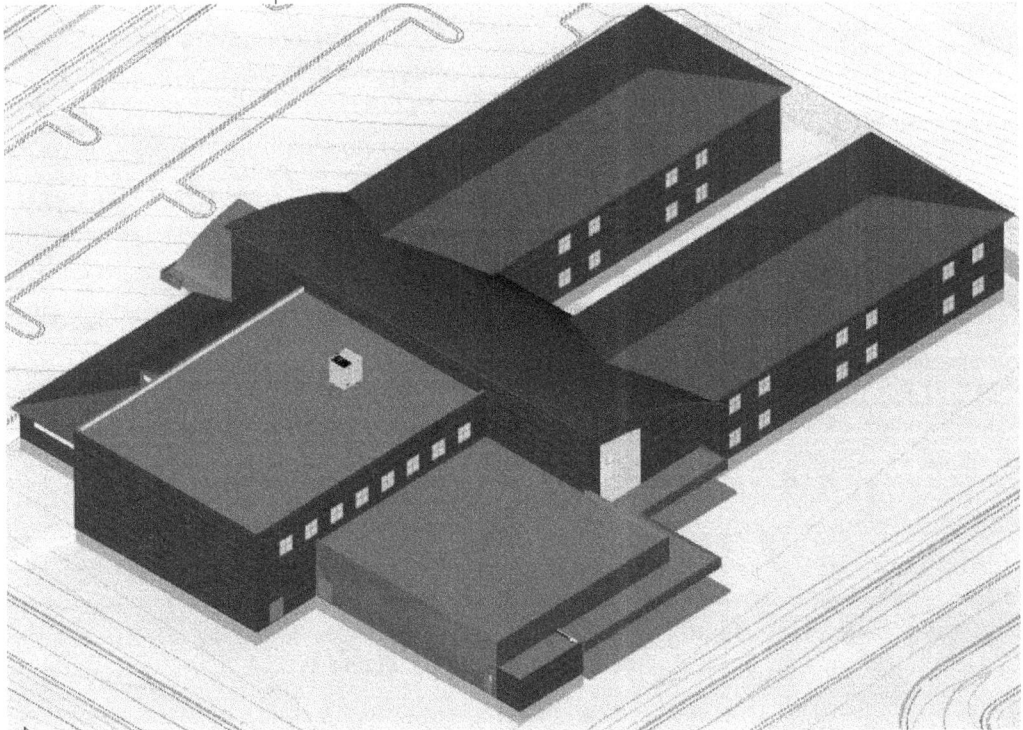

Figure 4–14

8. In the Selection Inspector window, click **Save Selection** and name the set **Metal Roofs**.

9. Close the Selection Inspector window.

10. Press <Esc> or, in the *Home* tab>Select & Search panel,

click ⌖ (Select None) to clear the selection of the rooftops.

11. In the *Home* tab>Select & Search panel, expand ⌐ (Select

Box) and click ⌖ (Select).

12. In the Scene View, click on the terrain surface surrounding the building. Then expand the Properties window to review the surface properties, as shown in Figure 4–15. Review each of the available tabs in the Properties window to review all of the surface properties.

Figure 4–15

13. Press <Esc> to clear the surface selection.

14. In the *Home* tab>Select & Search panel, click (Select). In the model, select any one of the visible windows.

15. In the *Home* tab>Select & Search panel, click (Select Same) and select **Same Type** from the list.

16. Save the selection as **All Windows**.

17. Save the model.

4.3 Using the Selection Tree

The selection tree can be used to select very specific information in the model, right down to the material if required. The selection tree includes all of the models in the project and all of the geometry in every model, as shown in Figure 4–16.

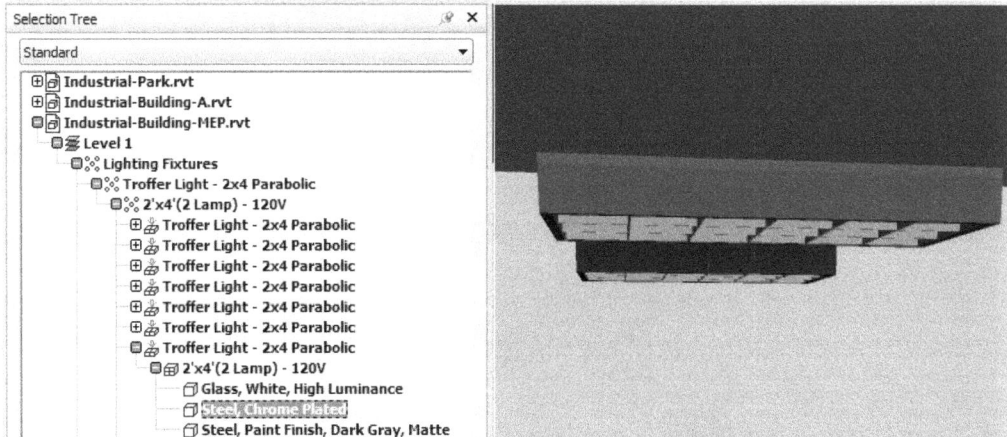

Figure 4–16

When you select items in the model, they display in the Selection Tree. Similarly, if you select items in the Selection Tree, they highlight in the model.

- In the *Home* tab>Select & Search panel, click 🗐 (Selection Tree) or press <Ctrl>+<F12>.

- The Selection Tree is a window, and can therefore be docked and set to auto-hide.

- In the Selection Tree, hold <Ctrl> or <Shift> to select multiple items.

- To zoom in on a selected item, right-click on it in the Selection Tree and then select **Focus on Item**.

- You can save selections when they are highlighted in the Selection Tree. In the *Home* tab>Select & Search panel, click ⌾ (Save Selection).

- Press <Esc> to remove items from the selection set.

Selection Resolution

You can select items at the various levels of the hierarchy shown in the Selection Tree by setting the Selection Resolution. In the *Home* tab, expand the Select & Search panel title to display the drop-down list shown in Figure 4–17, or right-click on an item in the Selection Tree to select from the menu.

To cycle through selection options, hold <Shift> and click on an item to cycle through the resolutions. It helps to have the Selection Tree open to see how this works.

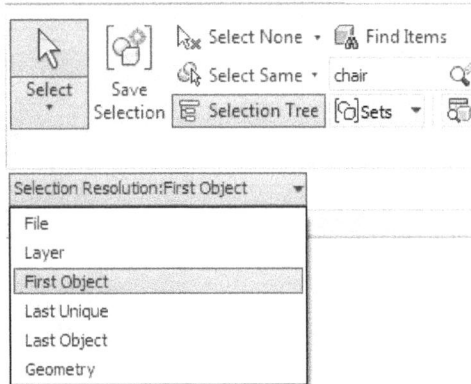

Figure 4–17

Selection Resolution Options

The Selection Resolution options (shown in Figure 4–18) are as follows:

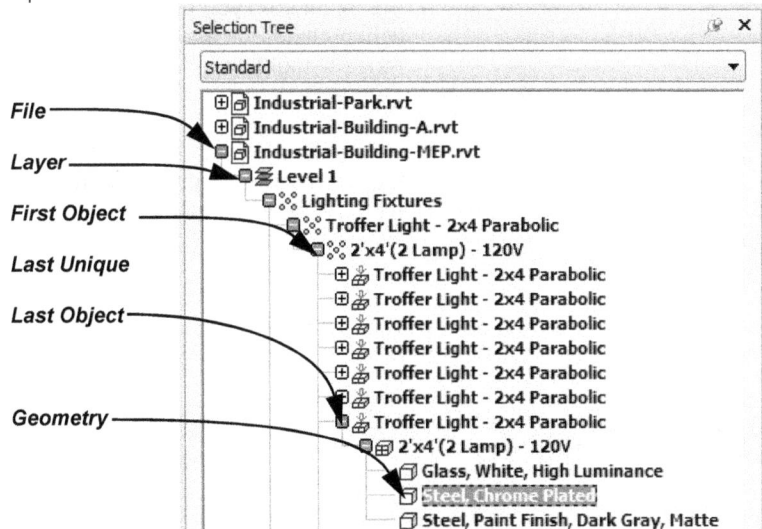

Figure 4–18

- **File:** Selects all of the elements in a file.

- **Layer:** Selects all of the elements on a specific layer. For the example shown in Figure 4–19, selecting the door on the first floor selects all of the other elements on that layer, in this case the windows and those items you can see such as the first floor interior walls.

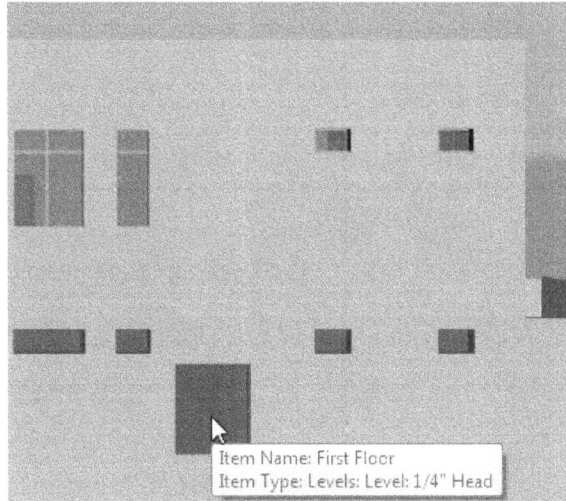

Item Name: First Floor
Item Type: Levels: Level: 1/4" Head

Figure 4–19

- **First Object, Last Object** and **Last Unique** are based on their location below the level, but typically each option selects the exact item you pick, such as a specific wall, column, or lighting fixture in an Autodesk Revit model. AutoCAD-based models might be different because of the underlying geometry.

- **Geometry:** Selects the base geometry of the item, such as the material of a lighting fixture, or a line, polyline, or arc element in an AutoCAD project.

Hint: Selection Options

There are several options that can help you be more precise in selecting and viewing items. These are found in the Options Editor in the **Interface>Selection** pane, as shown in Figure 4–20

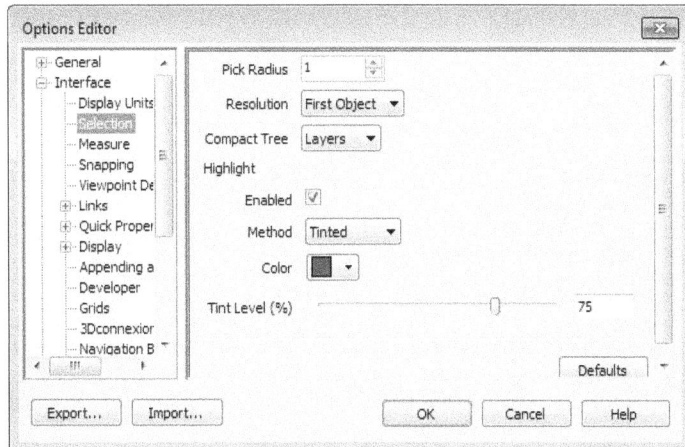

Figure 4–20

- **Pick Radius:** Sets the size (in pixels) of the point where you click the cursor to select an element.

- **Resolution:** Establishes the default pick order.

- **Compact Tree:** Establishes the default presentation of the Selection Tree.

- **Highlight:** Sets the method (Tinted, Shaded, Wireframe) and color of selected items.

Setting the Viewing Order

The Selection Tree can be very complex, depending on the number of models included in the project and the number of items within each model. There are at least three ways to view the information, as shown in Figure 4–21.

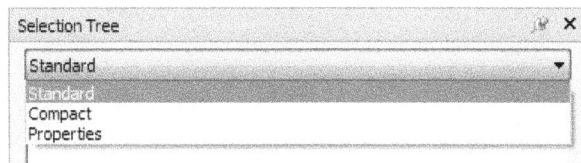

Figure 4–21

- **Standard:** Displays all of the nodes from *File* to *Geometry*.

- **Compact:** Displays only the nodes for *File* and *Layers*

- **Properties:** Displays all of the properties of every item in the model by category. For example, in an Autodesk Revit model, each room is considered a category, and you can find properties such as the Area of the room. When you select the room, all of the related items (such as the exterior wall and windows) are selected, as shown in Figure 4–22.

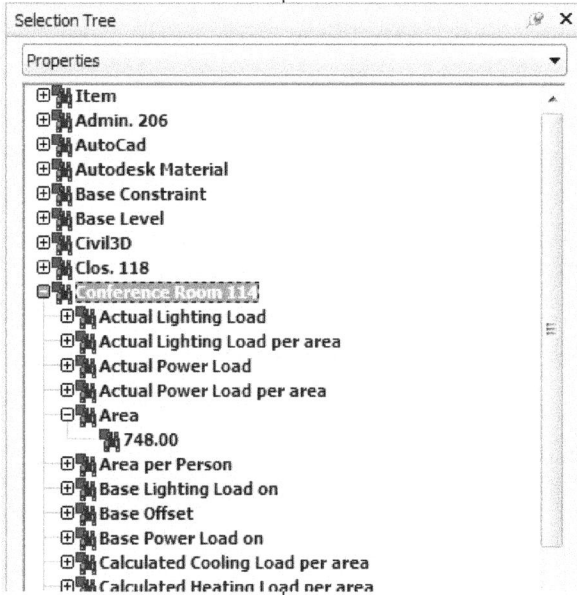

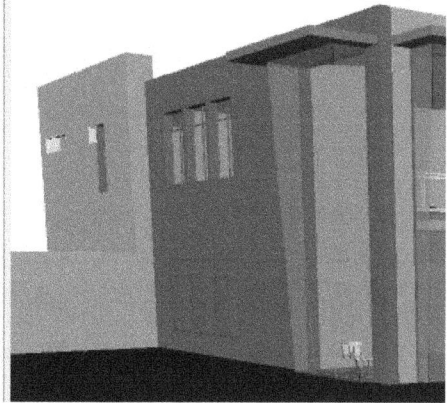

Figure 4–22

- **Sets**: Only available when you have saved selections in the project, and displays those sets.

Practice 4b

Use the Selection Tree

Practice Objectives

- Change the Selection Resolution.
- Use the Selection Tree to familiarize yourself with the model.

Estimated time for completion: 5 minutes

In this practice you will become more familiar with the model shown in Figure 4–23 by using the selection tree to select features and focus on them. You will also change the selection resolution to make selecting individual items much easier.

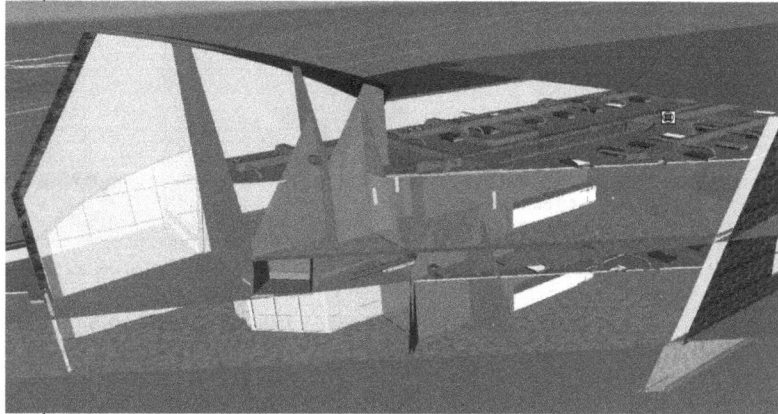

Figure 4–23

Task 1 - Change the Selection Resolution.

1. In the *Analyze* practice files folder, open **NewElementarySchool-Tree.nwf**.

2. In the Saved Viewpoints window, click **NE-View**.

3. In the *Home* tab>Select & Search panel, ensure that ⌖ (Select) is active.

4. Pin the Selection Tree open.

5. In the Scene View, click on the lower flat roof, as shown in Figure 4–24. Only that one roof should be selected.

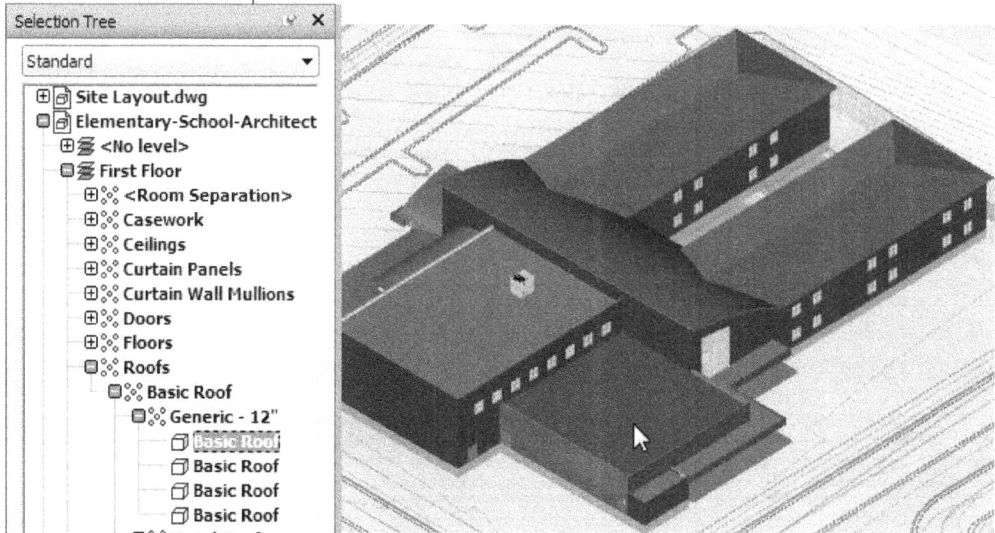

Selection Tree

Standard

⊞ Site Layout.dwg
⊟ Elementary-School-Architect
  ⊞ <No level>
  ⊟ First Floor
    ⊞ <Room Separation>
    ⊞ Casework
    ⊞ Ceilings
    ⊞ Curtain Panels
    ⊞ Curtain Wall Mullions
    ⊞ Doors
    ⊞ Floors
    ⊟ Roofs
      ⊟ Basic Roof
        ⊟ Generic - 12"
          Basic Roof
          Basic Roof
          Basic Roof
          Basic Roof

Figure 4–24

6. Click away from any elements or press <Esc> to clear the selection.

7. In the Home tab, expand the Select & Search panel title.

8. Expand the Selection Resolution drop-down list and note which method is selected.

9. Change Selection Resolution to **File**.

10. Select the same roof again and note how the entire building is now selected.

11. Clear the selection, change the *Selection Resolution* to **Layer**, and then reselect the same roof. Note that only the first floor elements are selected, as shown in Figure 4–25.

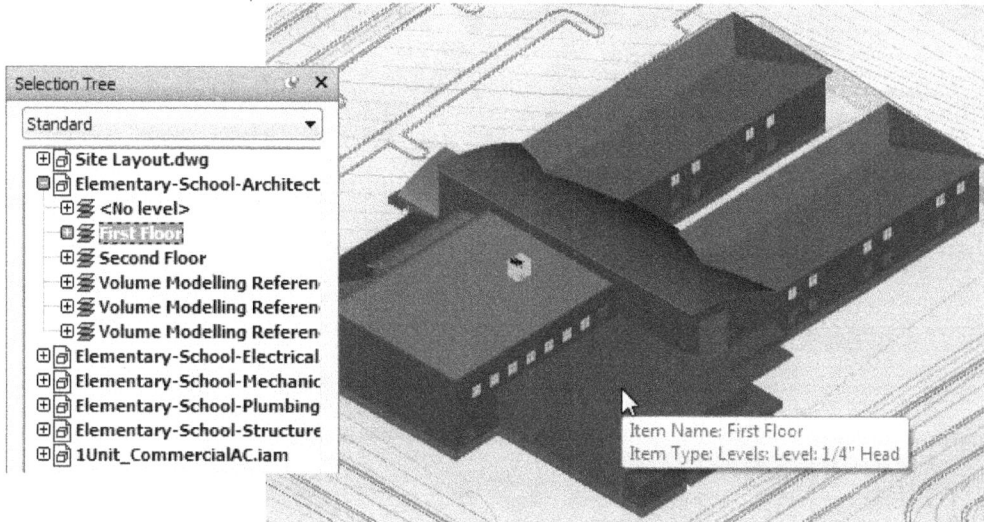

Figure 4–25

12. Once you have tested all of the selection resolution methods, reset the resolution to **First Object**.

13. Unpin the Selection Tree.

14. Save the file.

Task 2 - Fix a selection set.

---

1. In the *Home* tab>Select & Search panel, expand the Sets drop-down list and select **AC Unit**.

2. Hover the cursor over the Selection Tree. Note that some but not all of the elements in the AC Unit are selected, as shown in Figure 4–26. Also note that other elements that are not in the AC unit file were also selected. This occurs because the set was created using the Select Box tool.

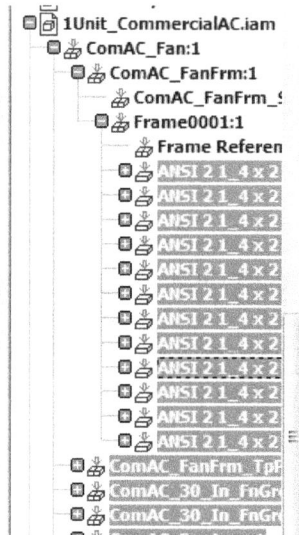

Figure 4–26

3. In the Selection Tree, select **1Unit_Commercial AC.iam** (the top level node).

4. In the Sets window, right-click on **AC Unit** and then select **Update**.

Task 3 - Use the Selection Tree to select objects.

---

1. In the Selection Tree, expand **Elementary-School-Architectural.rvt>First Floor** and select **Doors**. Note what is selected in the Scene View .

2. Now expand **Doors** and select **Double Door**. Right-click and select **Focus on Item**.

3. In the Selection Tree, still in the **Doors** node, select **SINGLE**, right-click and select **Focus on Item**.

4. Select **Curtain Wall Sgl Glass**, right-click and select **Focus on Item**.

Note that the Scene is panned to center the curtain wall in the view.

5. With the **Curtain Wall Sgl Glass** item still selected, right-click and select **Selection Inspector** to make it visible.

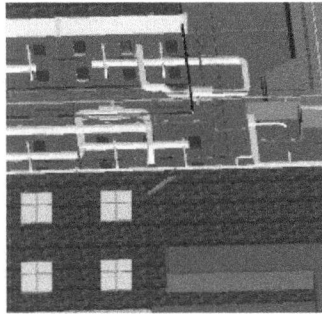

6. In the Selection Inspector window, click ▷ (Show Item) next to **Curtain Wall Sgl Glass**. Note that the view zooms in and centers on the curtain wall, but that there is a brick wall in front of the window blocking your view.

7. Close the Selection Inspector window.

8. In the Saved Viewpoints window, click **Section-2ndFloorUtilities**.

9. In the Selection Tree window, click on **Elementary-School-Electrical.rvt**, the electrical components display as shown in Figure 4–27. Then, click on **Elementary-School-Mechanical.rvt** to display the mechanical ducts, as shown in Figure 4–28.

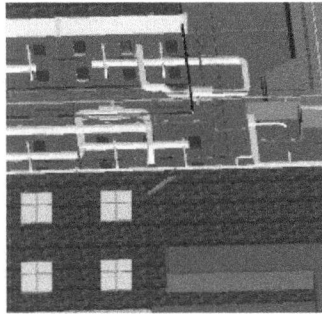

Figure 4–27

Figure 4–28

10. Continue selecting different items in the Selection Tree window to become more familiar with the model.

11. Press <Esc> to clear the selection.

12. In the Saved Viewpoints window, click **NE-View** to return to it.

13. In the Selection Tree, expand **Elementary-School-Architectural.rvt>First Floor>Windows>4x4 Adjustable** and select **6' SQ**. Note that only one window is selected in the Scene View.

14. In the *Home* tab>Select & Search panel, expand (Select Same) and select **Same Name**. All of the **4x4 Adjustable-6' SQ** windows are selected in the model.

15. In the *Home* tab>Select & Search panel, click (Save Selection). Enter **Gym Windows** for the name.

16. Save the model.

4.4 Finding Items and Saving Search Sets

Due to the large amount of information that can be stored in an Autodesk Navisworks project, the tools that help you find objects become very important. You can use Quick Find for simple searches or Find Items for more complex searches. The items you find can be saved to a search set.

The advantage of a search set over a saved set is that as new models are appended, the search set updates automatically to include new objects, while saved sets do not update automatically. Figure 4–29 shows an example of search sets.

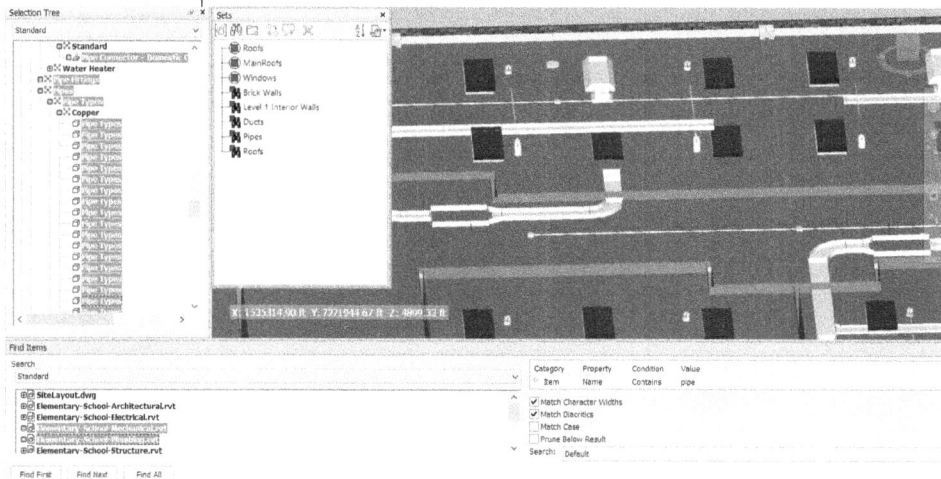

Figure 4–29

• Searches are based on information stored in item properties.

Using Quick Find

You can use Quick Find to do a search based on a text string. For example, in a Civil 3D model, type "road" (as shown in

Figure 4–30) and press <Enter>, or click the ^{Q} (Quick Find) button. The first related item in the Selection Tree is highlighted, as shown in Figure 4–31.

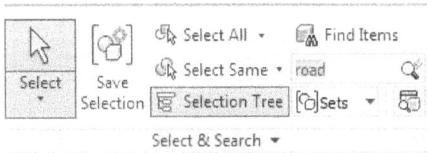

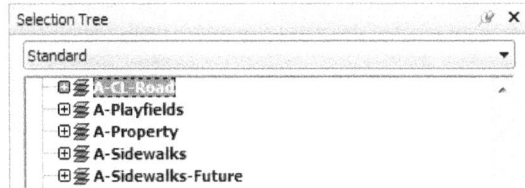

| Figure 4–30 | Figure 4–31 |

- Repeatedly pressing <Enter> or clicking the button will continue to the next item through the entire Selection Tree.

- Quick Find drills down to the geometry level with each click, before moving to the top level of the next related item.

How To: Use the Find Item Dialog Box.

1. In the *Home* tab>Select & Search panel, click (Find Items).
2. In the Find Items dialog box, in the left pane, drill down to the level where you want to start searching. This list is the same as the Selection Tree.
3. In the right pane, expand each drop-down list and select the *Category*, *Property*, *Condition*, and *Value* to specify which rules you want active in the search, as shown in Figure 4–32.
   - **Category:** A list that corresponds to the tabs in Properties
   - **Property:** A list of properties within the selected category.
   - **Condition:** How you want to search.
   - **Value:** What you want to search for based on the condition.

The options available in each drop-down list depend on the items that you are investigating.

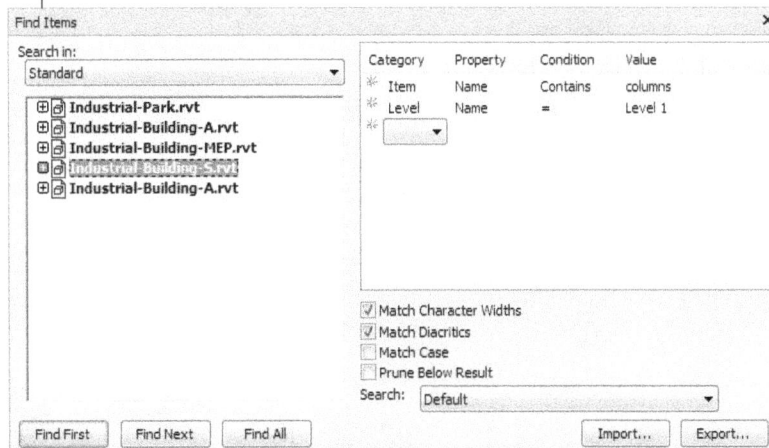

Figure 4–32

4. Select the Matching options below the right pane, or by right-clicking and selecting the appropriate **Ignore** statements.
5. Click **Find First**, **Find Next**, or **Find All**, as required.

Working with Conditions

The Conditions that are available depend on whether the property you select is text based (as shown in Figure 4–33), or number based (as shown in Figure 4–34)

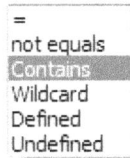

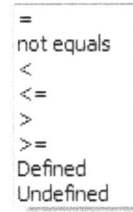

| Figure 4–33 | Figure 4–34 |

- Additional rows are automatically an "and" statement: both conditions must be matched to return any selections.

- If you want to change a row to an "or" statement, right-click on the row and select **Or Condition**. The row is distinguished by a **+** sign, as shown in Figure 4–35.

Category	Property	Condition	Value
Item	Name	Contains	Column ▾
Level	Name	=	Level 1
+Base C...	Elevation	=	10'-0"

Figure 4–35

- To search for the opposite of a condition, right-click on the row and select **Negate Condition**.

- To remove a row from the list, right-click on it and select **Delete Condition**.

- You can also right-click and select **Delete All Conditions** to start over.

How To: Save Searches

1. In the Find Items window, create a search condition and click **Find All**.

2. In the Sets window, click 🔍 (Save Search), or right-click and select **Save Search**.

3. Type in a name for the search. The icon indicates that it is a search set, as shown in Figure 4–36.

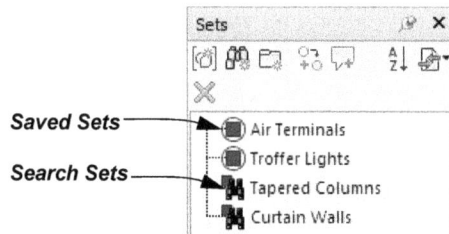

Figure 4–36

- Search sets update when new geometry is added to the model that matches the search.

- Click ⊕ (Duplicate) to make a copy of a search set to use as the base for another search set.

Practice 4c

Find Items and Save Search Sets

Practice Objectives

- Create a search criteria.
- Save a search set for later use.

Estimated time for completion: 10 minutes

In this practice you will run a quick search to find all of the HVAC ducts. Then, you will create a save set based on the type of walls (interior vs. exterior) for use later, as shown in Figure 4–37.

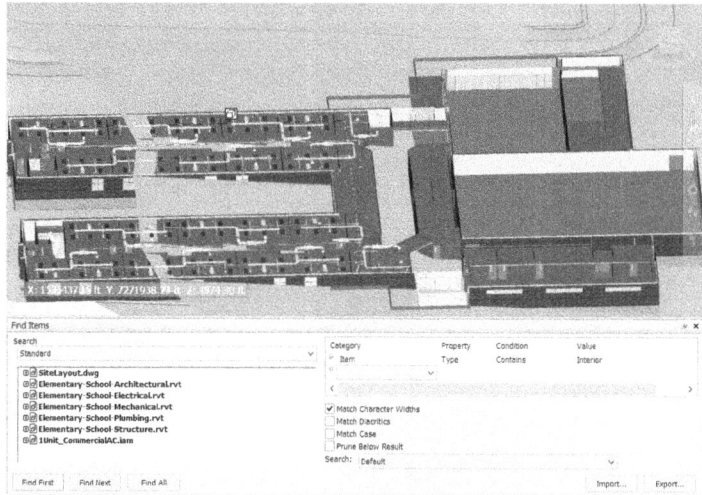

Figure 4–37

Task 1 - Do a quick search.

1. In the *Analyze* practice files folder, open **NewElementarySchool-Sets.nwf**.

2. In the Saved Viewpoints window, click **Section-1stFloorUtilities**.

3. Pin the Properties window open so that it is displayed for the next step.

4. In the *Home* tab>Select & Search panel, next to the

   (Quick Find) button, type **Ducts** and press <Enter>. Note that all of the ducts in the project are now selected.

5. Review the duct's properties in the Properties window, as shown in Figure 4–38.

6. Click the ⚲ (Quick Find) button or press <Enter>. Only one duct is selected. Note that there are more properties for individual ducts than for the group of ducts as shown in Figure 4–39.

Figure 4–38

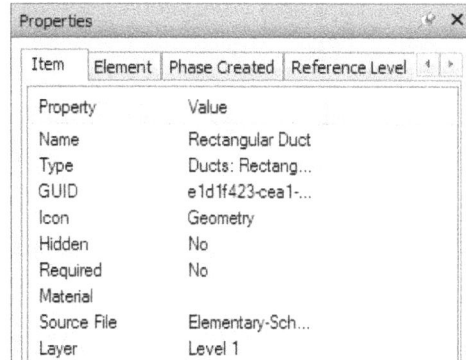

Figure 4–39

7. Continue to press <Enter> to cycle through the ducts in the model, reviewing each duct's properties.

8. Save the file.

Task 2 - Use the Find Items window for an advanced search.

1. Open and pin the Find Items window so that it is docked on the bottom of the screen.

   • If the Find Items window is not open, in the *Home* tab>

   Select & Search panel, click ⬚ (Find Items).

2. In the Find Items window, in the left pane, click on **Elementary-School-Architectural.rvt**.

Expand the width of the columns as needed to see the information.

3. In the right pane, do the following, as shown in Figure 4–40:
   - Under *Category*, select **Material**.
   - Under *Property*, select **Name**.
   - Under *Condition*, select **Contains**.
   - Under *Value*, type **Brick**
     (Note: Ensure that you capitalize **Brick** or clear the checkmark from **Match Case**.)

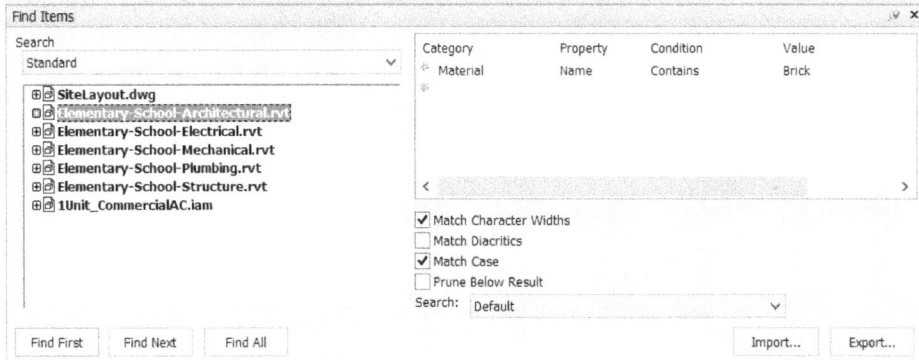

Figure 4–40

4. Leave the Matching options below the right pane set to the defaults.

5. Click **Find First**, **Find Next**, and then **Find All** and note what is selected in the model.

Task 3 - Save search sets

1. In the Sets window, click 🔍 (Save Search).

2. Type **Brick Wall** for the search. Note that the icon indicates that it is a search set, as shown in Figure 4–41.

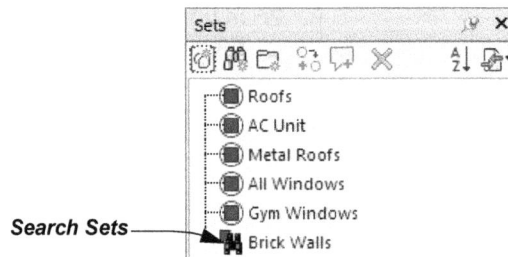

Figure 4–41

3. In the Find Items window, overwrite the information to create another search set with the criteria shown in Figure 4–42.

Category	Property	Condition	Value
✳ Item	Type	Contains	Interior
✳			

Figure 4–42

4. In the Sets window, save the search and name it **Interior Walls**.

5. In the Find Items window, create another search using the following criteria:
   - Under *Category*, select **Item**.
   - Under *Property*, select **Name**.
   - Under *Condition*, select **Contains**.
   - Under *Value*, type **Duct**.

6. Click **Find First**. A dialog box displays, as shown in Figure 4–43. Click **OK**.

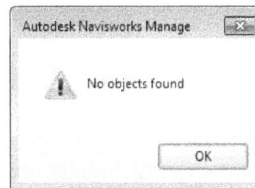

Figure 4–43

7. In the Find Items window, in the left pane, select **Elementary-School-Mechanical.rvt** and then click **Find All**. The ducts now display as shown in Figure 4–44.

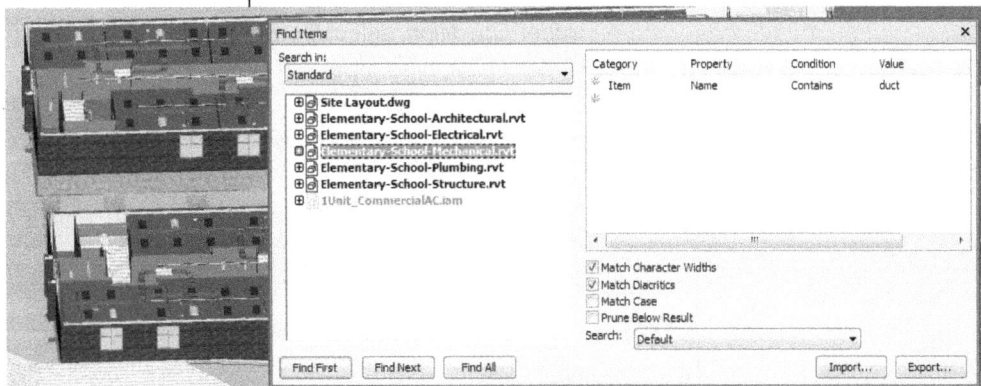

Figure 4–44

8. In the Sets window, click 🔍 (Save Search).

9. Type in **Ducts** for the search name.

10. Open the saved viewpoint **Section - 2ndFloorUtilities**.

11. Zoom in on the lower left corner of the building so that the pipes are displayed as shown in Figure 4–45.

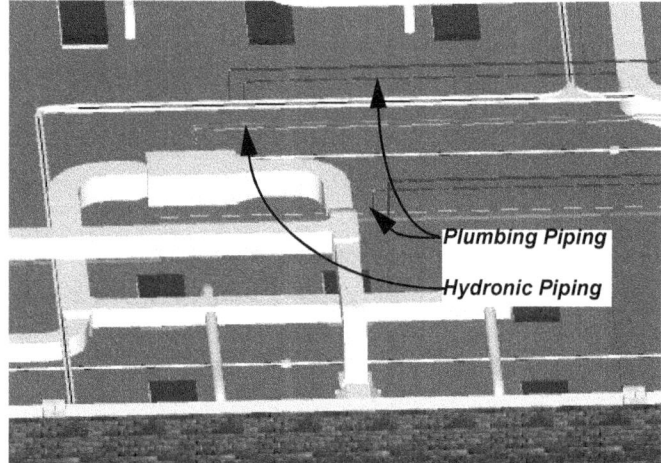

Plumbing Piping

Hydronic Piping

Figure 4–45

12. In the Find Items window, in the left pane, select the **Elementary-School-Mechanical.rvt** and **Elementary-School-Plumbing.rvt** files.

13. In the right pane, set the following, as shown in Figure 4–46:
   - Under *Category*, select **Item**.
   - Under *Property*, select **Name**.
   - Under *Condition*, select **Contains**.
   - Under *Value*, type **pipe**.

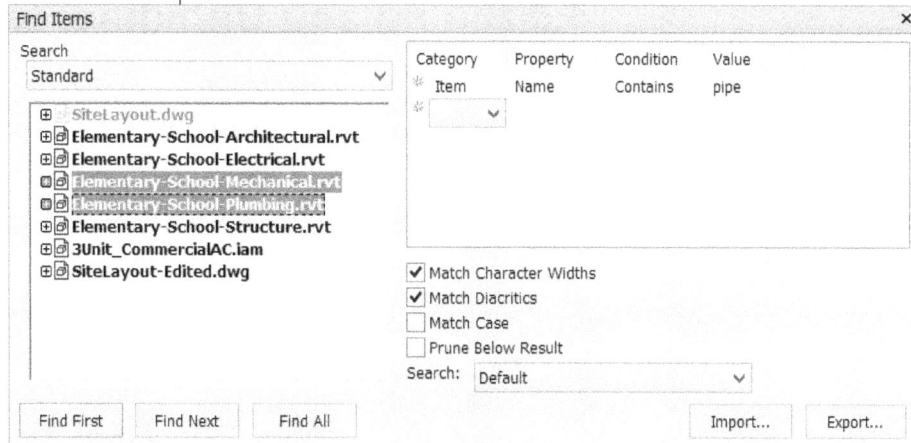

Figure 4–46

14. Click **Find All**. Pipes in both the mechanical and plumbing should highlight.

15. In the Sets window, click 🔍 (Save Search).

16. Type **Pipes** for the search name.

17. As you have time, create separate saved searches for piping in the mechanical and plumbing files.

18. Save the model.

4.5 Hiding and Unhiding Items

As you work in a model, it can help to hide items that are in the way or to isolate them so that you can investigate them more thoroughly. In the example shown in Figure 4–47, the brick walls are hidden to make viewing interior features easier.

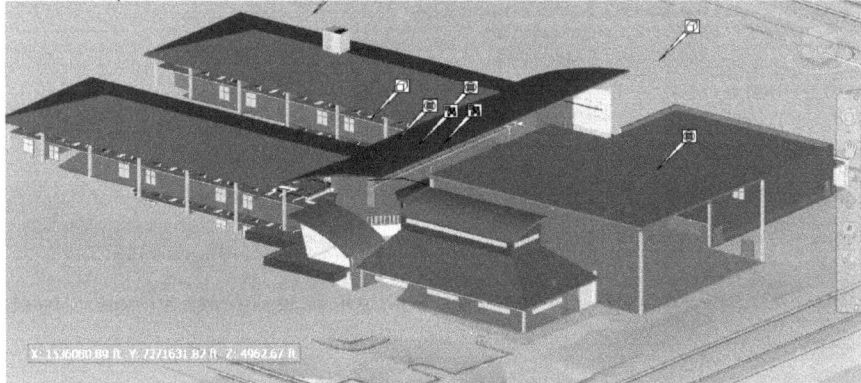

Figure 4–47

*   Having Saved Sets and Search Sets can be very helpful when you want to hide and unhide elements.

How To: Hide Items

1. Select individual items in a scene or, in the Sets dialog box, click on a Saved Set or Search Set.

2. In the *Home* tab>Visibility panel, click (Hide).
3. Note that the selected items are removed from the scene and are grayed out in the Selection Tree, as shown in Figure 4–48.

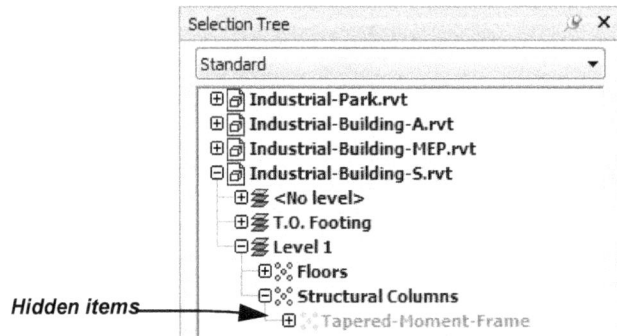

Figure 4–48

How To: Isolate Items

1. Select individual items in a scene or, in the Sets dialog box, click on a Saved Set or Search Set.

2. In the *Home* tab>Visibility panel, click 🗔 (Hide Unselected).
3. Any items that are not in the selection are hidden.

Unhiding Items

*   To unhide everything in the project that has been hidden, in

    the *Home* tab>Visibility panel, click 🗔 (Unhide All).

*   To unhide only specific hidden items, select them in the Selection Tree, right-click and select **Hide**, as shown in Figure 4–49. This toggles off the checkmark and unhides the items.

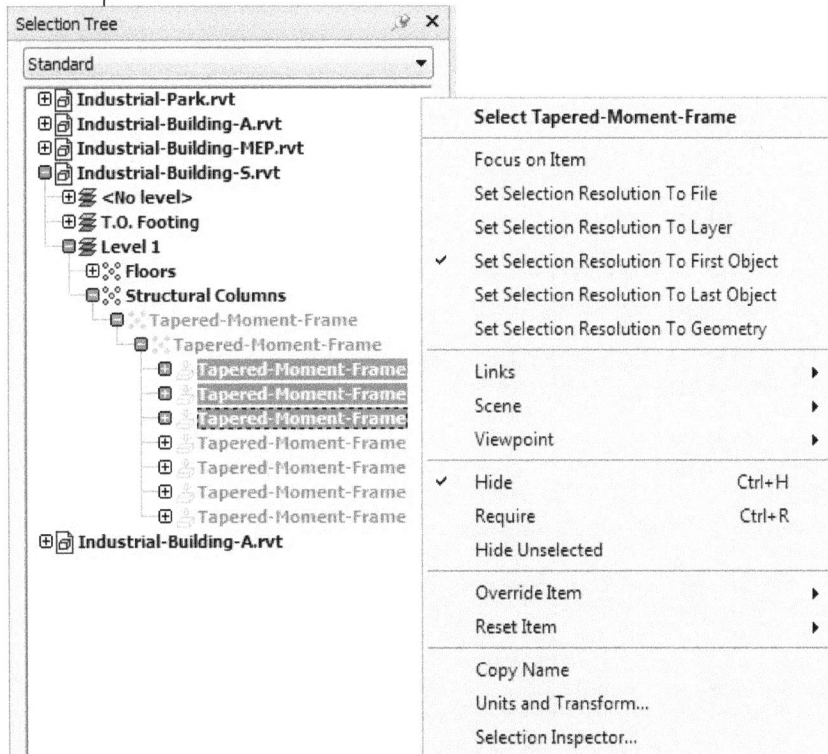

Figure 4–49

Hint: Required Items

To keep selected items displayed as you navigate through a model, you can select items and, in the *Home* tab>Visibility

panel, click ⬛ (Require). This can be helpful when you are using very complex models so you do not lose the items when the scene regenerates.

- To toggle this option off, expand ⬛ (Unhide All) and select

  ⬛ (Unrequire All).

Practice 4d

Hide and Unhide Objects in a Model

Practice Objectives

- Hide objects in the scene.
- Unhide hidden objects.

Estimated time for completion: 10 minutes

In this practice you will test out hiding sets of elements and use the Selection Tree to hide other elements as shown in Figure 4–50.

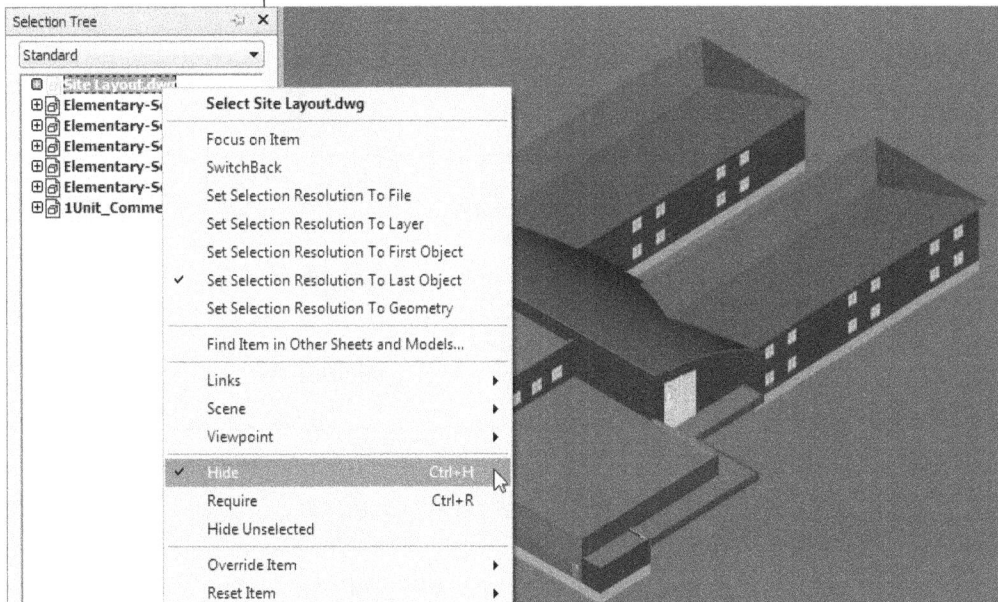

Figure 4–50

Task 1 - Hide walls

1. In the *Analyze* practice files folder, open **NewElementarySchool-Hide.nwf**.

2. Open the Saved Viewpoint **NE-View**.

3. In the Sets window, select **Brick Walls**.

4. In the *Home* tab>Visibility panel, click (Hide)

5. In the Sets dialog box, select **Interior Walls**.

6. Note that the selected items are removed from the scene and grayed out in the Selection Tree as shown in Figure 4–51.

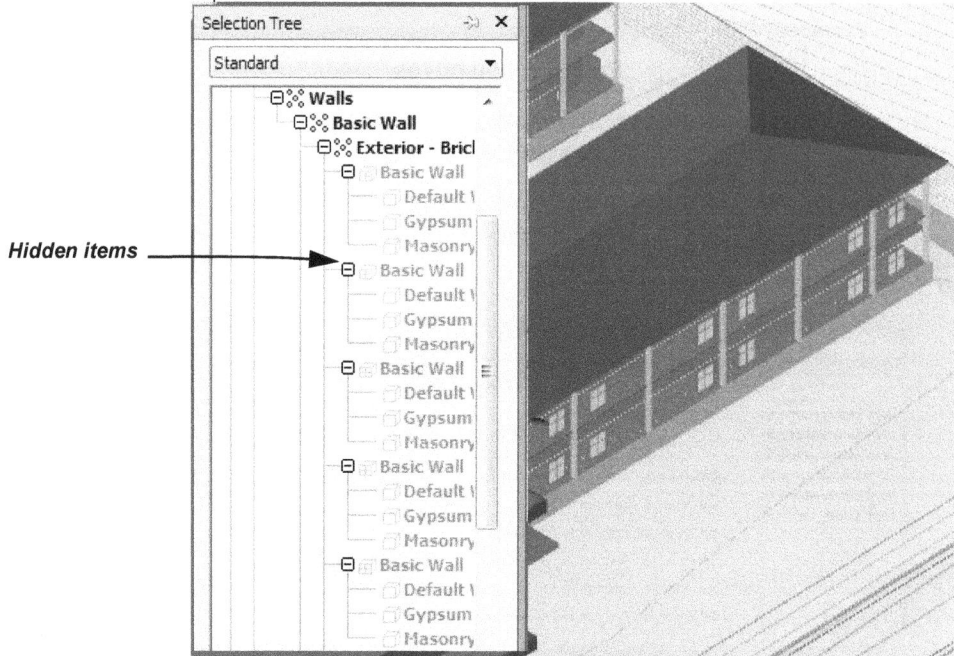

Hidden items

Figure 4–51

Task 2 - Hide site elements

1. Select one of the site elements.

2. In the *Home* tab>Visibility panel, click ⬜ (Hide Unselected). All of the building elements are hidden.

3. In the *Home* tab>Visibility panel, click ⬛ (Unhide All).

4. With the site element still selected, in the *Home* tab>Visibility panel, click ⬛ (Hide). Only the selected site element is hidden.

5. In the Selection Tree, select **Site Layout.dwg**. Right-click and select **Hide**. All of the site elements are hidden.

6. Save the model.

Chapter Review Questions

1. Which selection tool would you use to clear the current selection while simultaneously selecting everything that is not in the current selection?

   a. (Select All)

   b. (Select None)

   c. (Invert Selection)

   d. (Select Same)

2. Once a section set is saved, you cannot make any changes to it.

   a. True

   b. False

3. To view the properties of more than one element, which tool do you need to use?

   a. (Selection Inspector)

   b. (Quick Properties)

   c. (Properties)

4. Which Selection Resolution would you use to select the base geometry of an item, such as the material of a lighting fixture?

   a. File

   b. Layer

   c. First Object, Last Object, and Last Unique

   d. Geometry

5. How would you ensure that objects in the model that absolutely need to be visible do not disappear?

   a. Create a save set

   b. Create a search set

   c. In the *Home* tab>Visibility panel, click (Require)

   d. You cannot make items remain visible.

Command Summary

Button	Command	Location
Selection Tools		
	Invert Selection	• **Ribbon:** *Home* tab>Select & Search panel> expand Select All
	Manage Sets	• **Ribbon:** *Home* tab>Select & Search panel
	Save Selection	• **Ribbon:** *Home* tab>Select & Search panel
	Select	• **Ribbon:** *Home* tab>Select & Search panel • **Quick Access Toolbar** • **Navigation Bar** • **Shortcut:** <Ctrl>+<1>
	Select All	• **Ribbon:** *Home* tab>Select & Search panel
	Select Box	• **Ribbon:** *Home* tab>Select & Search panel> expand Select
	Select None	• **Ribbon:** *Home* tab>Select & Search panel> expand Select All
	Select Same	• **Ribbon:** *Home* tab>Select & Search panel
	Selection Inspector	• **Ribbon:** *Home* tab>Select & Search panel
	Selection Tree	• **Ribbon:** *Home* tab>Select & Search panel • **Shortcut:**<Ctrl>+<F12>
Properties and Options		
Options	Options	• **Application Menu**
	Properties	• **Ribbon:** *Home* tab>Display panel
	Quick Properties	• **Ribbon:** *Home* tab>Display panel
Find Tools		
	Find Items	• **Ribbon:** *Home* tab>Select & Search panel

	Quick Find	• **Ribbon:** *Home* tab>Select & Search panel
	Save Search	• **Window:** *Sets*

Visibility Tools

	Hide	• **Ribbon:** *Home* tab>Visibility panel
	Hide Unselected	• **Ribbon:** *Home* tab>Visibility panel
	Require	• **Ribbon:** *Home* tab>Visibility panel
	Select	• **Quick Access Toolbar** • Navigation Bar • **Ribbon:** *Home* tab>Select & Search panel
	Select Box	• **Quick Access Toolbar** • **Ribbon:** *Home* tab>Select & Search panel> expand Select
	Unhide All	• **Ribbon:** *Home* tab>Visibility panel
	Unrequire All	• **Ribbon:** *Home* tab>Visibility panel expand Unhide All

Communication: Review and Markup a Model

The next step in the BIM workflow is communication. BIM was originally created as a way to increase communication and reduce RFI's. In this chapter, you learn how to measure the model and turn those measurements into redlines to communicate to other team members what corrections need to be made. You also learn how to markup a scene using text, tags, and other drawing tools.

Learning Objectives in this Chapter

- Use measure tools to review information in the model.
- Convert measurements to redline dimensions.
- Markup scenes for review using text and drawing tools.
- Add tags and comments to elements in a model.

BIM Workflow: Communicate

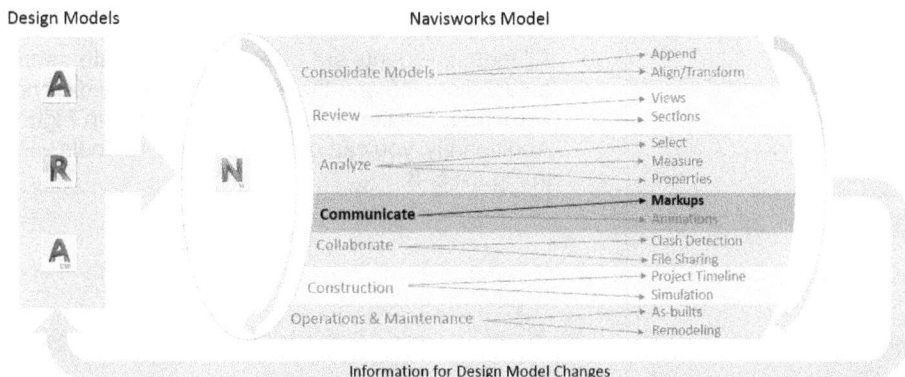

Design Models · Navisworks Model

Consolidate Models — Append, Align/Transform
Review — Views, Sections
Analyze — Select, Measure, Properties
Communicate — **Markups**, Animation
Collaborate — Clash Detection, File Sharing
Construction — Project Timeline, Simulation
Operations & Maintenance — As-builts, Remodeling

Information for Design Model Changes

5.1 Using Measuring Tools

Measuring distances (as shown in Figure 5–1), angles, and areas in a model is a critical part of using the Autodesk® Navisworks® software. This information can be included in redline views sent to the architect or engineer as a request for information, or to the construction superintendent to clarify a situation.

Figure 5–1

- There are a variety of measuring tools and options to help you get the most accurate measurements.

- All measurements are based on coordinate geometry. The actual distance and the X-, Y-, and Z-axis distances can be seen near the item measured, as shown in Figure 5–2. Additionally, you can open the Measure Tools window, shown in Figure 5–3.

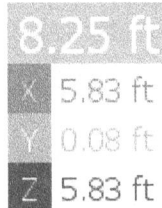 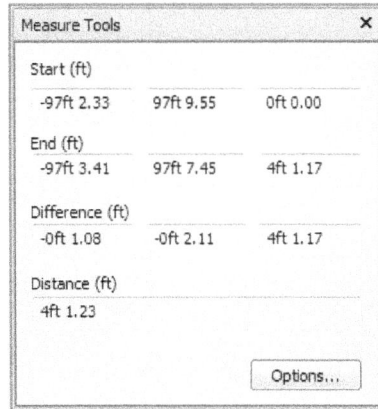

Figure 5–2   **Figure 5–3**

- To open the Measure Tools window, in the *Review*

  tab>Measure panel, in the panel title, click ⬃ (Measure Options).

How To: Measure Distances

1. In the *Review* tab>Measure panel, expand ⬒ (Measure) and click one of the measurement options.
2. Select the first point. The cursor displays a box that recognizes 3D surfaces (as shown in Figure 5–4 and Figure 5–5) and 2D lines and points.

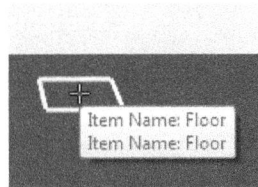   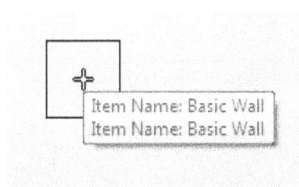

Figure 5–4   **Figure 5–5**

Measurement Options

- ⬒ **(Point to Point):** Select two points to display the distance between them.

- ◿ **(Point to Multiple Points):** Select the first point and then a second point. Then select additional points and the measured distance of each point is based on the original first point.

Point to Multiple Points is similar to using a baseline dimension.

- ![Point Line icon] **(Point Line):** Select the first point and then additional points. The measured distance includes all selections along the path.

- ![Accumulate icon] **(Accumulate):** Select two points and then two more points, continuing as needed. The measured distance of all of the sets of points are added together.

- Any time you want to clean up a view with measurements, in the *Review* tab>Measure panel, click ![Clear icon] (Clear).

How To: Measure Angles

1. In the *Review* tab>Measure panel, expand ![Measure icon] (Measure) and click ![Angle icon] (Angle).
2. For the first point, select the first plane of the angle.
3. For the second point, select a vertex point.
4. For the third point, select the second plane of the angle. The dimension displays as shown in Figure 5–6

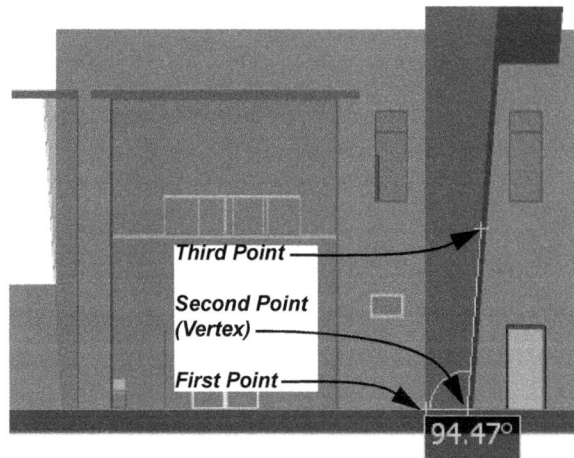

Figure 5–6

How To: Measure Areas

1. In the *Review* tab>Measure panel, expand ⬌ (Measure) and click ◺ (Area)
2. Select at least three points to display the area.
3. Continue selecting points as required, as shown in Figure 5–7.

Figure 5–7

How To: Measure the Shortest Distance Between Two Items

1. Select an item, then hold <Ctrl> and select a second item.

2. In the *Review* tab>Measure panel, expand ⬌ (Measure) and click ⬌ (Shortest Distance).
3. The distance displays as shown in Figure 5–8.

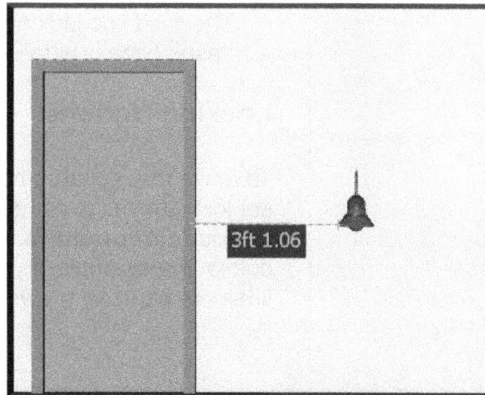

Figure 5–8

Working with the Locking Options

Many times you need to ensure that you are measuring exactly what you are expecting. The Lock options can help you focus the measuring tools to a specific plane. For example, in Figure 5–9, when measuring from the finish floor to the ceiling, toggle on the Z-axis lock so that the other axes are not included in the distance.

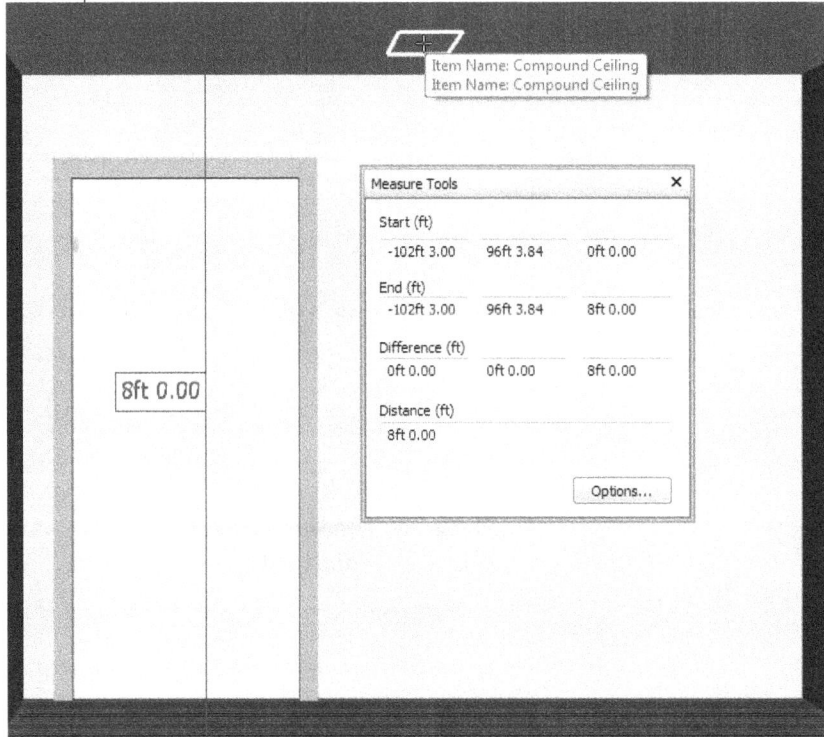

Figure 5–9

- The solid line indicates the locked measurement, while the dashed line is where the cursor is actually positioned.

Locking Options

To make the measurements as accurate as possible, it helps to set lock options in some circumstances. When you use any of the lock options, the measurement matches the specific lock colors. For example, if you use the Z-axis lock, the measurement lines are blue, as shown in Figure 5–9 (above).

In the *Review* tab>Measure panel, expand **Lock** and click an option from the list:

- ⬜ **(None):** No lock is applied

- ↳ˣ **(X Axis)**, ↳ʸ **(Y Axis)**, ↳ᶻ **(Z Axis):** The measurement is locked to the specified axis. The color of each lock line matches the axis color shown in the gizmo, HUD icon, and other locations.

    - Note: When using the X-axis direction, the measurement is based on the rotation of the viewpoint and changes if you change the viewpoint.

- ↳ **(Perpendicular):** The measurement is locked to the plane of the first selected point, and moves perpendicular to that plane.

- ⫽ **(Parallel):** The measurement is locked to the plane of the first selected point and moves parallel to it. This is most useful when using the Area tool.

Measurements of 3D models are based on the surface areas of the items. Sometimes, it can help to see these exact planes as you measure, as shown in Figure 5–10. In the *Viewpoint* tab> Render Style panel, expand **Mode** and click ⬚ (Hidden Line).

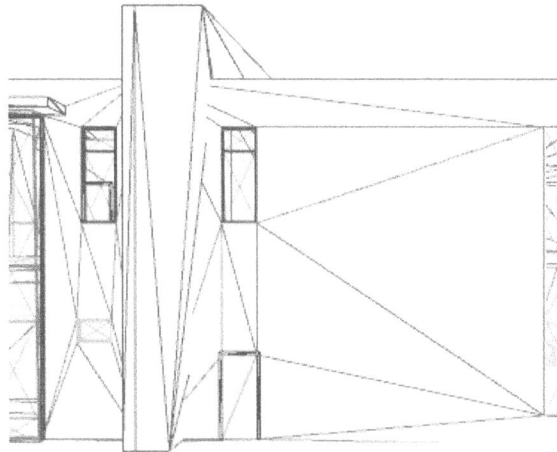

Figure 5–10

Hint: Measuring and Snapping Options

Many of the default options can be modified to fit your company standards or to help you get more precise measurements. These include setting up the color and thickness of the visual dimensions, as well as tools to clarify what you are measuring.

To open the Options Editor, in the Measure Tools window or Application Menu, click **Options**. In the Options Editor, expand **Interface** and select **Measure,** as shown in Figure 5–11.

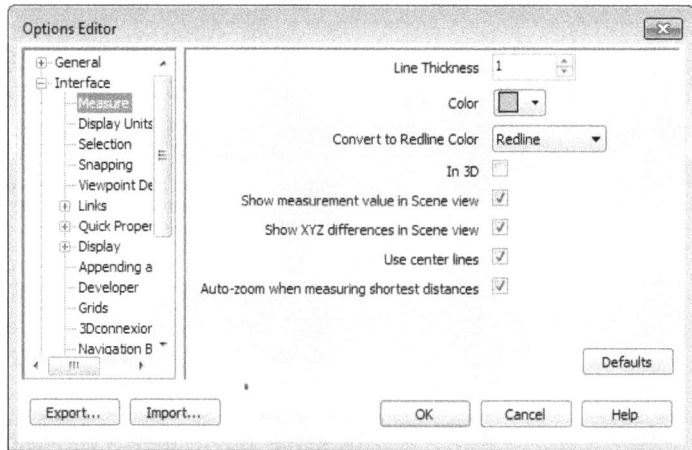

Figure 5–11

Snapping options are also important, especially the **Snap to Vertex** or **Snap to Edge** settings, as shown in Figure 5–12.

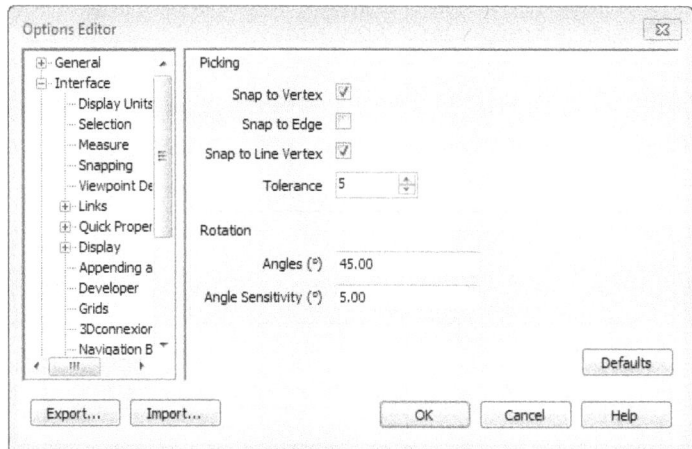

Figure 5–12

Converting Measurements to Redlines

As you are measuring items, you might want to use the measured distance as a redline dimension, as shown in Figure 5–13. To do this, in the Review tab>Measure panel, click ⟍ (Convert to Redline).

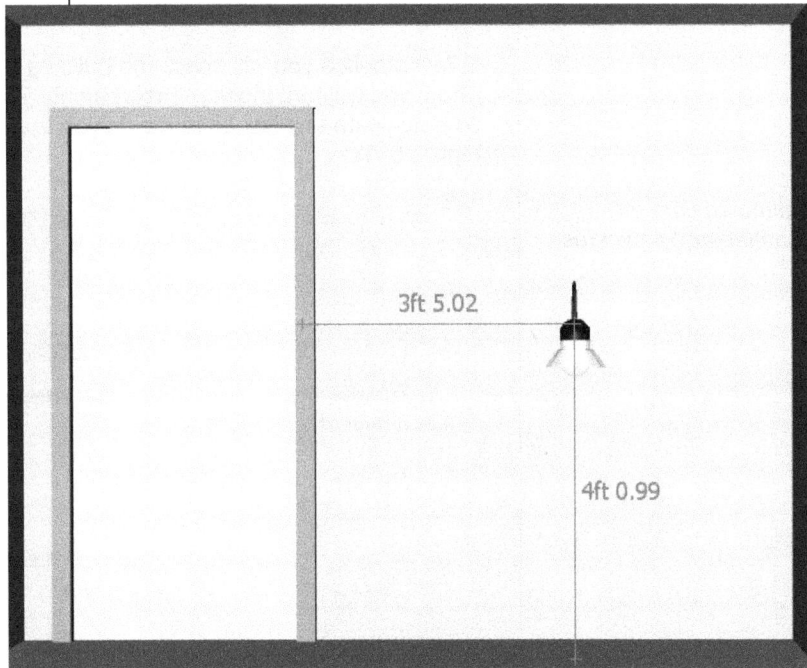

Figure 5–13

- Each measurement must be converted separately.

- When the first redline is added, a viewpoint is also automatically created in the Saved Viewpoints dialog box. Rename the view to help you retrieve it later.

- The view can be used with additional redline tools as well.

Practice 5a

Use Measuring Tools

Practice Objectives

- Measure the model.
- Convert measurements into redlines.

In this practice you will check the building model for accuracy. Then, you will turn those measurements into redlines to communicate any issues to the design team, as shown in Figure 5–14.

Estimated time for completion: 15 minutes

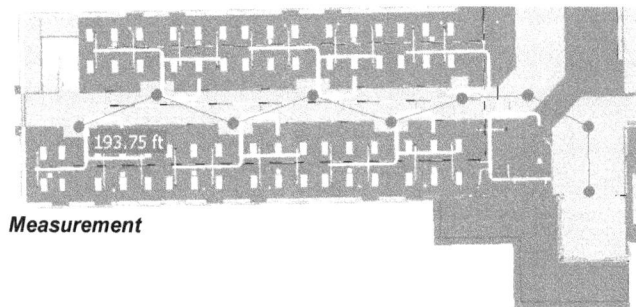

Measurement

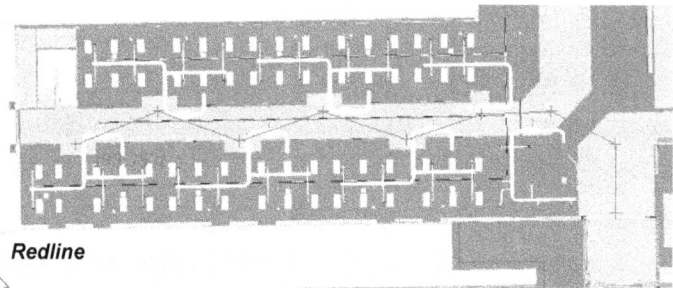

Redline

Figure 5–14

Task 1 - Measure distances.

1. In the *Markup* practice files folder, open **NewElementarySchool-Measure.nwf**.

2. In the Saved Viewpoints window, click **AC Unit**.

3. In the *Review* tab>Measure panel, expand (Measure) and click (Point to Point).

If the units display in units that you are not expecting, in the Options Editor> Interface, check the Display Units option.

4. In the Scene view, select the two points shown in Figure 5–15 to display the height of the AC unit.

Note that four distance values are displayed: Actual (yellow), X (red), Y (green), and Z (blue).

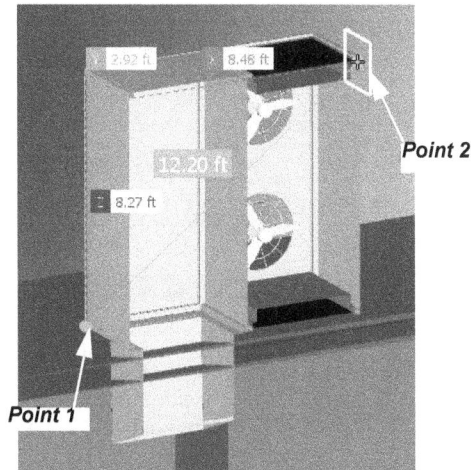

Figure 5–15

5. In the *Review* tab>Measure panel, expand 🔒 (Lock) and click ⊿ (X Axis).

6. In the Scene view, select the same two points that you used in Step 4. Note that only the X (red) value is displayed this time, as shown in Figure 5–16.

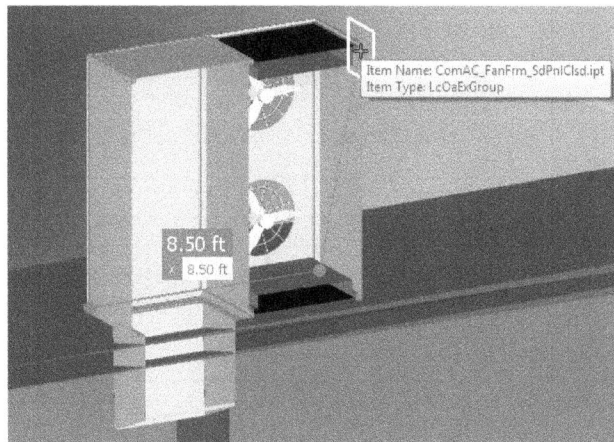

Figure 5–16

7. In the *Review* tab>Measure panel, click ✂ (Clear).

8. In the Saved Viewpoints window, click **Section-1stFloorUtilities**.

9. In the scene view, click **Top** on the ViewCube to display a plan-like view.

10. Save the viewpoint as **Egress Check**.

11. In the *Review* tab>Measure panel, expand ⬜ (Measure) and click ⬜ (Point to Multiple Points).

12. In the *Review* tab>Measure panel, expand ⬜ (Lock) and click ⬜ (Parallel).

13. Select a point near the entry doors, and then another point near one of the door setbacks on the hall, as shown in Figure 5–17.

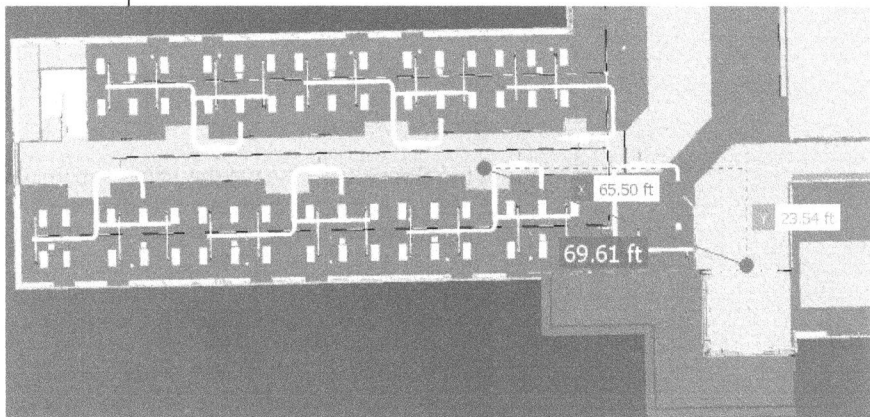

Figure 5–17

14. Select another point on the next door setback, as shown in Figure 5–18. Note that the first point is remembered. Test the distances for the other door setbacks to check them against egress requirements as well.

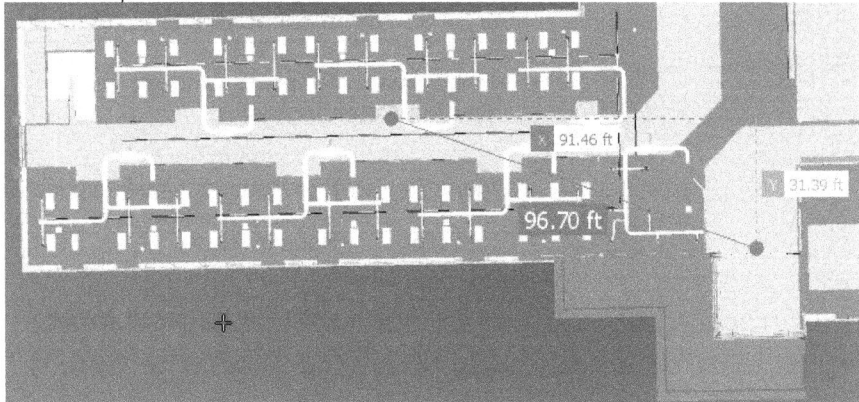

Figure 5–18

15. In the *Review* tab>Measure panel, click ⬚ (Clear) to clean up the view measurements.

16. In the *Review* tab>Measure panel, expand ⬚ (Measure) and select ⬚ (Point Line).

17. Starting at the entry, select the points shown in Figure 5–19.

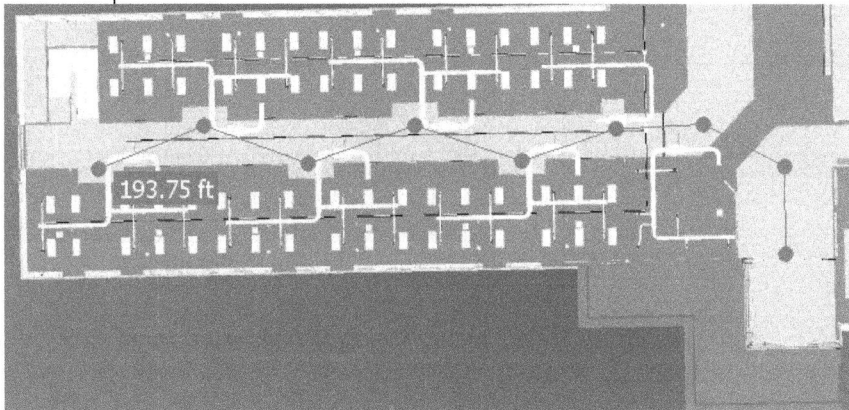

Figure 5–19

18. In the *Review* tab>Measure panel, click ⬚ (Convert to Redline).

19. The view is saved with the redlines included.

20. Save the file.

Task 2 - Convert measurements to redlines.

1. In the Saved Viewpoints window, click
   Section-RetainingWall.

2. In the *Review* tab>Measure panel, expand ⌷⌷⌷ (Measure)
   and click ⌷⌷⌷ (Point to Point).

3. In the *Review* tab>Measure panel, expand 🔓 (Lock) and
   click ⌷ᶻ (Z Axis).

4. In the Scene view, select the two points shown in Figure 5–20
   to display the height of the retaining wall.

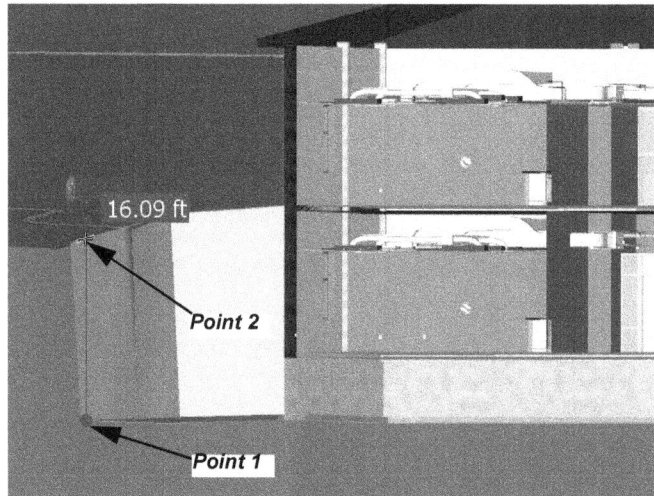

Figure 5–20

5. In the *Review* tab>Measure panel, click ⌷↘ (Convert to
   Redline).

6. Add two more vertical dimensions at other heights along the
   retaining wall and covert them to redlines as well.

Task 3 - Measure areas and angles.

1. In the Saved Viewpoints window, click **Hallway**.

2. Set the measurement lock to **Parallel**.

3. In the *Review* tab>Measure panel, expand ▭ (Measure) and click ◹ (Area).

4. Click in the center of the hall to select the floor for the points to be parallel to. Then, select the points shown in Figure 5–21 to display the area.

Figure 5–21

5. Convert the measurement to a redline.

6. If you have changed the zoom of the view, you are prompted to create a new saved viewpoint. Name it **Area of Hallway**.

7. In the *Review* tab>Measure panel, expand ▭ (Measure) and click △ (Angle).

8. in the Scene View, select the points indicated in Figure 5–22.

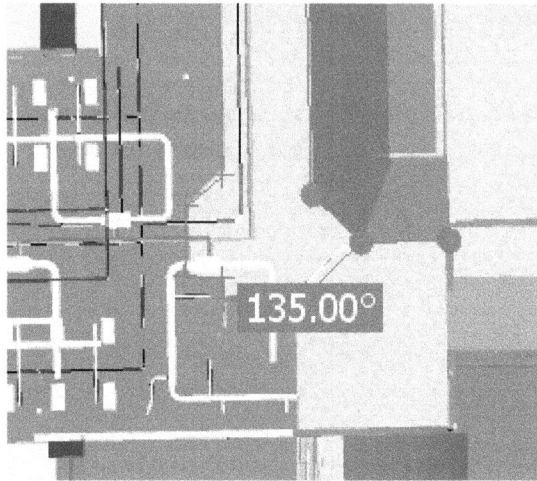

Figure 5–22

9. Click ▭ ✕ (Clear).

10. Save the file.

Task 4 - Measure shortest distances between two selections.

1. In the Saved Viewpoints window, click **Level2-Utilities**.

2. In the Quick Access Toolbar, click ⬉ (Select).

3. In the *Home* tab>Select & Search panel, expand the panel title and set the *Selection Resolution* to **Last Unique**.

4. In the Scene View, select the hall floor in the north wing. Then, hold <Ctrl> and select the hall floor in the south wing, as shown in Figure 5–23.

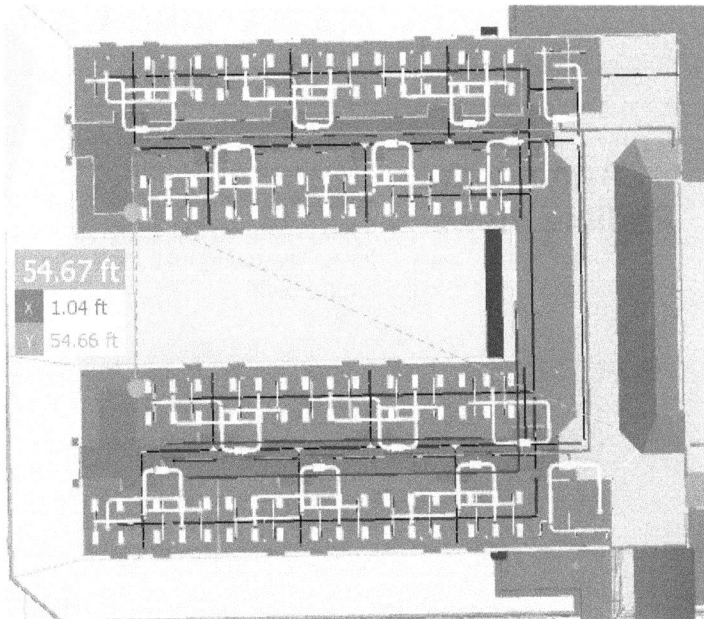

Figure 5–23

5. In the *Review* tab>Measure panel, click ⬚ (Shortest Distance).

6. Select two other floors and test another shortest distance.

7. In the *Review* tab>Measure panel, click ⬚ (Clear) to clean up the view measurements.

8. Save the model.

5.2 Marking Up Scenes for Review

Annotating Redline Views

Sometimes it is important to add comments or other geometry in addition to dimensions to fully communicate any questions you have regarding the design. In that case, you can mark up scenes for review using text, tags, and drawing tools, as shown in Figure 5–24.

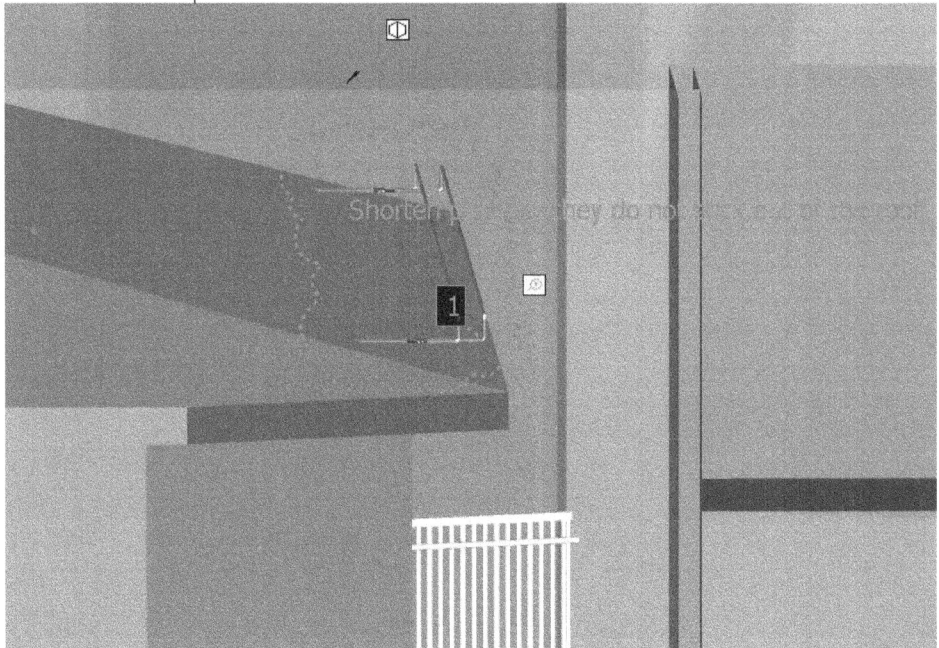

Figure 5–24

- Redlines are saved in a viewpoint.

- When you navigate away from the viewpoint the redlines disappear.

- A viewpoint is automatically added to the Saved Viewpoints window upon adding text or other redline geometry to the current view.

- If the Viewpoint is deleted, the redline is lost with it.

How To: Add Text to a Viewpoint

1. Open the saved viewpoint where you want to add the text.

2. In the *Review* tab>Redline panel, click 𝔸 (Text).
3. In the dialog box, type the text you want to add (as shown in Figure 5–25), and then click **OK**.

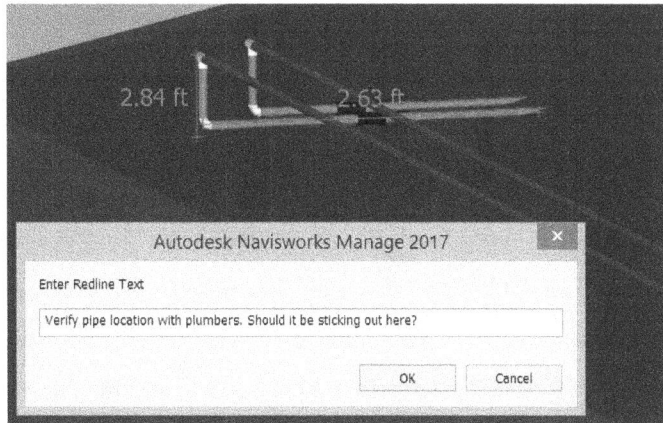

Figure 5–25

- Redline dimensions, text, and drawings cannot be moved,

  but they can be erased. To erase redlines, click ✐ (Erase) and draw a window around the entire redline item, as shown in Figure 5–26. If you select only part of the redline (as shown in Figure 5–27), the redline is not included in the deletion.

Figure 5–26

Figure 5–27

How To: Use the Draw Tools

1. Open the saved viewpoint where you want to add redlines.
2. In the *Review* tab>Redline panel, expand **Draw** and select the required tool:

The most recently-used tool remains on the top of the drop-down list.

- (Cloud): Click two points to create each arc of the cloud. The distance between the clicks determines the size of the arc.

- (Ellipse): Click and drag to create a bounding box. When you release the mouse button, the ellipse is created inside the bounding box you selected.

- (Freehand): Click and drag the cursor around to create lines. Release the mouse button to stop drawing.

- (Line): Click two points to place lines between them. The lines are individual, not connected.

- (Line String): Click to place the first point and then as many other points as needed. The lines are connected.

- (Arrow): Click to place the end point for the arrow line, and then click again to place where you want the arrow pointing.

Hint: Set the Redline Tools Color and Thickness

You can customize the Redline tools by changing the color and thickness in the *Review* tab>Redline panel, as shown in Figure 5–28.

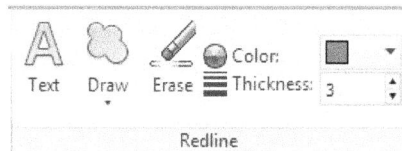

Figure 5–28

Adding Tags and Comments

The difference between adding text and a tag is that a tag places a marker in the Scene View, rather than text. Once the tags are placed, you can review the comments added to tags in the order that they were added. In addition, tags enable you to see who added or edited a comment and the date that it was added.

How To: Add Tags

1. Open the saved viewpoint where you want to add a tag.
2. In the *Review* tab>Tags panel, click (Add Tag).
3. Click a point for the beginning of the line.
4. Click a point to place the tag.
5. In the Add Comments dialog box type in the comment and click **OK**.

How To: Review Tags

1. In the *Review* tab>Comments panel, click (View Comments) to toggle the Comments window off and on. It can be resized or docked.
2. If there are a lot of comments, in the *Review* tab>Comments panel, type a search string in the Quick Find Comments area, as shown in Figure 5–29.

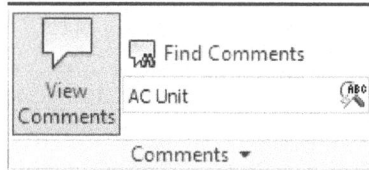

Figure 5–29

3. To step through the tags, in the *Review* tab>Tags panel, select the arrow buttons, or use one of the keyboard shortcuts below:

- **(First Tag):** <Ctrl>+<Shift>+<Up Arrow>

- **(Previous Tag):** <Ctrl>+<Shift>+<Left Arrow>

- **(Next Tag):** <Ctrl>+<Shift>+<Right Arrow>

- **(Last Tag):** <Ctrl>+<Shift>+<Down Arrow>

Hint: Merging Project Files

Since there might be multiple people reviewing and marking up the model, it might be necessary to merge redlines. When project files are merged, redlines from other users are copied into one file without creating duplicates.

You can use either of the following methods to merge redlines:

- In the *Home* Tab>Project panel, expand ⬜ (Append) and click ⬜ (Merge).

- In the Quick Access Toolbar, expand 📂 (Open), and then click **Merge**.

Practice 5b

Mark up Scenes for Review

Practice Objectives

- Add text to communicate a question regarding the design.
- Create redline geometry to draw attention to specific parts of the design.
- Merge project files.

In this practice you will redline the model to communicate questions and issues to the appropriate teams, as shown in Figure 5–30. You will then merge in another Autodesk Navisworks file and review additional markups.

Estimated time for completion: 10 minutes

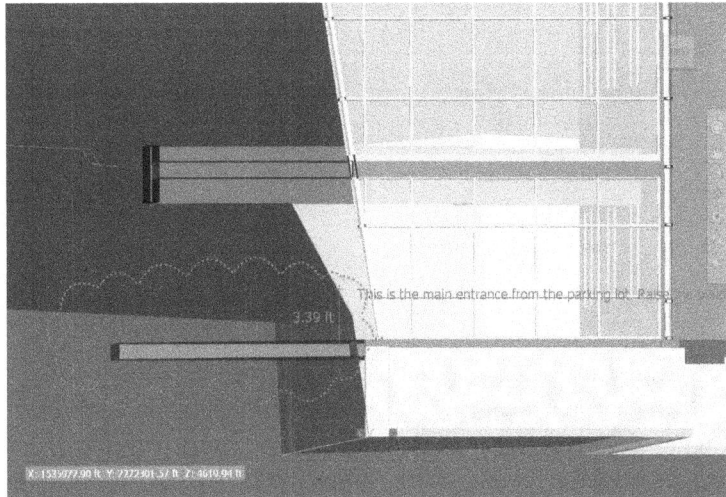

Figure 5–30

Task 1 - Add redline dimensions and text to the entrance section.

1. In the *Markup* practice files folder, open **NewElementarySchool-Markup.nwf**.

2. In the Saved Viewpoints window, click **Section-EntrancePlatform**.

3. Add a point to point measurement from the base of the entrance floor to the cut of the topography and turn it into a redline, as shown in Figure 5–31.

4. The Saved Viewpoints window displays. Click on the new view and name it **Entrance Elevation Change Comments**.

5. In the *Review* tab>Redline panel, click $\mathbb{A}$ (Text).

6. Click on the edge of the redline dimension.

7. In the dialog box type the following (as shown in Figure 5–31) and then click OK:

   This is the main entrance from the parking lot. Raise the building elevation to accommodate surface elevations.

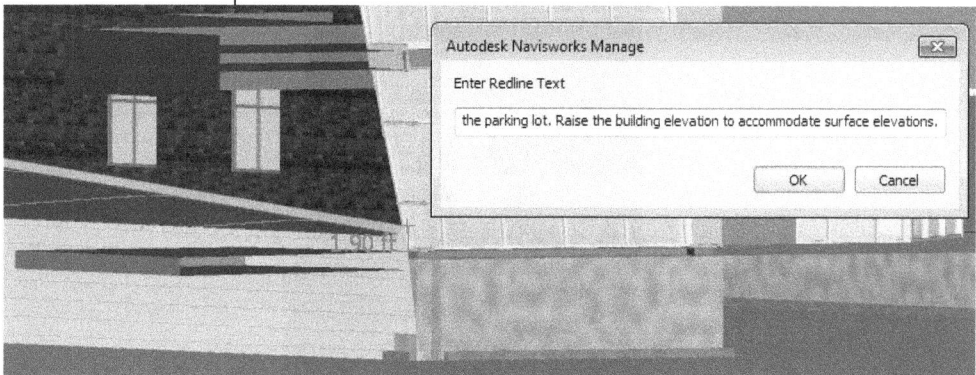

Figure 5–31

8. Without changing the viewpoint, in the *Review* tab>Redline panel, expand **Draw** and click $\mathbb{O}$ (Cloud).

The distance between the clicks determines the size of the arc.

9. In the Scene view click points in a clockwise direction to create each arc of the cloud, as shown in Figure 5–32. The redline information is automatically saved with the viewpoint.

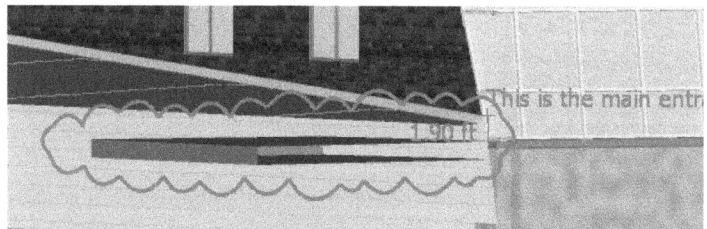

Figure 5–32

10. Save the file.

Task 2 - Use Redline Graphics and Tags.

1. In the Saved Viewpoints window, click **NE-View**.

2. Save the viewpoint as **NE-View-Comments**.

3. In the *Review* tab>Redline panel, expand **Draw** and click

   ◯ (Ellipse).

4. In the Scene view click and drag to draw the bounding box around the AC Unit, as shown in Figure 5–33. When you release the mouse button, the ellipse is created inside the bounding box you selected, as shown in Figure 5–34.

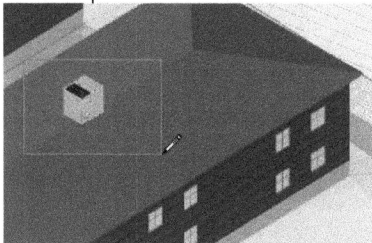

Figure 5–33

Figure 5–34

5. In the *Review* tab>Tags panel, click 🏷 (Add Tag).

6. Click a point on the AC Unit for the beginning of the line.

7. Click a point on the ellipse to place the tag.

8. In the Add Comments dialog box, type in the following comment (as shown in Figure 5–35) and then click **OK**:

   This is the worst place to put an AC Unit. Please move to flat roof.

Figure 5–35

9. In the *Review* tab>Redline panel, expand **Draw** and click

   ◹ (Arrow).

10. In the Scene view, click the AC Unit for the start point, then click the center of the flat roof to place the arrow, as shown in Figure 5–36.

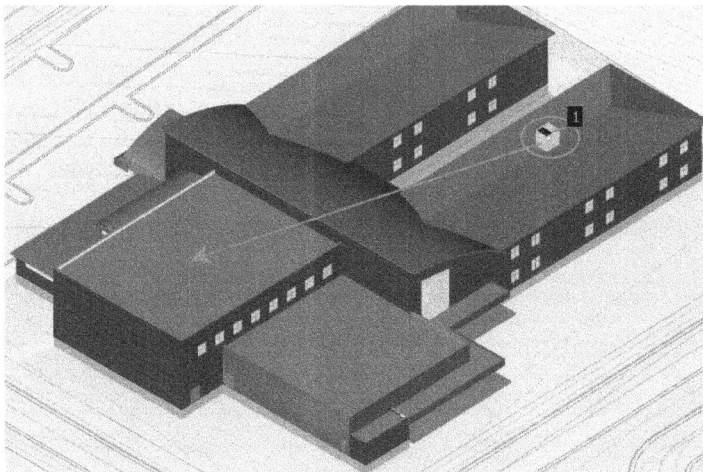

Figure 5–36

11. In the *Review* tab>Tags panel, click 🏷 (Add Tag).

12. Click a point for the beginning of the line where you placed the arrow.

13. Click a point to place the tag, as shown in Figure 5–37.

14. In the Add Comments dialog box type **New location of AC Unit** in the comment (as shown in Figure 5–37) and click **OK**.

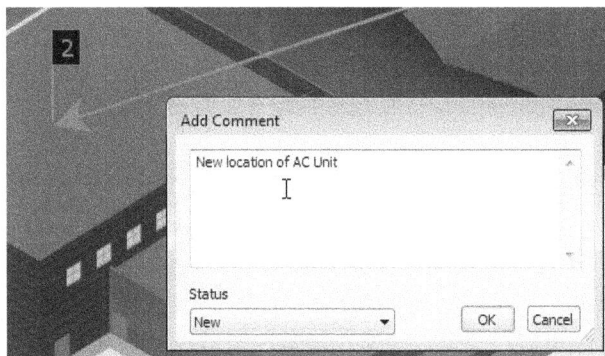

Figure 5–37

15. Add an additional tag to the AC Unit with the following comment: **AC Unit is much too small for building. Replace with larger unit.**

16. Open the Comments window.
    - The Comments window is probably at the bottom of the screen. If it is not displaying, in the *Comments* tab>Tags panel, click 🗩 (View Comments).

17. In the Comments window title bar, toggle off 📌 (Auto Hide) to force the window to always display.

18. Step through the tags in the *Review* tab>Tags panel by selecting the arrow buttons:
    - ◁Ⅰ (First Tag)
    - ◁ (Previous Tag)
    - ▷ (Next Tag)
    - Ⅰ▷ (Last Tag)

19. Save the file.

Task 3 - Merge Files and Review Comments.

1. In the *Home* tab>Project panel, expand 🗋 (Append) and click 🗋 (Merge).

2. In the Merge dialog box, select **NewElementarySchool-Markup-Mechanical.nwf** and then click Open.

3. In the Saved Viewpoints window. select **NE View-Mechanical Redline**.

4. Open the Comments window and review the comments in this viewpoint, as shown in Figure 5–38.

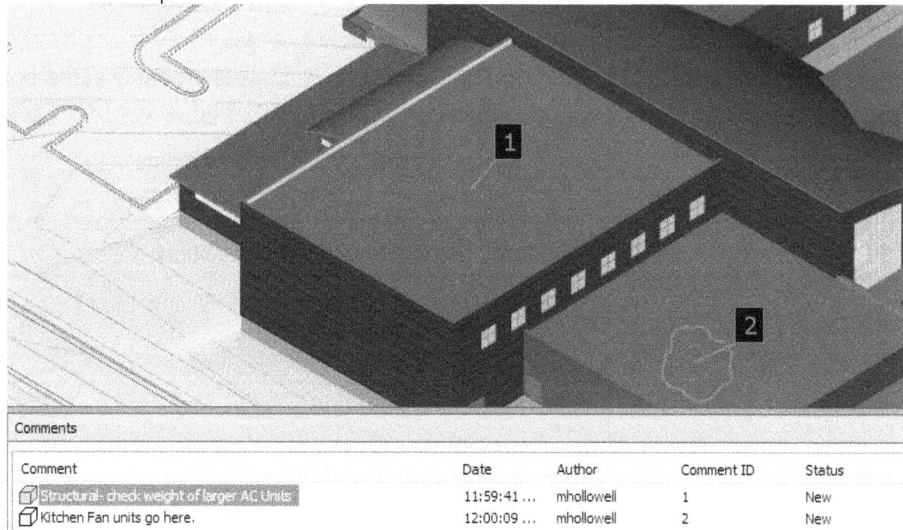

Comment	Date	Author	Comment ID	Status
Structural- check weight of larger AC Units	11:59:41 …	mhollowell	1	New
Kitchen Fan units go here.	12:00:09 …	mhollowell	2	New

Figure 5–38

5. Save the file.

Chapter Review Questions

1. How do you make measurements as accurate as possible?

   a. Zoom in really close as you pick a point.

   b. Use one of the Lock options found in the *Review* tab> Measure panel.

   c. It is not possible to make measurements accurate in the Autodesk Navisworks software. You can only get them close to find an approximate dimension.

   d. Draw lines from the points you want to measure, and then dimension the lines.

2. How do you ensure that a measurement remains visible?

   a. In the *Review* tab>Measure panel, click 🖉 (Convert to Redline).

   b. Take a screen shot and add the image to the file.

   c. Put the dimension in a tag.

   d. Manually draw the dimension with the Draw and Text tools.

3. You can convert more than one measurement to a redline at a time.

   a. True

   b. False

4. What happens when you place a dimension, text, or some other redline geometry in the Scene View, and then zoom in/out?

   a. The redlines seem to change size with the view.

   b. Nothing. The Redline remains the same size (percentage of the screen) no matter how much you zoom in/out.

   c. The Redline disappears if the view was not saved.

5. How do you move a redline?

   a. Select the redline and use the gizmo to move it.

   b. Select the redline and click **Move** on the *Redline* contextual tab.

   c. In the *Review* tab>Measure panel, click **Clear**.

   d. Redlines cannot be moved. They must be erased and redrawn in the new location.

Command Summary

Button	Command	Location
Measuring Tools		
	Accumulate	• **Ribbon:** *Review* tab>Measure panel> expand Measure
	Angle	• **Ribbon:** *Review* tab>Measure panel> expand Measure
	Area	• **Ribbon:** *Review* tab>Measure panel> expand Measure
	Clear	• **Ribbon:** *Review* tab>Measure panel
	Convert to Redline	• **Ribbon:** *Review* tab>Measure panel
	None	• **Ribbon:** *Review* tab>Measure panel> expand Lock
	Parallel	• **Ribbon:** *Review* tab>Measure panel> expand Lock
	Perpendicular	• **Ribbon:** *Review* tab>Measure panel> expand Lock
	Point Line	• **Ribbon:** *Review* tab>Measure panel> expand Measure
	Point to Multiple Points	• **Ribbon:** *Review* tab>Measure panel> expand Measure
	Point to Point	• **Ribbon:** *Review* tab>Measure panel> expand Measure
	Shortest Distance	• **Ribbon:** *Review* tab>Measure panel
	X Axis	• **Ribbon:** *Review* tab>Measure panel> expand Lock
	Y Axis	• **Ribbon:** *Review* tab>Measure panel> expand Lock
	Z Axis	• **Ribbon:** *Review* tab>Measure panel> expand Lock

Redline Tools

	Add Tag	• **Ribbon:** *Review* tab>Redline panel
	Arrow	• **Ribbon:** *Review* tab>Redline panel, expand Draw
	Cloud	• **Ribbon:** *Review* tab>Redline panel, expand Draw
	Color	• **Ribbon:** *Review* tab>Redline panel
	Ellipse	• **Ribbon:** *Review* tab>Redline panel, expand Draw
	Erase	• **Ribbon:** *Review* tab>Redline panel
	Find Comments	• **Ribbon:** *Review* tab>Comments panel
	Freehand	• **Ribbon:** *Review* tab>Redline panel, expand Draw
	Line	• **Ribbon:** *Review* tab>Redline panel, expand Draw
	Line String	• **Ribbon:** *Review* tab>Redline panel, expand Draw
	Text	• **Ribbon:** *Review* tab>Redline panel
	Thickness	• **Ribbon:** *Review* tab>Redline panel
	View Comments	• **Ribbon:** *Review* tab>Comments panel

Chapter 6

Collaboration: Clash Detection

The collaboration stage of the BIM workflow is meant to ensure that all of the disciplines are on the same page. For example, it is important that HVAC ductwork does not interfere with the electrical or structural parts of the building, while at the same time, civil engineers need to be sure that they are bringing utilities into a building at the right location for interior connections to be made. In this chapter you learn how to run clash tests to ensure that everything is properly aligned.

Learning Objectives in this Chapter

- Run a clash test.
- Review clash test results.
- Fix clashes in the model.
- Communicate clash results using reports.

BIM Workflow: Collaborate

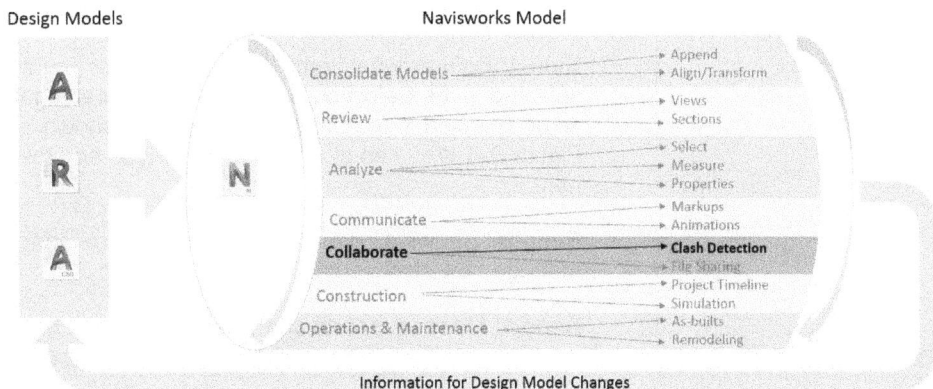

Design Models   Navisworks Model

Consolidate Models — → Append
→ Align/Transform

Review — → Views
→ Sections

Analyze — → Select
→ Measure
→ Properties

Communicate — → Markups
→ Animations

Collaborate — → **Clash Detection**
→ File Sharing

Construction — → Project Timeline
→ Simulation

Operations & Maintenance — → As-builts
→ Remodeling

Information for Design Model Changes

6.1 Overview of the Clash Detective

The Clash Detective eliminates the tedious manual process of inspecting and identifying interference clashes in a 3D project model. This process helps to keep construction costs down by reducing the number of change orders that caused by objects occupying the same space. You can run clash tests using traditional 3D geometry, or using point clouds generated from laser scans. In addition, you can check stationary objects (buildings) against moving objects (cranes) to ensure that construction equipment does not collide with anything on the project site. When you are doing a clash test, consider the following:

- Always run a clash test on the most up-to-date 3D models.

- Rerun existing clash tests before creating a new test.

- Rules can be created to ignore certain clashes.

- You can minimize the number of clashes that must reviewed at a time by working with groups.

- Clash test parameters can be saved and used on other projects.

The Clash Detective Window is shown in Figure 6–1. The top pane is where you can manage all of the clash tests and displays a list of previously-created clash tests. The bottom pane includes four tabs, which are as follows:

- **Rules:** Configure the rules or assumption of items to be ignored when a clash test is run. You can create new rules, edit existing rules, or delete rules, as required.

- **Select:** Defines what items the test includes. The items selected in the Selection A pane are compared against the items selected in the Selection B pane, as shown in Figure 6–1. You can also set the clash type and tolerance here.

- **Results:** Shows a list of the clashes that were found. You can manage how clashes are handled in this tab.

- **Report:** Manage reports and what they include here.

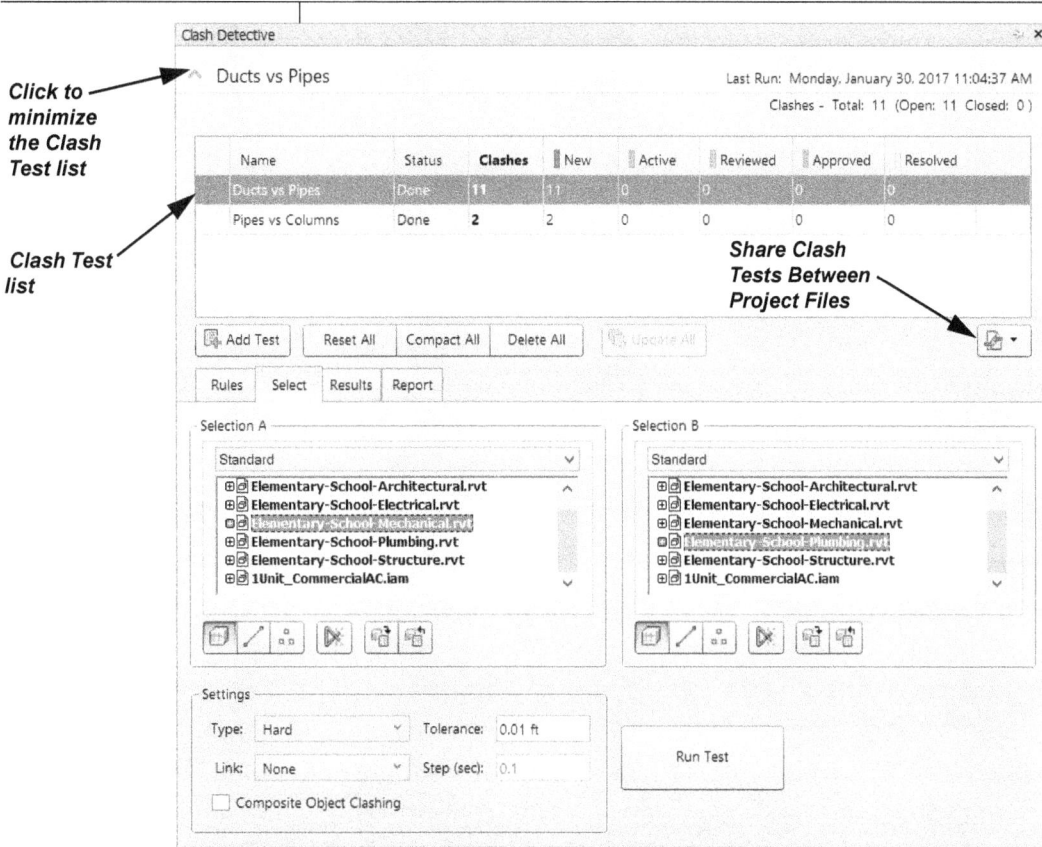

Figure 6–1

How To: Set up and Run a Clash Test

1. In the *Home* tab>Tools panel, click 🐾 (Clash Detective) or press <Ctrl>+<F2>.

2. In the Clash Detective window, click 🖳 (Add Test). A new test is loaded in the top pane with tabs where you can set up the test in the lower panes, as shown in Figure 6–2.

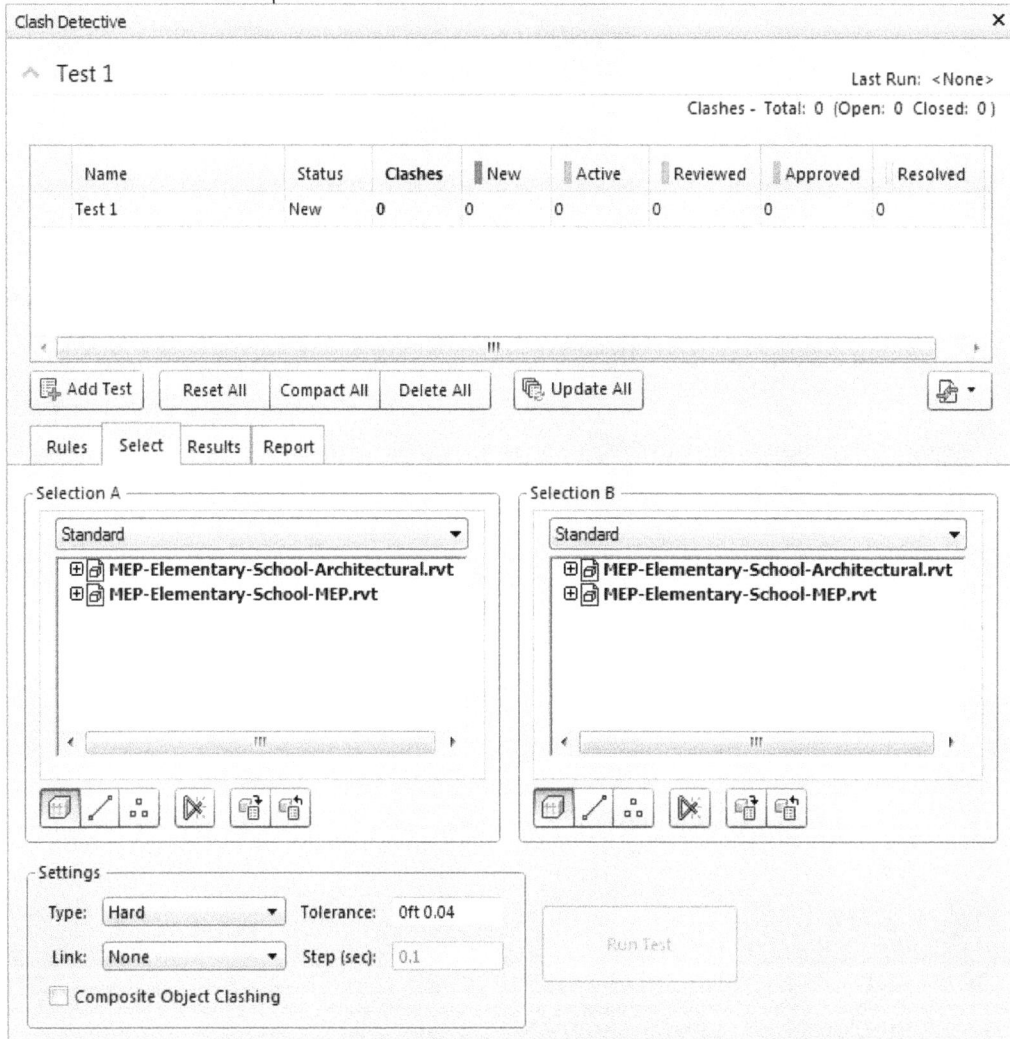

Figure 6–2

3. Type in a name for the new test. You can come back and rename the clash test later, if required.

4. Select the *Rules* tab and select any of the ignore clashes options, as shown in Figure 6–3

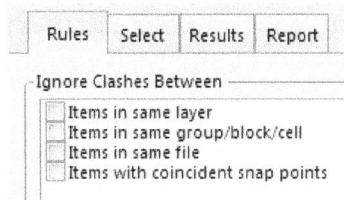

Figure 6–3

5. Select the *Select* tab to set up the clash criteria.
6. Click **Run Test**.
7. The *Results* tab opens displaying a list of clashes and the scene view zooms in on the first clash, as shown in Figure 6–4. Review the results.

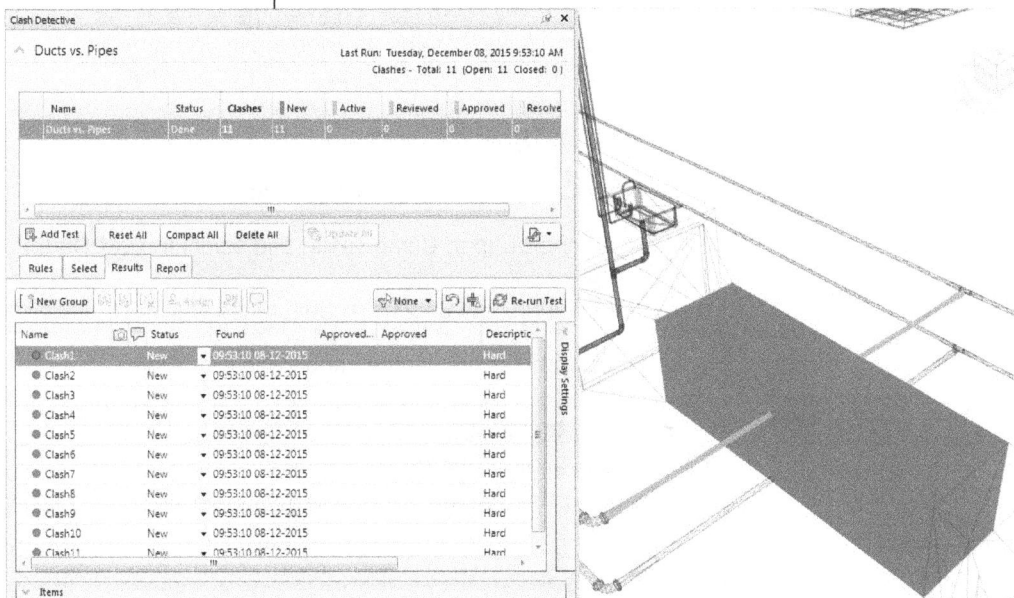

Figure 6–4

8. In the *Report* tab, create a report that can be viewed by others, as required.
9. After reloading files that have been modified, in the Clash Detective window, click **Update All** to re-run the clash test to ensure that everything has been corrected.

Importing and Exporting Clash Tests

Clash tests can be shared between project files. If you set up a clash test to check all of the objects on a specific layer against all of the objects on another layer, you can reuse that test on every project that uses the same standard layer names and definitions.

- Clash Tests are saved as .XML files.

How To: Export Clash Tests

1. In the Clash Detective window, in the Test pane, expand

   (Import/Export Clash Tests) and select **Export Clash Tests**.
2. In the Export dialog box, navigate to the location where you want to save the file.
3. Name the file and click **Save**.

- By default, the clash test is named the same as the Autodesk Navisworks file that you are working in. Rename it to fit a standard so that it can be used in other projects.

How To: Import Clash Tests

1. In the Clash Detective window, in the Test pane, expand

   (Import/Export Clash Tests) and select **Import Clash Tests**.
2. In the Import dialog box, navigate to the location of the saved file.
3. Select the file you want to import and click **Open**.

> **Hint: Customizing Clash Tests**
>
> You can edit the .XML file to suit other projects. When you do this, using standard naming conventions are the key to making them work.

6.2 Setting up Clash Tests

Rules Tab

Use the *Rules* tab to filter out things that you do not want checked, as shown in Figure 6–5. This helps to eliminate false positives and makes the results more meaningful. For example, you might not want to check things that were originally created in the same file, as they are tested separately. For this example, in the *Ignore Clashes Between* pane, you would select the **Items in the same file** option.

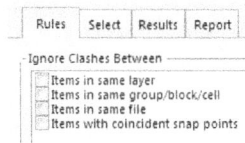

Figure 6–5

- Click **New** to add other options from the Rule Editor.

- Click **Edit** to modify an existing rule.

- Click **Delete** to remove the rule from the list.

Select Tab

The Selection A and Selection B panes enable you to select which items are compared against each other. The format drop-down list in each pane enables you to select the format in which the items are listed, as shown in Figure 6–6. The formats are as follows:

- **Standard:** Provides the same list groups according to the appended files found in the Selection Tree.

- **Compact:** A simplified version of the Standard list.

- **Properties:** Lists objects according to their properties, such as the same name, material, area name, etc.

Using the Sets option makes clash tests easier to share and reuse.

- **Sets:** These are the sets that are listed in the Sets window, and can be either saved sets or search sets. Using a search set ensures that all of the objects in newly appended files are selected for the clash test.

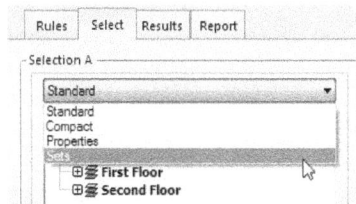

Figure 6–6

Next you can select the types of geometry to compare. Select from the following geometry types, which are located below the selection panes, as shown in Figure 6–7:

- ⬚ **(Surfaces):** These are the 3D triangles most 3D objects are made out of. This is the default setting.

- ╱ **(Lines):** These represent linear objects that have centerlines, such as pipes.

- ⬚ **(Points):** These are point clouds that are created using laser scan data.

- ⬚ **(Self-Intersect):** Clash tests a selection against itself.

Hold <Ctrl> to select multiple items.

- ⬚ **(Use Current Selection):** Selects anything in the selection list that is already selected in the Scene View.

- ⬚ **(Select in Scene):** Enables you to select items in the Scene view to populate the selection list.

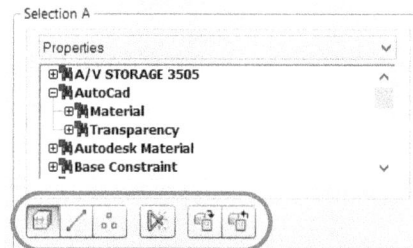

Figure 6–7

Clash Settings

Clash Settings are used to set the type of clash to run and the tolerance factor for the clash, as shown in Figure 6–8. There are four clash types, as follows:

- **Hard:** Two objects reside in the same space or intersect each other.

- **Hard (Conservative):** A more thorough method than Hard that returns two objects that might clash. You might receive false positives using this method, but it is a more thorough test.

- **Clearance:** Two objects are within the tolerance distance of each other. When using this method, hard clashes are also detected.

- **Duplicates:** Two objects are the same type and reside in the same position.

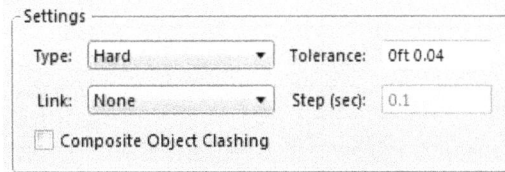

Figure 6–8

It is possible to run a clash test against construction equipment or other items that might move on site. To do this, link the clash test to a TimeLiner schedule or an object animation scene using the Settings area>Link drop-down list. Then, set the period of time between clash tests in the *Step (sec)* field. Since multiple clash tests are run at set intervals throughout the simulation sequence, it does take more time to complete a clash test with a link.

If a clash test is taking too much time to finish, you can stop the test by clicking **Cancel** in the Working dialog box, shown in Figure 6–9. The progress bar displays how much of the model was tested. All of the clashes that were found before the test was canceled are reported, and the test displays a *Partial* status in the Clash list, as shown in Figure 6–10.

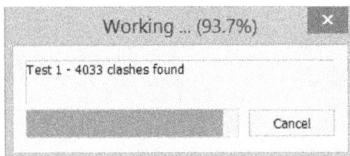

Figure 6–9

Figure 6–10

How To: Select Items to Test

1. In the *Selection A* column, expand the *Search in:* drop-down list and select the format of how you want to view the potential items, as shown in Figure 6–11.

   - Create and use Sets if you expect to recheck the same clashes when models are updated.

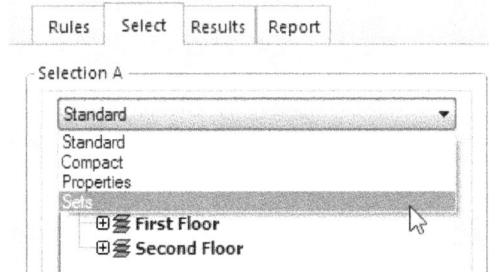

Figure 6–11

2. Select the items or sets you want to compare.

   - Hold <Ctrl> or <Shift> to select multiple options.

3. Repeat the process in the *Selection B* column.
4. Specify the geometry types and settings you want to use.

Practice 6a

Create Clash Tests

Practice Objective

- Check for clashes between objects.

Estimated time for completion: 5 minutes

In this practice you will check the model for clashes against the structural columns and pipes, as shown in Figure 6–12.

Figure 6–12

Task 1 - Create a simple clash test.

---

1. In the *Clash Detection* practice files folder, open **NewElementarySchool-Simple.nwf**.

2. In the Saved Viewpoints window, click **SW Isometric**.

If the Clash Detective is not already displayed, in the Home tab>Tools panel, click (Clash Detective).

3. In the Clash Detective window click (Add Test).

4. Select the name, and then click on it again to rename it. Type **Structure vs Pipes** for the name, as shown in Figure 6–13.

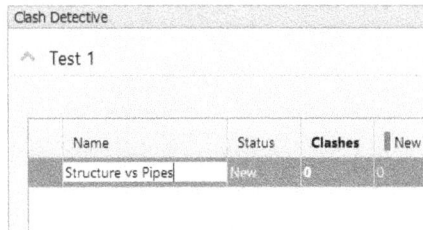

Figure 6–13

---

5. In the *Rules* tab, clear all of the *Ignore Clashes Between* options, as shown in Figure 6–14

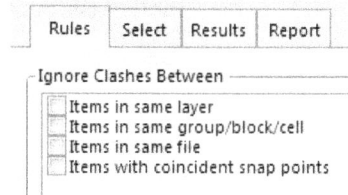

| Rules | Select | Results | Report |

Ignore Clashes Between
- Items in same layer
- Items in same group/block/cell
- Items in same file
- Items with coincident snap points

Figure 6–14

6. In the *Select* tab, set up the clash criteria.

7. In the Selection A pane, select **Standard** from the list format drop-down list. Then select **Elementary-School-Structure.rvt**.

8. In the Selection B pane, select **Sets** from the list format drop-down list. Then select the **Pipes** search set.

9. Click **Run Test**.

10. The *Results* tab displays a list of clashes and the scene view zooms in on the first clash. Click the down arrow next to Items to minimize the Items pane, as shown in Figure 6–15. Review the results.

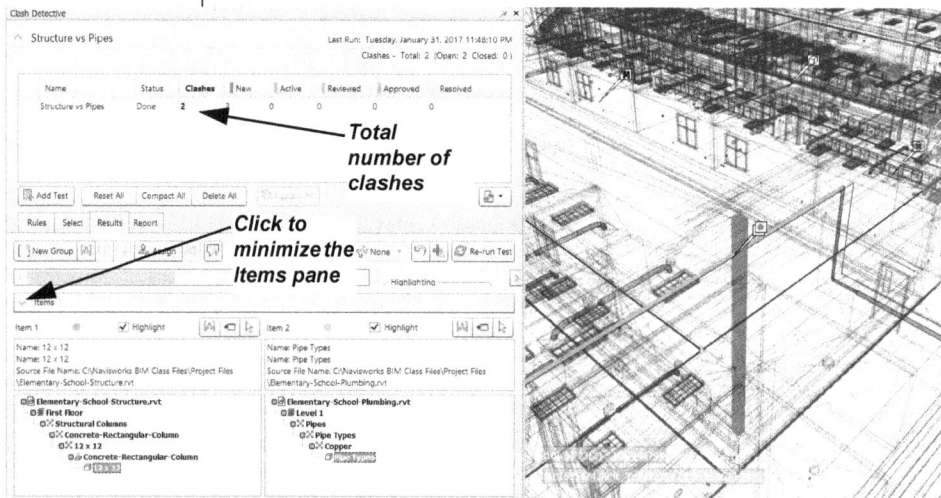

Figure 6–15

11. Save the file.

Task 2 - Run a clash test on pipes and ducts.

1. In the Clash Detective window, click ▣ (Add Test).

2. Select the name, and then click on it again to rename it. Type **Pipes vs Ducts** for the name.

3. In the *Rules* tab, clear all of the *Ignore Clashes Between* options.

4. In the *Select* tab, set up the clash criteria.

5. In the *Selection A* pane, select **Sets** from the list format drop-down. Then select **Pipes** search set.

6. In the *Selection B* pane, select **Sets** from the list format drop-down. Then select the **Ducts** search set.

7. In the *Settings* area, change the Type to **Clearance** and set the *Tolerance* to **0.2 ft** so that you check for things that are less than a quarter of an inch part.

8. Click **Run Test**.

9. The *Results* tab displays a list of clashes and the scene view zooms in on the first clash, as shown in Figure 6–16. Review the results.

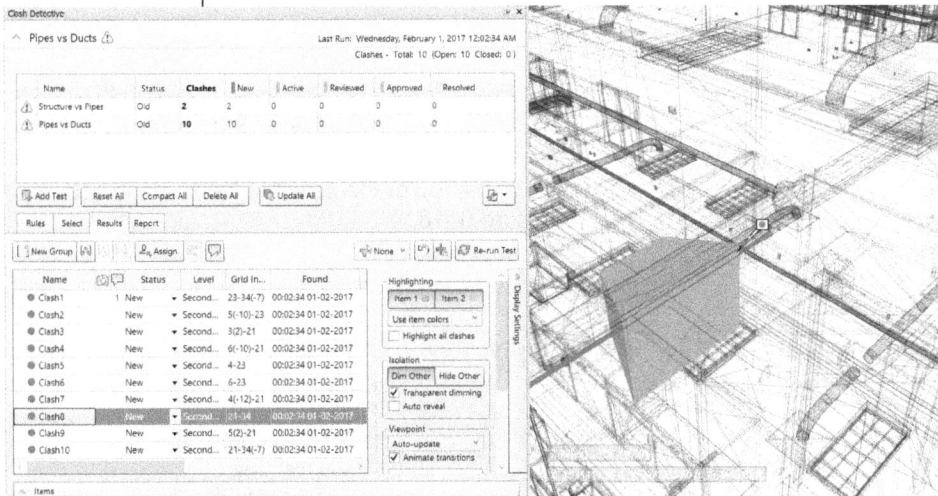

Figure 6–16

10. Save the file.

6.3 Reviewing Clash Results

The *Results* tab of the Clash Detective window enables you to review the clashes that were found during each clash test. Selecting a clash test in the top pane displays a list of clashes in the bottom pane, as shown in Figure 6–17. Use this pane to:

- View clash results and change how they display.

- Set the status of a clash.

- Add comments to each clash.

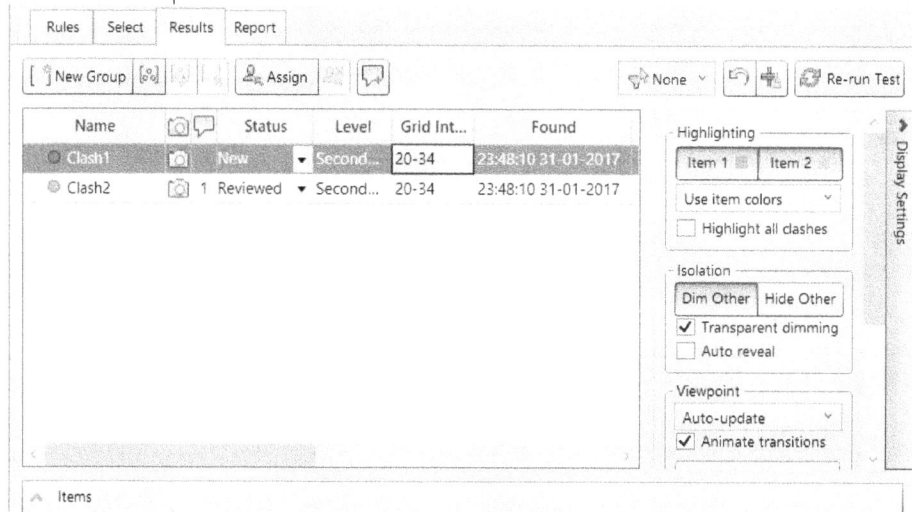

Figure 6–17

- Click the arrow next to the Items title to display or hide the tests at the top or the selected items at the bottom, as shown in Figure 6–18.

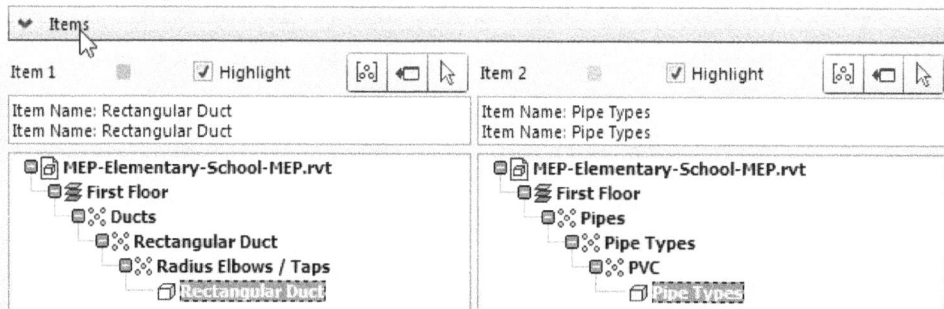

Figure 6–18

Viewing Clashes

Click on a clash to zoom to it in the Scene view. If you Pan or Zoom the Scene view while a clash is selected, the view is saved and the Camera icon displays (as shown in Figure 6–19) to indicate that there is a saved viewpoint available.

Figure 6–19

Display Settings

The Display Settings panel (shown in Figure 6–20) enables you to set how clashed items and other items display in the Scene view. Each of the clash items can be set to their own color, and you can fade or completely hide everything else in the Scene view. By isolating clashed items, you can get a cleaner picture of the corrections that need to be made.

• Click on the Display Settings title to open the panel.

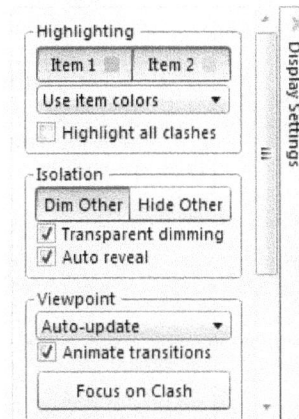

Figure 6–20

Highlighting

Highlighting can help you see which items are clashing, as shown in Figure 6–21.

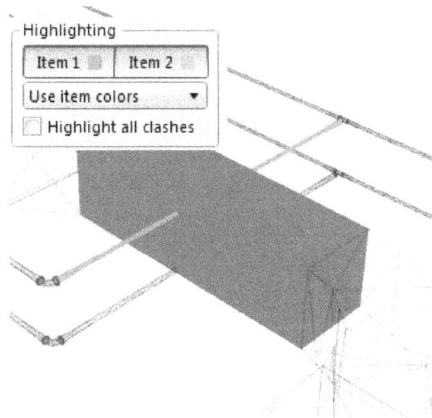

Figure 6–21

- Select the **Item 1** and **Item 2** buttons to toggle the highlighting on and off.

- In the drop-down list, use the **Use item colors** option to display the highlight colors, or use the **Use status color option** to display both items using the color defined for the status options.

- Select **Highlight all clashes** to display all clashes. This can be especially helpful if you have more than one item clashing with the same item (as shown in Figure 6–22), or if you want to see an overview of all of the clashed areas.

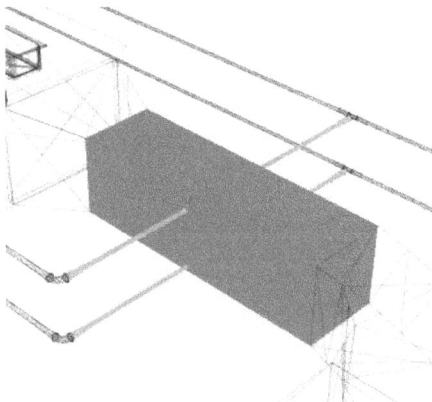

Figure 6–22

Isolation

By default, all of the other elements around the clashing elements are dimmed and display in wireframe, as shown in Figure 6–22 (above). You can change this behavior in the Isolation area, shown in Figure 6–23. In the *Isolation* area, click **Hide Other** to display only the items in the current clash. This automatically toggles off the **Transparent dimming** option.

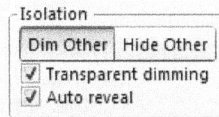

Figure 6–23

- If neither option is selected, the clash items are highlighted but the other elements display in the current Render Style Mode.

- **Auto reveal** temporarily hides any elements that might be obscuring the clash. It is a good idea to have this selected.

Viewpoint

In the *Viewpoint* area, you can specify how the viewpoint displays when you select clashes, as shown in Figure 6–24.

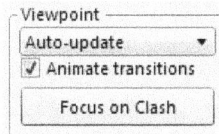

Figure 6–24

The *Viewpoint* area options are as follows:

- **Auto-update:** Automatically zooms in on an appropriate viewpoint and saves any changes you make to the viewpoint.

- **Auto-load:** Automatically zooms in on the default viewpoint, but does not save it as a new viewpoint if you navigate away.

- **Manual:** Does not change the viewpoint when you select clashes. You might want to use this option to display each clash in the context of the overall view.

- **Animate transitions:** Zooms out from the existing clash to the full model and then back in on the selected clash. This can help you locate a specific clash in the model.

- **Focus on Clash:** Zooms in on the clash again if you have moved away from it. This also turns on the 3rd Person avatar by default.

You can right-click on a camera icon in the *Results* tab to load or save a viewpoint other than the automatic viewpoint. You can also specify **Focus on Clash** or delete the selected viewpoint or all viewpoints.

Hint: Clash Detective Options

You can specify how viewpoints display and animate when you select clashes, how clash tests are imported and exported, and set the default custom highlight colors.

To access these options, in the Application Menu, click **Options**. In the Options editor, expand **Tools>Clash Detective**, as shown in Figure 6–25.

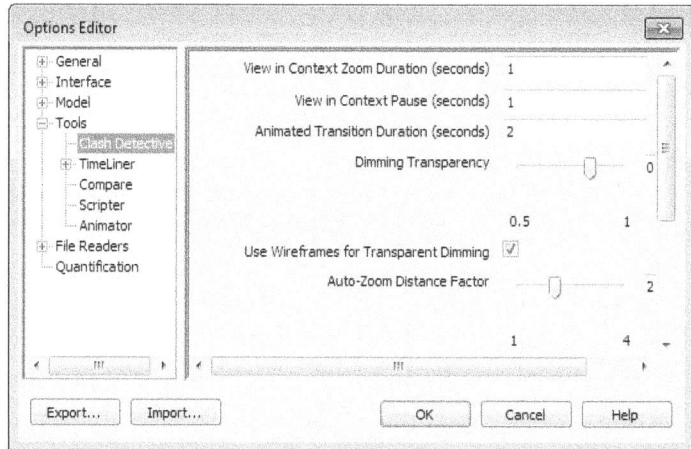

Figure 6–25

6.4 Assigning Clash Fixes

Assigning and Commenting

Clashes are most often found between different disciplines that do not work together. For example, electrical cable trays, plumbing pipes, and ducts might be modeled by separate firms trying to occupy the same space in a plenum. You can assign responsibility for a clash (as shown in Figure 6–26) and add comments.

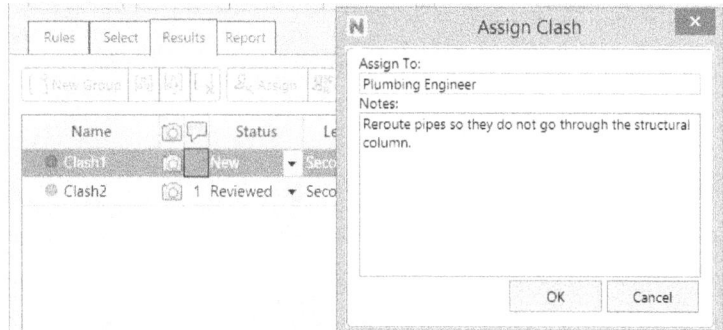

Figure 6–26

How To: Assign and Comment on Clashes

1. In the Clash Detective>*Results* tab, select a clash or clash group.
2. Click ⚃ (Assign) or 💬 (Add Comment).
3. In the Assign Clash dialog box, enter a name in the *Assign To* field, and then add any notes, as shown in Figure 6–26 (above).
   - Alternatively, in the Add Comment dialog box, type in the comment as shown in Figure 6–27.

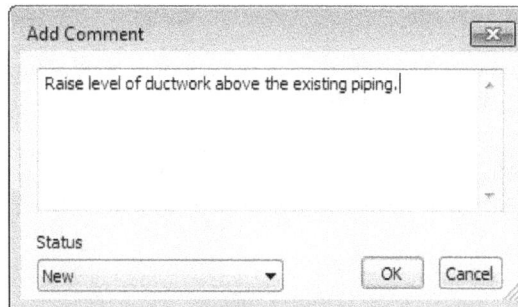

Figure 6–27

4. Click **OK**.

- To remove an assignment, select the clash and click

  ⚊̲ͯ (Unassign).

- Comments and assignments are typically included in any clash test reports.

- To view the comments in the Autodesk Navisworks software, in the *Review* tab>Comments panel, click 🗩 (View Comments) to open the Comments window, shown in Figure 6–28.

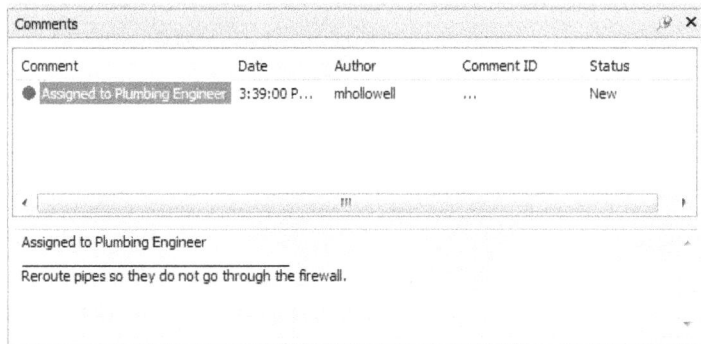

Figure 6–28

Setting the Clash Status

The Clash Status changes automatically as you work through the project. You can also manually apply a clash status, as shown in Figure 6–29.

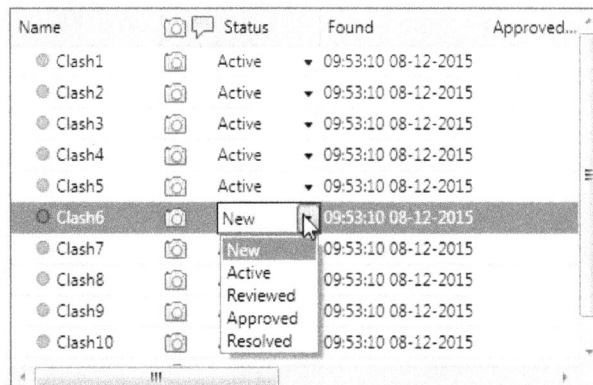

Figure 6–29

Each status displays a different color dot beside the name. The number of clashes for each status also displays in the Test pane, as shown in Figure 6–30.

Name	Status	Clashes	New	Active	Reviewed	Approved	Resolved
Ducts vs. Pipes	Done	7	2	5	0	0	0
Walls vs. Pipes	Done	0	0	0	0	0	0
Structure vs. MEP	New	0	0	0	0	0	0

Figure 6–30

The clash statuses are as follows:

- **New:** The first time a clash has been detected.

- **Active:** A Clash test has been run again, and the clash is still unresolved.

- **Reviewed:** The clash has been reviewed, but not modified.

- **Approved:** The clash is approved to remain as is. The user who approved and the time of approval are logged.

- **Resolved:** The clash was in a previous run of the test, but is no longer found and is assumed to be resolved.
  - If a clash is manually changed to Resolved, when the test is run again and the clash still exists, the clash is assigned a New status.

- **Old:** When a model is updated since the test was run, this is a reminder that the current test does not reflect the information in the updated model. Clash tests show this status.

6.5 Clash Grouping

Grouping Clashes

Grouping related clashes together can save everyone time. For example, a series of pipes might be going through a fire-rated wall. Each intersection of pipe and wall is considered one clash. You can group these clashes together (as shown in Figure 6–31) so that they can all be addressed at the same time.

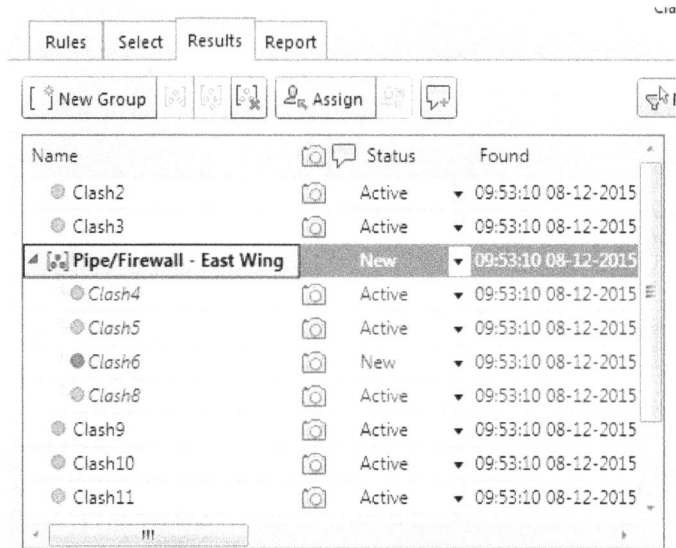

Figure 6–31

You can create groups in any of the following three ways:

- Click [⚲] (New Group) and then drag and drop clashes into the group.

- Select several clashes and click [⚲] (Group Selected Clashes).

- In the *Results* tab, select the clashes, right-click on them, and then select **Group,** as shown in Figure 6–32.

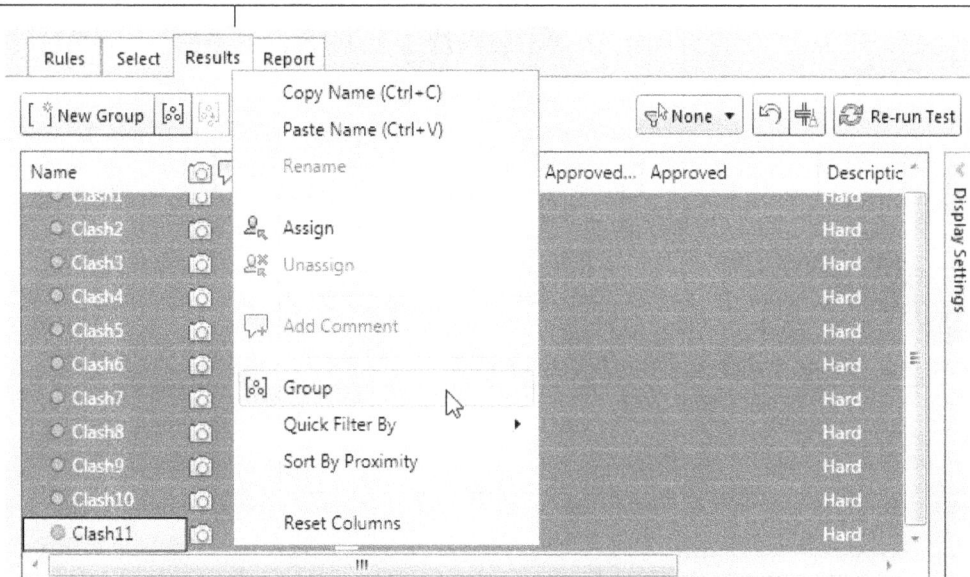

Figure 6–32

- Use <Ctrl> or <Shift> to select multiple names.

- You can rename the groups to make them easily recognizable. Click twice on the name or right-click and select **Rename**.

- To remove a clash from a group, select it and click

  [icon] (Remove from Group).

- To ungroup, select the group title and click [icon] (Explode Group).

6.6 Sharing Clash Test Results

The *Reports* tab of the Clash Detective window enables you to create a text file, HTML report, or XML report to communicate the details of the clash tests. You can also save a list of viewpoints for later review. The *Reports* tab is broken into the following three areas, as shown in Figure 6–33:

It is a good practice to keep reports as short and as easy to read as possible. Do this by only including the required information in the report.

- **Contents:** Provides a list of selectable attributes that can be included in the report.

- **Include Clashes:** The clash status is used to select which clashes are included in the report. Groups can also be used to control the report contents.

- **Output Settings:** Sets the type and format of the report.

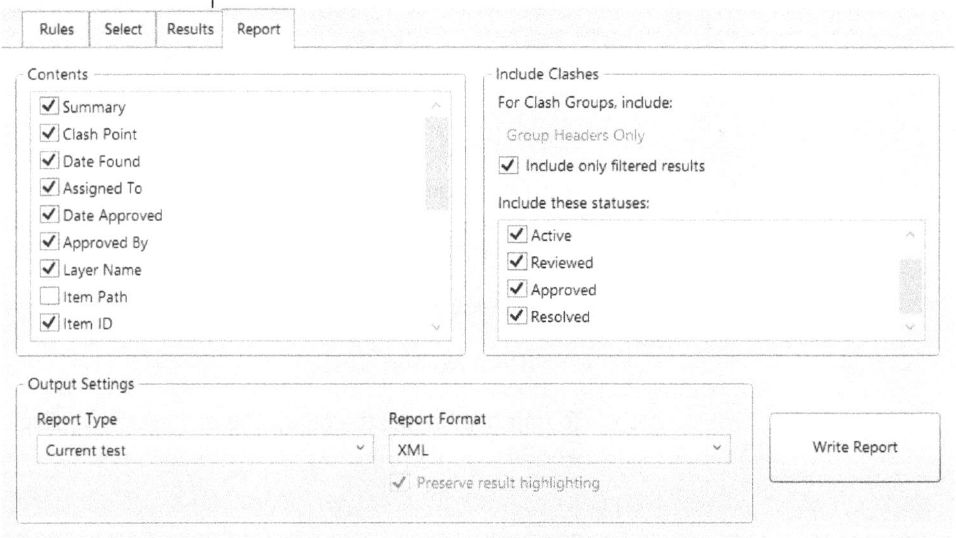

Figure 6–33

Output Settings

There are several types of reports and formats to chose from, as listed below:

Report Type

There are three report types, as shown in Figure 6–34:

- **Current Test:** Run a report on the currently-selected clash test.

- **All Tests (Combined):** Combine all of the clash tests into a single report.

- **All Tests (Separate):** Create reports for all of the clash tests, with a separate report for each clash test.

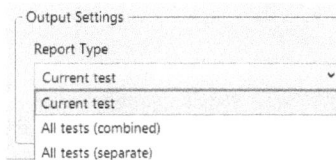

Figure 6–34

Report Format

There are several report formats available for the clash test results. When a report is written, a .JPEG file is created for each Scene view that contains a clash. These image files are automatically saved to a folder located in the same directory as the report. The following report formats are available:

- **XML:** Includes images and details for clashes in an .XML file.

- **HTML:** Includes images and details for clashes in an .HTML file.

- **HTML (Tabular):** Includes details for clashes in a table which can be opened and edited in Microsoft Excel 2007 or later.

- **Text:** Includes the details for clashes in a text file with references to the image filenames.

- **As Viewpoint:** Creates a saved viewpoint for each clash and places all of the clash viewpoints within one folder in the Saved Viewpoints window. Comments containing the details of each clash are added to the viewpoint automatically.

This is helpful for sharing the clash results with anyone using the Autodesk Navisworks Freedom software.

How To: Write a Clash Test Report

1. Open the Clash Detective window.
2. Select the clash test you want to create a report for.
3. In the *Report* tab, do the following, as shown in Figure 6–35:
   - In the *Contents* area, select any information that you want to include in the report.
   - In the *Include Clashes area,* select the grouping level and statuses that you want to include in the report.
   - In the *Output Settings* area, select the type and format of the report that you need.

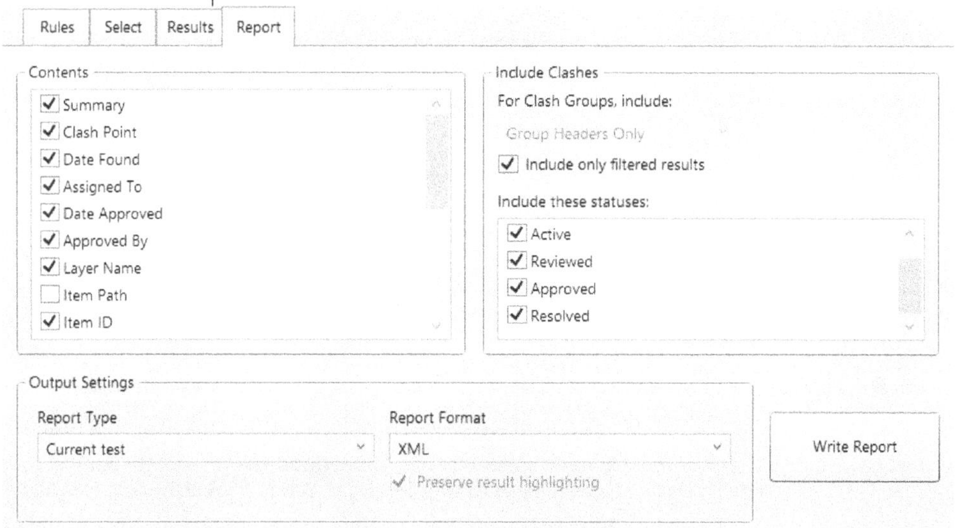

| Rules | Select | Results | Report |

Contents
- ☑ Summary
- ☑ Clash Point
- ☑ Date Found
- ☑ Assigned To
- ☑ Date Approved
- ☑ Approved By
- ☑ Layer Name
- ☐ Item Path
- ☑ Item ID

Include Clashes

For Clash Groups, include:

Group Headers Only

☑ Include only filtered results

Include these statuses:
- ☑ Active
- ☑ Reviewed
- ☑ Approved
- ☑ Resolved

Output Settings

Report Type
Current test

Report Format
XML

☑ Preserve result highlighting

Write Report

Figure 6–35

4. Click **Write Report**.

6.7 Incorporating Model Updates

Incorporating changes to the source models in the Autodesk Navisworks software can be done very easily, depending on the file format you are using. Remember, the following file formats are used in the Autodesk Navisworks software:

- **Navisworks (.NWD):** The current state (or "snapshot") of a project, with all of the model geometry and redlines included.
- **Navisworks File Set (.NWF):** Includes links to the original files that form an Autodesk Navisworks model and redlines.
- **Navisworks Cache (.NWC):** Snapshots of each original file that are created automatically when you open or append files from other software.

The .NWF format are the files you should work with most often as updating this model is the easiest.

- Since the .NWF files include links to the source files, you can simply overwrite the original source file with the latest version of the source file.

- If the source files are on your server, you can chose to keep the .NWF file updated at all times.

- If you are sharing files with team members outside of your office, you can also copy files from an external server or email.

How To: Incorporate Updated Models in Clash Tests

1. In Windows Explorer, navigate to the Project Files. Paste the updated models into the directory, overwriting the original source files.
2. In the Autodesk Navisworks software, on the *Home* Tab>

   Project panel, click (Refresh) to force a refresh of the model to the latest file version.
3. If the files do not update in the Autodesk Navisworks model, close the file, delete the (.NWC) file, and then re-open the Autodesk Navisworks model.
4. In the Clash Detective window, click (Update All) to re-run all of the clash tests.

Practice 6b

Review Clash Tests

Practice Objectives

- Review clash tests for clashes between objects.
- Assign clashes to individuals for correcting.

Estimated time for completion: 15 minutes

In this practice you will review the clash tests ran in the previous practice. Then you will assign clashes to specific team members for corrections, as shown in Figure 6–36. Finally, you will create reports to share the results with others.

Figure 6–36

Task 1 - Review and group the results.

1. In the *Clash Detection* practice files folder, open **NewElementarySchool-Review.nwf**.

2. In the Clash Detective window, select the **Pipes vs Ducts** clash test.

3. Select the *Results* tab. Review several of the clashes by clicking on them one at a time.

At first glance, all but one clash includes the same pipe.

4. In the *Results* tab, select **Clash1**. Hold <Shift> and select **Clash10** to select all of the clashes from 1 to 10. Hold <Ctrl> and select **Clash8** to clear it, as shown in Figure 6–37.

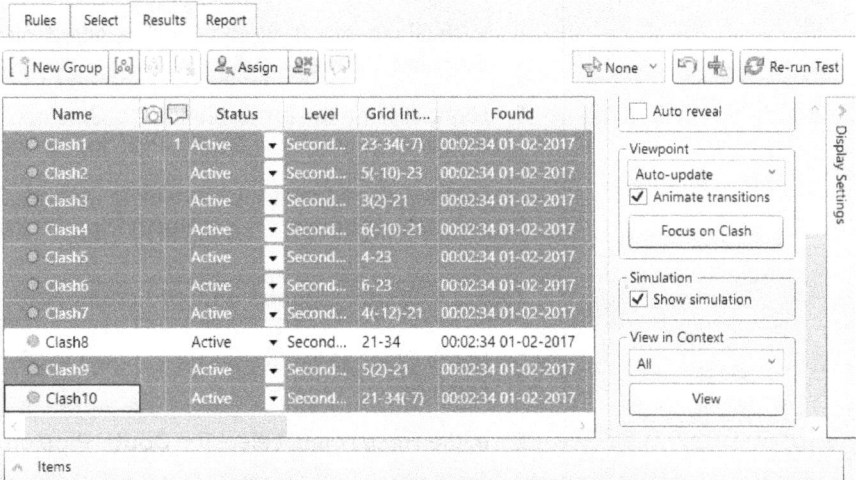

Figure 6–37

5. In the *Results* tab, click (Group Selected Clashes). The results are shown in Figure 6–38. Note how the number of clashes in the clash list has been reduced to 2.

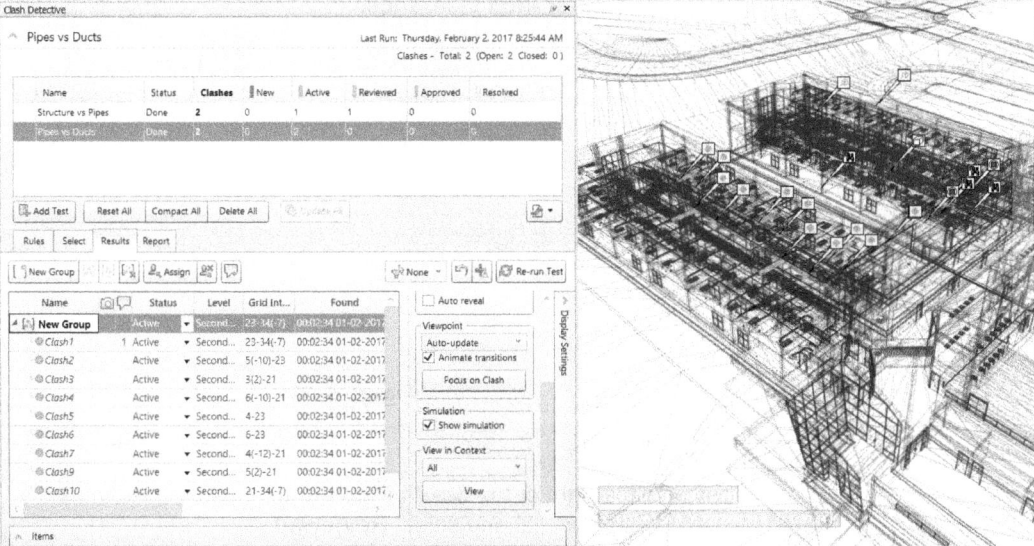

Figure 6–38

With the clashes grouped, note that the clashes do not all include the same pipe.

6. In the New Group, hold <Ctrl> and select Clashes 1, 3, 5, and 6.

7. Click (Remove from Group).

8. With Clashes 1, 3, 5, and 6 still selected, click ⬚ (Group Selected Clashes).

9. Right-click on the group containing Clashes 1, 3, 5, and 6 and select **Rename**. Type **South Pipe** for the name.

10. Right-click on the group containing Clashes 2, 4, 7, 9, and 10 and select **Rename**. Type **North Pipe** for the name.

Task 2 - Assign clashes and add comments.

1. In the Clash Detective window, select the Pipes vs Ducts clash test.

2. In the *Results* tab, select the **South Pipe** group.

3. Click ⚲ (Assign).

4. In the Assign Clash dialog box, in the *Assign To* field, type **Jessica**, and then enter the following in the *Notes* field, as shown in Figure 6–39:

   • **Reroute pipe above the ductwork and ensure a quarter inch clearance.**

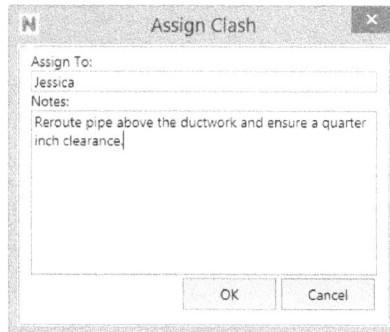

Figure 6–39

5. Click **OK**.

6. To the right of the **South Pipe** group, expand the Status drop-down list and select **Reviewed**.

7. In the *Results* tab, select the **North Pipe** group.

8. Click ⚲ (Assign).

9. In the Assign Clash dialog box, in the *Assign To* field, type **Jessica**, and then enter the following in the *Notes* field, as shown in Figure 6–40:

- **Reroute pipe above the ductwork and ensure a quarter inch clearance.**

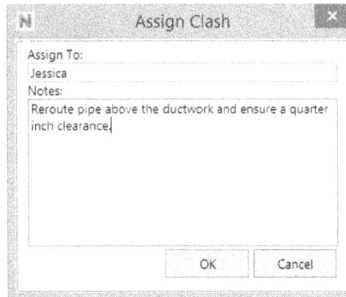

Assign Clash

Assign To:
Jessica
Notes:
Reroute pipe above the ductwork and ensure a quarter inch clearance.

OK   Cancel

Figure 6–40

10. Click **OK**.

11. To the right of the **North Pipe** group, expand the Status drop-down list and select **Reviewed**.

12. In the *Results* tab, select **Clash8**.

13. Click (Assign).

14. In the Assign Clash dialog box, in the *Assign To* field, type **Jessica**, and then enter the following in the *Notes* field:

- **Reroute pipe to the right of the ductwork and ensure a quarter inch clearance.**

15. Click **OK**.

16. To the right of **Clash8**, expand the Status drop-down list and select **Reviewed**.

17. In the Clash Detective window, select the **Structure vs Pipes** clash test.

18. In the *Results* tab, select **Clash1**.

19. Click (Assign).

20. In the Assign Clash dialog box, in the *Assign To* field, type **Sam**, and then enter the following in the *Notes* field:

- **Reroute pipe to the left of the column and ensure a quarter inch clearance.**

21. Click **OK**.

22. To the right of **Clash1**, expand the Status drop-down list and select **Reviewed**.

23. In the *Results* tab, select **Clash2**.

24. Click ⊡ (Add Comment).

25. In the Add Comment dialog box, type **Should this pipe be moved or removed?**.

26. In the Status drop-down list, select **Active**, as shown in Figure 6–41.

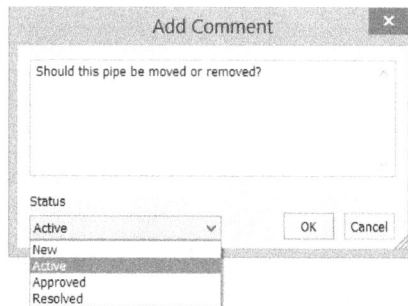

Figure 6–41

27. Click **OK**.

28. To see the comments in the Autodesk Navisworks software, in the *Review* tab>Comments panel, click ⊡ (View Comments). The Comments window displays, as shown in Figure 6–42.

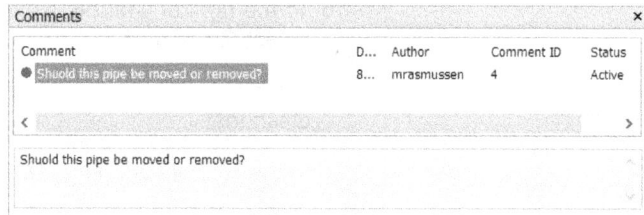

Figure 6–42

Task 3 - Create a clash report.

1. In the Clash Detective window, select the *Report* tab.:

2. In the *Contents* area, select the following, as shown in Figure 6–43:
   - Summery
   - Clash Point
   - Assigned To
   - Status
   - Description
   - Comments
   - Image
   - Clash Group
   - Grid Location

3. In the *Include Clashes area,* uncheck the option to **Include only filtered results**. Ensure that all of the statuses are selected.

4. In the *Output Settings* area, for *Report Type,* select **All Tests (combined)**, and for *Report Format* select **HTML**.

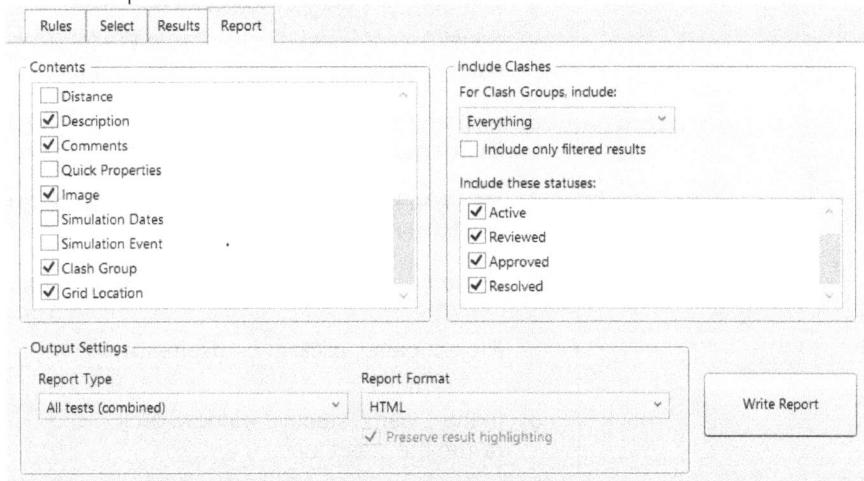

Figure 6–43

5. Click **Write Report**.

6. In the Save As dialog box, navigate to *C:\Navisworks BIM Practice Files\Clash Detection* and click **Save** to accept the default Filename.

7. In Windows Explorer, note the folder containing the images for the report and the HTML file, as shown in Figure 6–44.

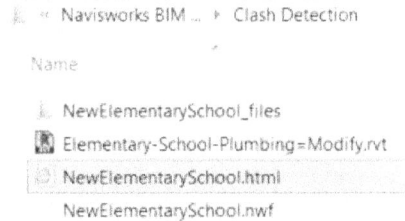

Navisworks BIM ... ▸ Clash Detection

Name

⬜ NewElementarySchool_files
🗎 Elementary-School-Plumbing=Modify.rvt
🗎 NewElementarySchool.html
NewElementarySchool.nwf

Figure 6–44

8. Open the HTML file to review the report.

9. Close the HTML file.

Task 4 - Update the appended plumbing model and re-run the clash tests.

---

1. In Windows Explorer, right-click on **Elementary-School-Plumbing=Modify.rvt** file and select **Copy**.

2. In Windows Explorer, navigate to *C:\Navisworks BIM Practice Files\Project Files*. Right-click in the folder window and select **Paste**.

3. Rename the *Elementary-School-Plumbing.rvt* file to **Elementary-School-Plumbing-Original.rvt**

4. Rename the **Elementary-School-Plumbing=Modify.rvt** file to **Elementary-School-Plumbing.rvt**

5. In the Autodesk Navisworks software, in the *Home* Tab> Project panel, click 🔄 (Refresh)

6. In the Clash Detective window, click ⬚ Update All (Update All) to re-run the clash tests.

7. Review the clashes individually. All of the clashes in the **Pipes vs Duct** clash test should display a status of **Resolved**. The clashes in the **Structure vs Pipes** clash test still need to be resolved.

Task 5 - Update the AutoCAD Civil 3D model.

In this task you will update the AutoCAD® Civil 3D® model to correct the elevation issues noted in the redlines. As the project point was not updated in the Autodesk® Revit® models to accommodate the new building elevation, you will also modify the elevations of the Autodesk Revit models to match the new surface elevations.

1. In Windows explorer, navigate to the *Project Files\Civil Files\Source Drawings\Surfaces* practice files folder.

2. Rename **SiteLayout.dwg** to **SiteLayout-Original.dwg**.

3. Rename **SiteLayout-Edited.dwg** to **SiteLayout.dwg**.

4. In the Autodesk Navisworks software, in the *Home* Tab> Project panel, click ⟳ (Refresh).

5. In the Saved Viewpoints window, click **Section-EntrancePlatform**.
   - Note: If the surface does not change, it might be necessary to delete the .NWC file that was created when the original file was loaded into the model.

You should see that the surface has been updated so that the building pad is now at elevation 4615.2, with the entrance platform meeting the proposed finish ground. You will need to transform all of the Autodesk Revit and Autodesk® Inventor® files to adjust the elevation of the building to match.

6. In the Selection Tree window, select all of the files except **SiteLayout.dwg**.

7. Right-click on any one of the selected files and select **Override Item>Override Transform**.

8. In the Override Transform dialog box, enter **3.2** in the *Z value* and click **OK**.

Chapter Review Questions

1. What are the different types of clashes that you can run? (Select all that apply.)

    a. Hard

    b. Soft

    c. Partial

    d. Clearance

2. Clash test parameters can be saved and used on other projects.

    a. True

    b. False

3. In the Clash Detective window, what would you use the *Rules* tab for?

    a. Use Rules to include the things you want to check.

    b. Use Rules to set the clearance tolerance.

    c. Use Rules to filter out things you do not want checked.

    d. Use Rules to change the colors of clashing items.

4. What is the purpose of Groups in the Clash Detective?

    a. To hide non-clashing items easily.

    b. To bring related clashes together.

    c. To run multiple clash tests at the same time.

    d. To view similar comments at the same time.

5. Where can you change the color of items that clash?

    a. In the Options dialog box.

    b. In the Clash Detective window, under Display Settings, in the *Isolation* Area.

    c. In the Clash Detective window, under Display Settings, in the *Highlighting* Area.

    d. In the Clash Detective window, in the Items pane.

Command Summary

Button	Command	Location
	Add Comment	• **Window:** Clash Detective>*Review* tab
	Add Test	• **Window:** Clash Detective
	Assign	• **Window:** Clash Detective>*Review* tab
	Clash Detective	• **Ribbon:** *Home* tab>Project Panel • **Hot Key:** <Ctrl>+<F2>
	Explode Group	• **Window:** Clash Detective>*Review* tab
	Group Selected Clashes	• **Window:** Clash Detective>*Review* tab
	Import/Export Clash Tests	• **Window:** Clash Detective
	New Group	• **Window:** Clash Detective>*Review* tab
	Remove from Group	• **Window:** Clash Detective>*Review* tab
	Unassign	• **Window:** Clash Detective>*Review* tab
	View Comment	• **Ribbon:** *Review* tab>Comments Panel

Practices to Prepare for Animator

There is a lot of work that goes into a project. In a classroom environment, you might not have time to create all of the viewpoints, sets, or search sets required for the class project. This chapter provides extra practice to help you test your skills. If you cannot complete a practice, go back and review the referenced chapter to refresh your memory on how to complete the task.

Learning Objectives in this Chapter

- Append a model.
- Transform a model.
- Create a Viewpoint.
- Create a selection set.
- Create a search set.

Practice 7a

Append Models

Practice Objectives

- Append a crane to the model.
- Transform the crane to the correct location.

Estimated time for completion: 5 minutes

This practice is a review of *Section 2.1: Consolidating the Model* and *Section 2.2: Aligning Models*. You will add a crane for later use, as shown in Figure 7–1.

Figure 7–1

Task 1 - Append a new model to the project.

1. In the *Extra Practice* practice files folder, open **NewElementarySchool-Append.nwf**.

2. In the *Home* Tab>Project panel, click ⬜ (Append).

3. In the Append dialog box, expand the *Files of type* drop-down list and set the file type to **SketchUp (*.skp)**.

4. Navigate to the *Animator* practice files folder, select **Mobile Crane.skp**, and click **Open**.

Task 2 - Transform the new model so it lines up.

You might not see the Crane because it was imported at the wrong location.

1. In the Selection Tree window, right-click on the newly appended Sketchup file and select **Units and Transform**.

2. In the Units and Transform dialog box, set the following values, as shown in Figure 7–2:
   - *Units:* **Centimeters**
   - *Origin (ft): X:* **1535779**, *Y:* **7272131**, *Z:* **4615**
   - Rotation: **76.5**

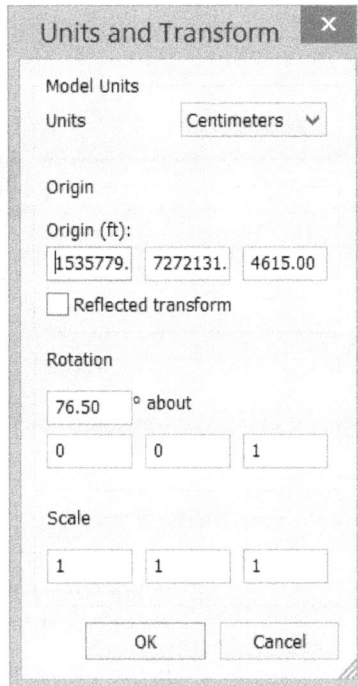

Figure 7–2

3. Click **OK**.

Practice 7b | Save Viewpoints

Practice Objective

- Save Viewpoints for easy navigation and communication.

Estimated time for completion: 20 minutes

This practice is a review of *Section 3.1: Saving and Retrieving Views*. In the model shown in Figure 7–3, you will create additional viewpoints and save them for later use.

Figure 7–3

Task 1 - Create a series of views around the building.

1. In the *Extra Practice* practice files folder open **NewElementarySchool-Views.nwf**.

2. In the *Viewpoint* tab>Camera panel, select the **Perspective** view.

3. Open the Saved Viewpoints window, if it is not already.

4. Pan and Orbit the model until the Scene view displays similar to that shown in Figure 7–4.

Figure 7–4

5. In the Viewpoint tab>Save, Load & Playback panel, click
   📷 (Save Viewpoint).

6. In the Saved Viewpoints window, type **Overview** for the
   name.

7. Repeat Steps 4 to 6 to create the following saved viewpoints,
   using the names and figure references provided:

   • Save the view shown in Figure 7–5 as **SE-Isometric**:

Figure 7–5

- Save the view shown in Figure 7–6 as **East Side**:

Figure 7–6

- Save the view shown in Figure 7–7 as **NE-Isometric**:

Figure 7–7

- Save the view shown in Figure 7–8 as **North Side**:

Figure 7–8

- Save the view shown in Figure 7–9 as **NW-Isometric**:

Figure 7–9

- Save the view shown in Figure 7–10 as **West Side**:

Figure 7–10

- Save the view shown in Figure 7–11 as **SW-Isometric**:

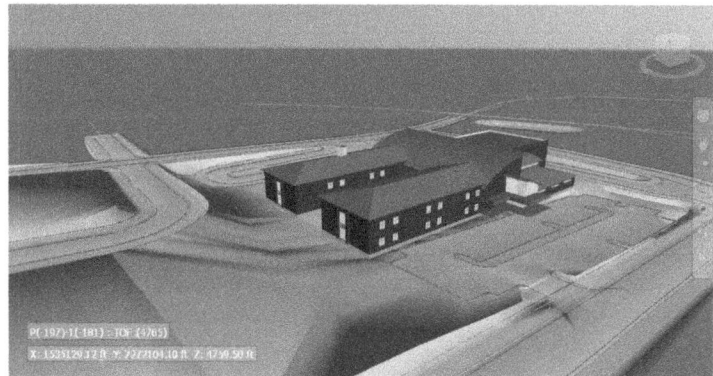

Figure 7–11

Task 2 - Create a series of views to walk into the building.

1. Pan and Orbit the model until the Scene view displays similar to that shown in Figure 7–12.

P(-33)·11(1) : TOF (4631)
X: 1535185.83 ft Y: 7272274.90 ft Z: 4626.21 ft

Figure 7–12

2. In the Viewpoint tab>Save, Load & Playback panel, click
   📷 (Save Viewpoint).

3. In the Saved Viewpoints window type **Front Entry** for the name.

4. In the Navigation Bar, click 👣 (Walk).

5. Click and drag the mouse forward until the Scene view displays similar to that shown in Figure 7–13.

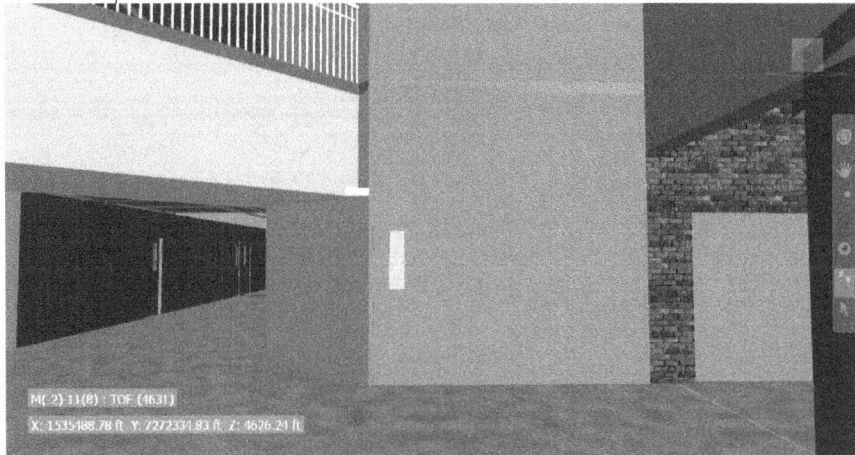

Figure 7–13

6. In the Viewpoint tab>Save, Load & Playback panel, click
   📷 (Save Viewpoint).

7. In the Saved Viewpoints window type **Turn1** for the name.

8. Pan and Orbit the model until the Scene view displays similar to that shown in Figure 7–14.

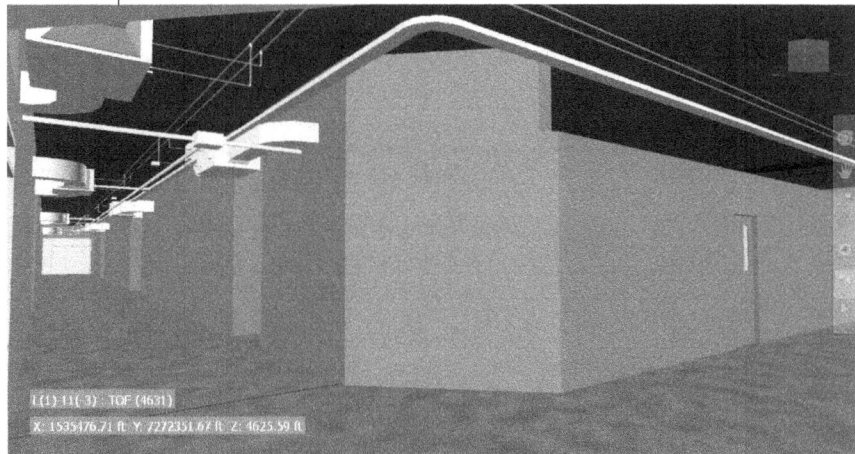

Figure 7–14

9. In the Viewpoint tab>Save, Load & Playback panel, click
   📷 (Save Viewpoint).

10. In the Saved Viewpoints window type **Turn2** for the name.

Practice 7c

Save Selection Sets

Practice Objectives

- Select items using the Selection Tree.
- Save selection sets for later use.

Estimated time for completion: 15 minutes

This practice is a review of *Section 4.1: Selecting Items*. You will create additional selection sets for later use using the model shown in Figure 7–15.

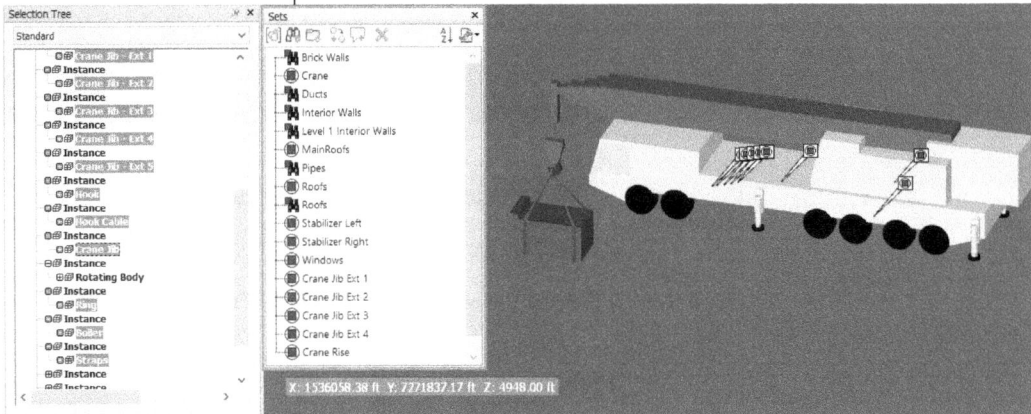

Figure 7–15

Task 1 - Select the crane.

1. In the *Extra Practice* practice files folder, open **NewElementarySchool-Select.nwf**.

2. In the *Home* tab, expand the Select & Search panel title to display the Selection Resolution drop-down list. Expand it and select **First Object**.

3. In the Selection Tree, select **Mobile Crane.skp**.

4. In the *Home* tab>Select & Search panel, click [icon] (Save Selection). Type **Crane** for the name.

Task 2 - Create selection sets for the crane stabilizers.

1. In the Selection Tree, expand **Mobile Crane.skp>Assembly** and select the first two **Instance** items, as shown in Figure 7–16. These are the right stabilizers.

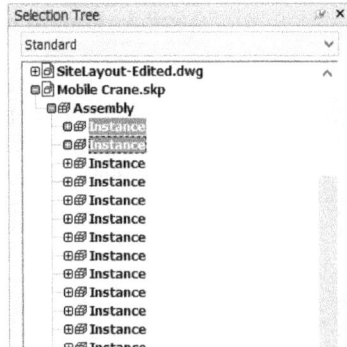

Figure 7–16

2. In the *Home* tab>Select & Search panel, click [icon] (Save Selection). Type **Stabilizer Right** for the name.

3. In the Selection Tree, expand **Mobile Crane.skp>Assembly** and select the third and forth **Instance** items, as shown in Figure 7–17. These are the left stabilizers.

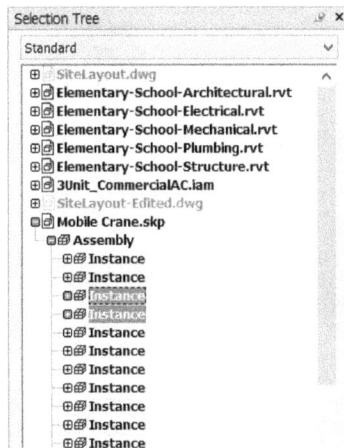

Figure 7–17

4. In the *Home* tab>Select & Search panel, click [icon] (Save Selection). Type **Stabilizer Left** for the name.

Task 3 - Create selection sets for animations.

1. In the Selection Tree, expand **Mobile Crane.skp>Assembly** and all of the **Instance** items. Select all of the items from the boiler to the first extender for the crane, as shown in Figure 7–18 and listed below. These will all move together.

- Crane Jib - Ext 1
- Crane Jib - Ext 2
- Crane Jib - Ext 3
- Crane Jib - Ext 4
- Crane Jib - Ext 5

- Hook
- Hook Cable
- Ring
- Boiler
- Straps

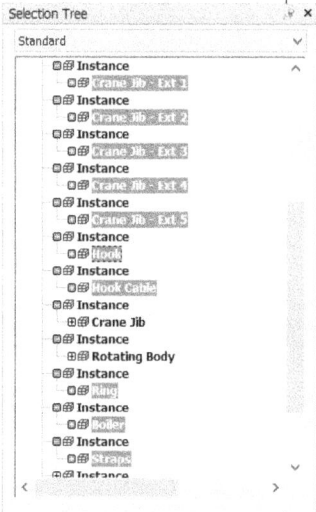

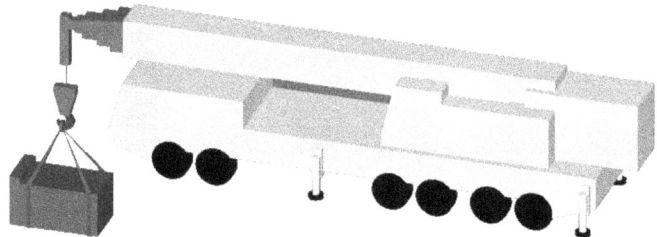

Figure 7–18

2. In the *Home* tab>Select & Search panel, click [⚙] (Save Selection). Type **Crane Jib Ext 1** for the name.

3. In the Sets window, select **Crane Jib Ext 1**.

4. In the Selection Tree, hold <Ctrl> and select **Crane Jib** to add it to the selection, as shown in Figure 7–19 and listed below. These will all move together.

- Crane Jib - Ext 1
- Crane Jib - Ext 2
- Crane Jib - Ext 3
- Crane Jib - Ext 4
- Crane Jib - Ext 5
- Hook

- Hook Cable
- Crane Jib
- Ring
- Boiler
- Straps

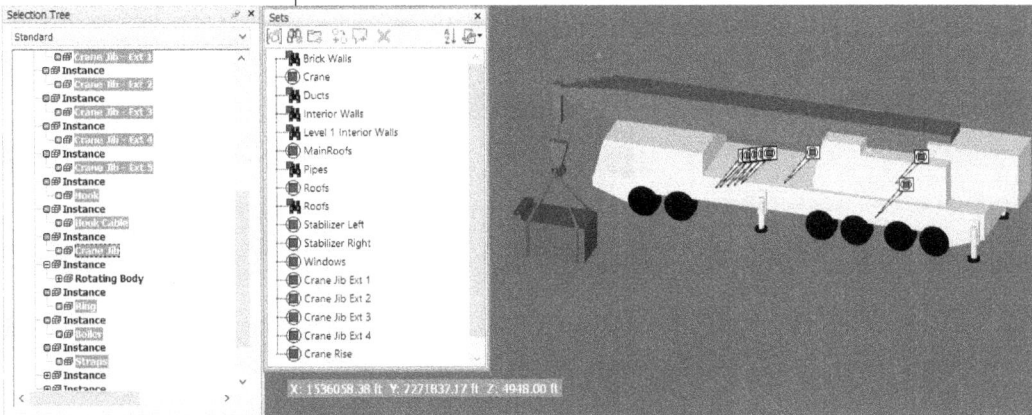

Figure 7–19

5. In the *Home* tab>Select & Search panel, click (Save Selection). Type **Crane Rise** for the name.

6. In the Sets window, select **Crane Rise**.

7. In the Selection Tree, hold <Ctrl> and select **Rotating Body** to add it to the selection, as shown in Figure 7–20 and listed below. These will all move together.

- Crane Jib - Ext 1
- Crane Jib - Ext 2
- Crane Jib - Ext 3
- Crane Jib - Ext 4
- Crane Jib - Ext 5
- Hook

- Hook Cable
- Crane Jib
- Rotating Body
- Ring
- Boiler
- Straps

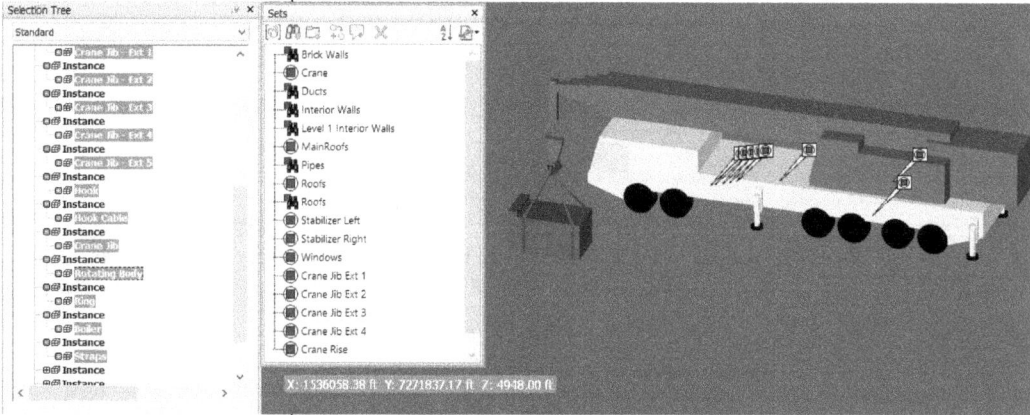

Figure 7–20

8. In the *Home* tab>Select & Search panel, click [icon] (Save Selection). Type **Crane Rotate** for the name.

9. In the Sets window, select **Crane Jib Ext 1**.

10. In the Selection Tree, hold <Ctrl> and clear the selection of **Crane Jib - Ext 1**, so that all that is selected are the parts shown in Figure 7–21 and listed below. These will all move together.

- Crane Jib - Ext 2
- Crane Jib - Ext 3
- Crane Jib - Ext 4
- Crane Jib - Ext 5
- Hook

- Hook Cable
- Ring
- Boiler
- Straps

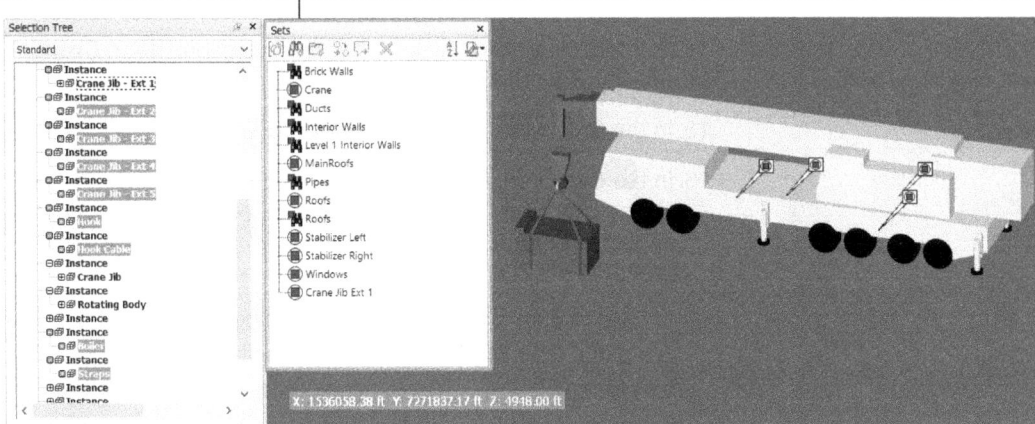

Figure 7–21

11. In the Sets window click [⊙] (Save Selection). Type **Crane Jib Ext 2** for the name.

12. In the Sets window, select **Crane Jib Ext 2**.

13. In the Selection Tree, hold <Ctrl> and clear the selection of **Crane Jib - Ext 2** so that all that is selected are the parts shown in Figure 7–22 and listed below. These will all move together.

- Crane Jib - Ext 3
- Crane Jib - Ext 4
- Crane Jib - Ext 5
- Hook

- Hook Cable
- Ring
- Boiler
- Straps

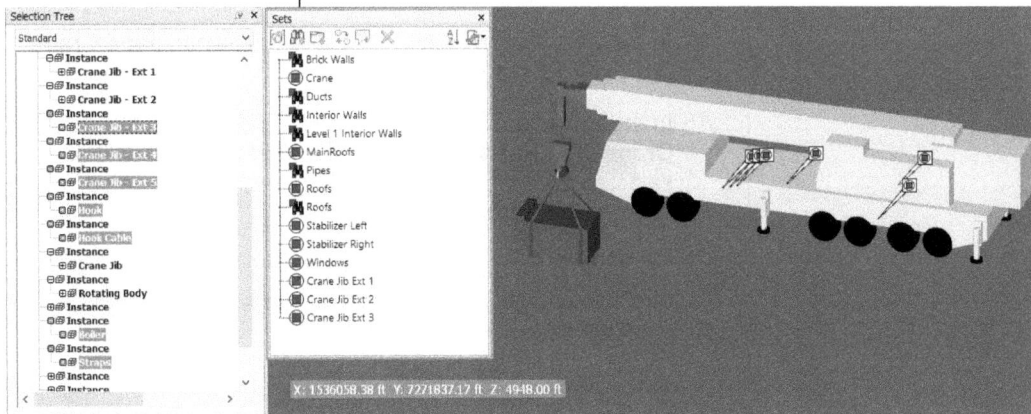

Figure 7–22

14. In the Sets window click ⌖ (Save Selection). Type **Crane Jib Ext 3** for the name.

15. In the Sets window, select **Crane Jib Ext 3**.

16. In the Selection Tree, hold <Ctrl> and clear the selection of **Crane Jib - Ext 3** so that all that is selected are the parts shown in Figure 7–23 and listed below. These will all move together.

- Crane Jib - Ext 4
- Crane Jib - Ext 5
- Hook
- Hook Cable
- Ring
- Boiler
- Straps

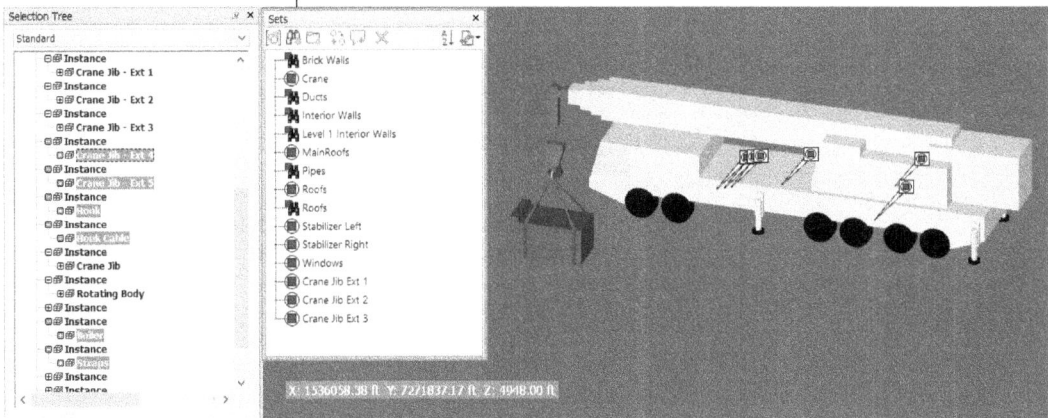

Figure 7–23

17. In the Sets window click ⌖ (Save Selection). Type **Crane Jib Ext 4** for the name.

18. In the Selection Tree, hold <Ctrl> and clear the selection of **Crane Jib - Ext 4** and **Crane Jib - Ext 5** so that all that is selected are the parts shown in Figure 7–24 and listed below. These will all move together.

- Hook
- Hook Cable
- Ring
- Boiler
- Straps

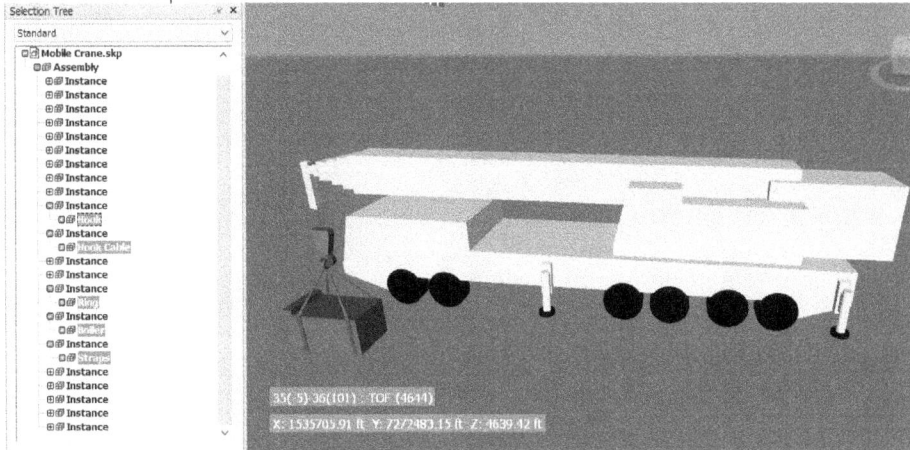

Figure 7–24

19. In the *Home* tab>Select & Search panel, click [⚙] (Save Selection). Type **Hook and Cable** for the name.

20. In the Sets window, select **Hook and Cable**.

21. In the Selection Tree, hold <Ctrl> and clear the selection of **Hook Cable** so that all that is selected are the parts shown in Figure 7–25 and listed below. These will all move together.

- Hook
- Ring

- Boiler
- Straps

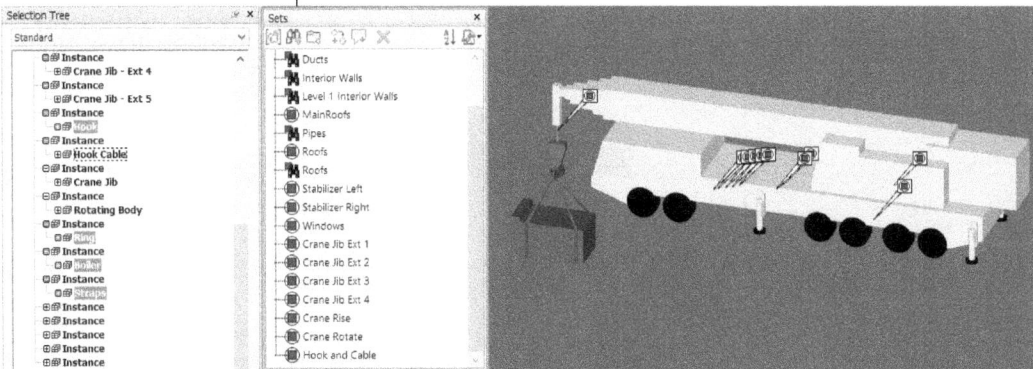

Figure 7–25

22. In the Sets window click [⚙] (Save Selection). Type **Hook** for the name.

23. In the Selection Tree, expand the eleventh Instance item and select **Hook Cable**, as shown in Figure 7–26

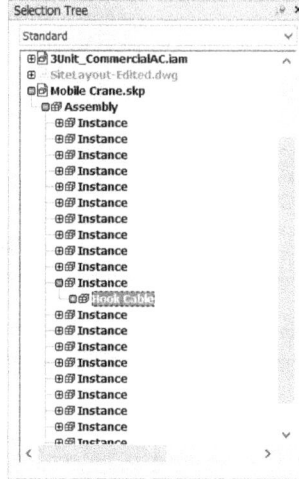

Figure 7–26

24. In the Sets window click (Save Selection). Type **Cable** for the name.

Practice 7d

Estimated time for completion: 10 minutes

Save Search Sets

Practice Objective

- Create a search set for easy selection of items with similar properties.

This practice is a review of *Section 4.4: Finding Items and Saving Search Sets*. You will create additional search sets for later use, as shown in Figure 7–27.

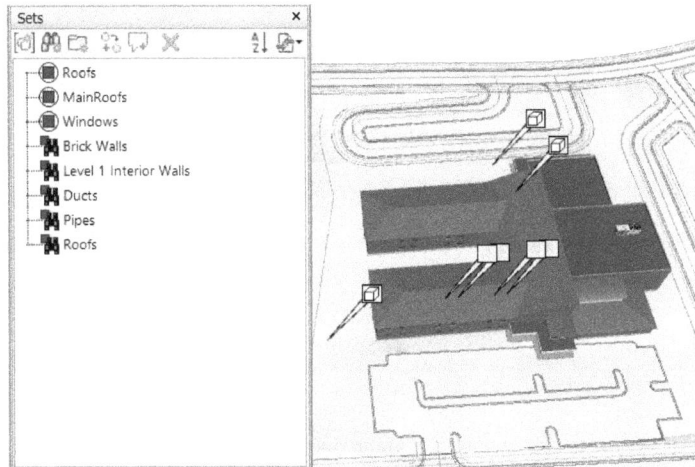

Figure 7–27

Task 1 - Create a search set for roofs.

1. In the *Extra Practice* practice files folder, open **NewElementarySchool-Search.nwf**.

2. In the *Home* tab>Select & Search panel, click (Find Items).

3. In the Find Items dialog box, in the left pane, do not select anything. This is the same as a select all on the files.

4. In the right pane, do the following, as shown in Figure 7–28.
   - Under *Category*, select **Item**.
   - Under *Property*, select **Name**.
   - Under *Condition*, select **Contains**.
   - Under *Value*, type **Roof**.
   - Clear all of the Matching options below the right pane.

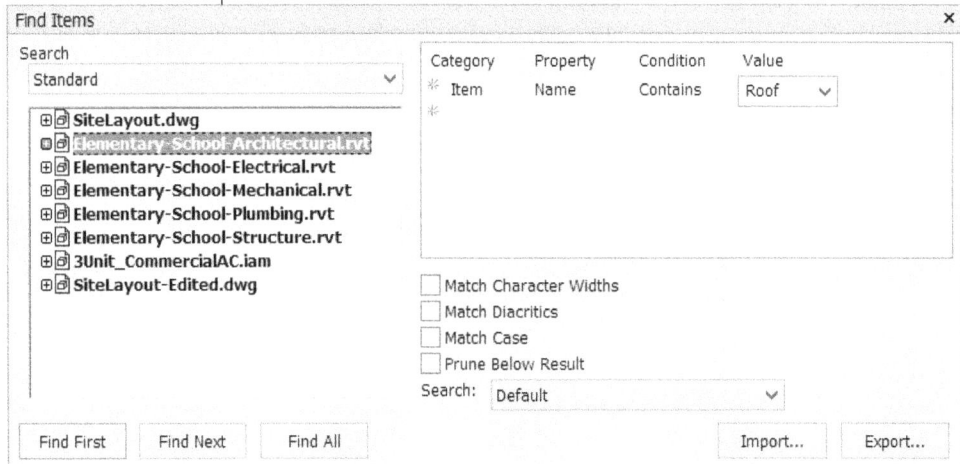

Figure 7–28

5. Click **Find All** and note what is selected in the model.

6. In the Sets window, click 🔍 (Save Search).

7. Type in **Roofs** for the search.

Task 2 - Create a search set for Boilers.

1. In the Find Items dialog box, in the left pane, click on a blank space to clear any selections.

2. In the right pane, do the following, as shown in Figure 7–29.
   - Under *Category*, select **Item**.
   - Under *Property*, select **Name**.
   - Under *Condition*, select **Contains**.
   - Under *Value*, type **Boiler**.
   - Clear all of the Matching options below the right pane.

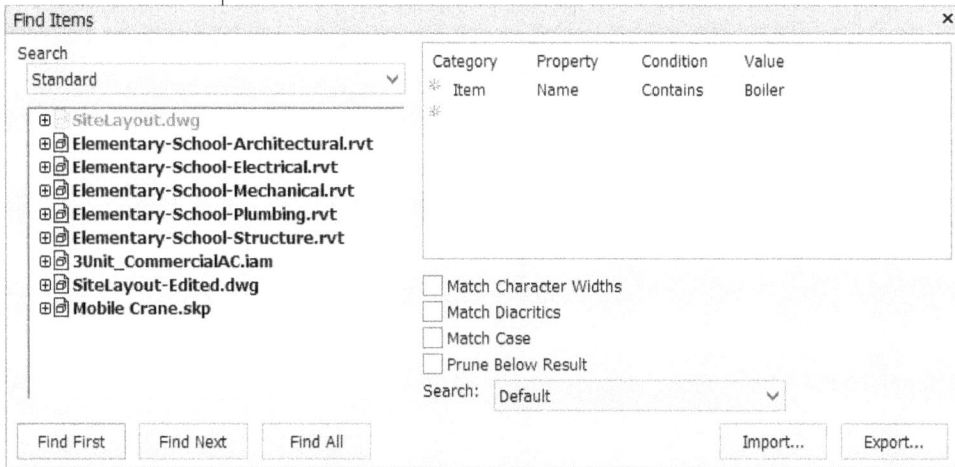

Figure 7–29

3. Click **Find All** to see what is selected in the model.

4. In the Sets window, click 🔍 (Save Search).

5. Type in **Boiler** for the search.

Communication: Animator

Communication is at the center of any great BIM workflow. Full communication ensures that all stakeholders fully understand how a project will look and function when it is complete. The Autodesk® Navisworks® Animator enables you to create movement in the model to show how objects interact with each other.

In this chapter you learn how to animate objects. You create a simple animation to orbit a model. Then you learn how to animate a crane to ensure that it has a full range of motion on the project site. Finally, you create AVI movies to share with others.

Learning Objectives in this Chapter

- Create an animation to tour a model.
- Modify the position, rotation, size, color, and transparency of objects to animate them.
- Create AVI files to share videos of a project with others.

BIM Workflow: Communicate

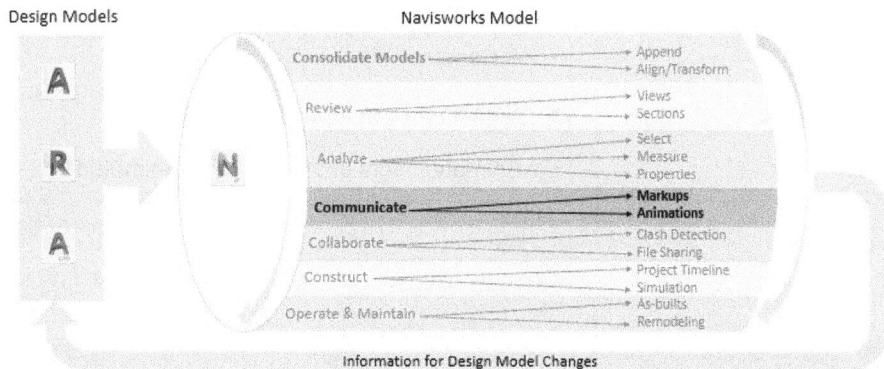

8.1 Creating Tours

You can create videos that simulate walking or flying through a model so that stakeholders can take a tour long before the structure is built.

Animator Window

Animator uses scenes along a timeline to create a slide show. The Animator window (shown in Figure 8–1) is broken into two key areas to reflect this: scenes are displayed on the left in the Tree pane, while the scene's placement in the animation is shown in the Timeline pane on the right. The Animator toolbar sits above the Tree and Timeline panes.

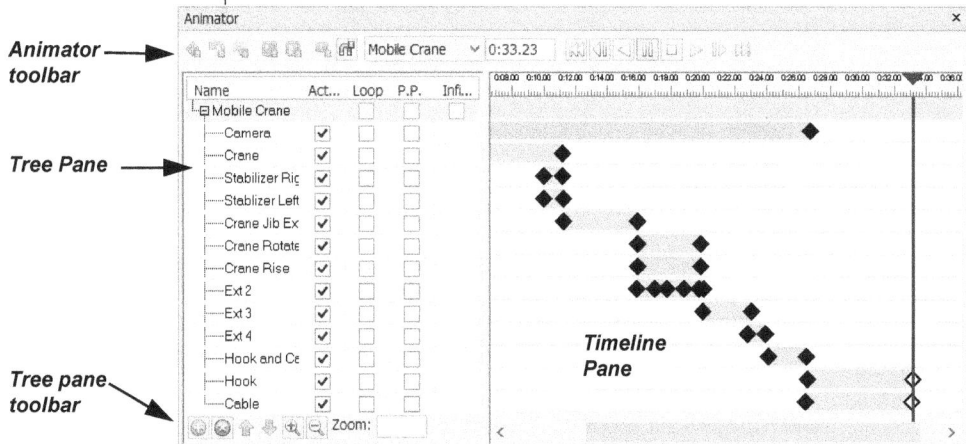

Figure 8–1

Tree Pane

You can add, view, and reorder scene components in the Tree pane. Scenes in the Tree pane can include:

- A Camera

- Section planes for sectional views

- Animation sets of objects to be animated

Each scene can only contain one camera, but, multiple Scene views or viewpoints can be added to the camera.

- When using multiple viewpoints, the animation can jump from view to view or transition smoothly between views.

- When only one viewpoint is added to the animation, the scene continuously focuses on one spot as objects are animated.

- If no viewpoint is added to the camera, then the current view is used during the animation.

The Tree pane tools do the following:

- 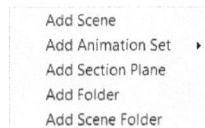 Opens a menu that enables you to add a Scene, Animation Set, Section Plane, Folder, or Scene Folder, as shown in Figure 8–2. You can also access these tools by right-clicking on a Scene in the Tree pane, as shown in Figure 8–3.

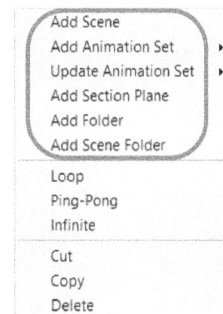

| Add Scene |
| Add Animation Set ▸ |
| Add Section Plane |
| Add Folder |
| Add Scene Folder |

Figure 8–2

Figure 8–3

- 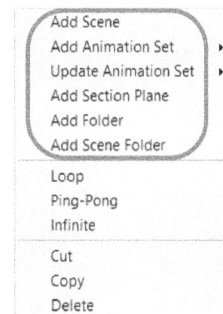 Deletes a Scene or Scene component.

- / Changes the order of the scenes and scene components by moving them up or down in the Tree.

- / Zooms in or out on the Timeline to make it easier to see the start, end, and duration of each item in the Tree pane.

- Zoom: 1/2   Sets how many seconds are displayed in the Timeline.

Timeline Pane

The Timeline pane is used to set when each keyframe displays in the animation, and how long the keyframe displays. A keyframe is a snapshot of a change to the model or the camera viewpoint. The animation bar indicates where on the Timeline the current keyframe falls. As the animation bar is moved, the Scene view is updated. The start and end diamonds can be dragged to a new location on the Timeline to change when a keyframe displays in the Scene view and the duration of the keyframe, as shown in Figure 8–4.

- In the Animator toolbar, click (Capture Keyframe) to add the current viewpoint of the camera to the animation.

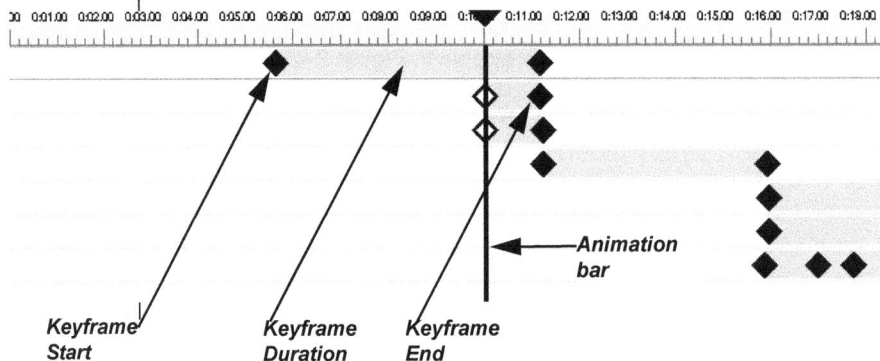

Keyframe Start   **Keyframe Duration**   **Keyframe End**   —**Animation bar**

Figure 8–4

- Right-click on a keyframe to display additional tools, as shown in Figure 8–5.

- **Edit:** Opens the Edit Key Frame dialog box (shown in Figure 8–6), which enables you to modify the keyframe focus, similar to modifying a Viewpoint.

- **Cut:** Removes a keyframe from the Timeline and saves it in a clipboard for later use.

- **Copy:** Saves a keyframe to the clipboard for later use without changing the original keyframe.

- **Delete:** Removes the keyframe.

- **Go to keyframe:** Moves the Animation bar to the selected keyframe, and changes the Scene view to that keyframe's view.

*If Cut or Copy are selected, right-clicking anywhere on the Timeline provides a Paste option. **Paste** enables you to place the last keyframe saved to the clipboard at the location which you right-click.*

- **Interpolate:** Creates a smooth transition between keyframes, as if panning or zooming in real-time.

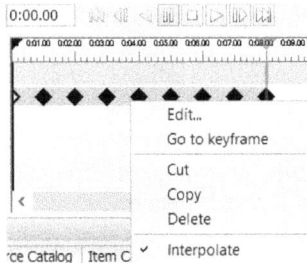

Figure 8–5

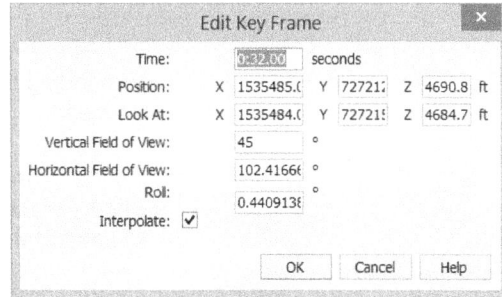

Figure 8–6

How To: Create a Simple Animation to Display the Model

1. In the *Home* tab>Tools panel, click (Animator) to open the Animator window.
2. In the Animator window, Tree pane, click (Add Scene).
3. Type a name for the scene.
4. In the Scene view, set the current view so that it is how you want the view to display in the keyframe, using saved Viewpoints as required.
5. Move the animation bar to the time that you want the scene to start.
6. Right-click on the scene name and select **Add Camera> Blank camera**.

7. In the Animator toolbar, click (Capture Keyframe). A black diamond displays in the Timeline to indicate the start of the keyframe.
8. Use the viewing tools (e.g., pan, orbit, saved viewpoints, etc.) to change the scene view to a new camera position.
9. Move the animation bar to where you want the scene to end.

Multiple keyframes can be added to the same camera.

10. On the Animator toolbar, click (Capture Keyframe). This sets the end of the keyframe and its duration, as shown in Figure 8–4.
11. Repeat Steps 2 to 10 until all of the necessary scenes are added to the Timeline.

Play Animations

The Animator toolbar contains a variety of tools. The tools found on the right of the Animator toolbar helps you review the animations:

- Orbit ⌄ **(Scene Picker):** Displays the active scene. Expanding this drop-down list provides a list of the available scenes.

- 0:36.25 **(Time Position):** Displays the current position of the black Animator bar in the Timeline pane. You can type a time to jump to that location in the Timeline.

- **(Rewind):** Moves the Animation bar to the beginning of the animation and changes the Scene view to match.

- **(Step Back):** Rewinds the animation one keyframe at a time.

- **(Reverse Play):** Plays the animation in reverse.

- **(Pause):** Pauses the animation.

- **(Stop):** Stops the animation, moves the Animation bar back to the beginning of the Timeline, and changes the Scene view to match.

- **(Play):** Starts the animation from the current position of the Animation bar.

- **(Step Forward):** Moves forward in the animation, one keyframe at a time.

- **(To End):** Fast forwards to the end of the animation.

In addition to the tools in the Animator toolbar, there are four columns in the Tree pane which sets the play options, as shown in Figure 8–7.

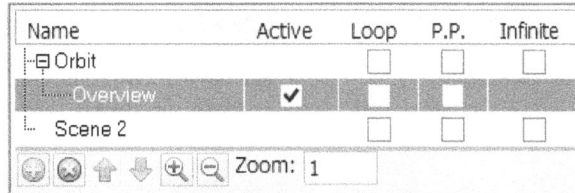

Figure 8–7

- **Active:** When checked, a scene component is active and is used in the animation. Clear the checkmark to make a scene component inactive.

- **Loop:** Causes the animation to automatically play again from the beginning once it reaches the end of the animation.

- **Ping-Pong (P.P.):** Causes the animation to play normally from beginning to end, and then plays in reverse until it returns to the beginning again.

- **Infinite:** Makes the scene play indefinitely, or until you click (Stop).

Practice 8a

Create a Simple Animation

Practice Objective

- Create a tour of the model using animator.

Estimated time for completion: 15 minutes

In this practice you will create an animation to tour the model, as shown in Figure 8–8.

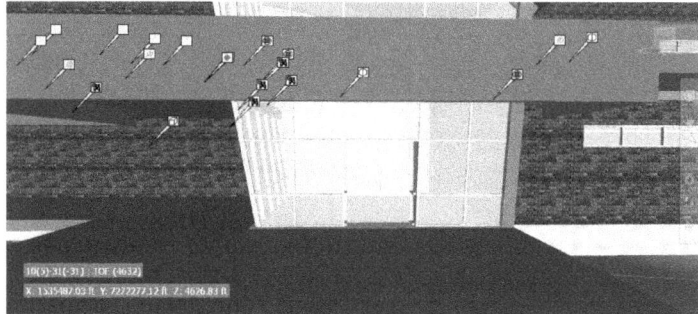

Figure 8–8

Task 1 - Create an animation that orbits around the model.

1. In the *Animator* practice files folder, open **NewElementarySchool-Orbit.nwf**.

2. In the Saved Viewpoints window, click **Overview**.

3. In the *Home* tab>Tools panel, click (Animator) to display the Animator window. Pin the window open to make it easier to work with it.

4. In the Animator window>Tree pane, click (Add Scene).

5. Click on the scene name and type **Orbit** for the name.

6. Ensure that the animation bar is at zero on the Timeline. If it is not, drag the animation bar to zero.

7. Right-click on the scene name and select **Add Camera> Blank Camera**.

8. Type **Overview** for the Camera name.

9. On the Animator toolbar, click (Capture Keyframe). A black diamond is added to the Timeline at zero to indicate the start of the keyframe.

10. Right-click on the new keyframe and ensure that **Interpolate** is checked. If it is not, select it to toggle it on.

11. Move the animation bar to **4** seconds on the Timeline.

12. In the Saved Viewpoints window, select the **SE-Isometric** viewpoint.

13. On the Animator toolbar, click (Capture Keyframe).

14. Repeat Steps 11 to 13 to create additional keyframes at the times and viewpoints listed below:
   - At **8** seconds, capture the **East Side** viewpoint.
   - At **12** seconds, capture the **NE-Isometric** viewpoint.
   - At **16** seconds, capture the **North Side** viewpoint.
   - At **20** seconds, capture the **NW-Isometric** viewpoint.
   - At **24** seconds, capture the **West Side** viewpoint.
   - At **28** seconds, capture the **SW-Isometric** viewpoint.
   - At **32** seconds, capture the **Overview** viewpoint.

15. On the Animator toolbar, click (Stop), and then click (Play) to play the animation from the beginning. Note how the animation moves through each of the viewpoints that you selected.

Task 2 - Create an animation that walks into the model.

---

1. Continue working in the same animation that was created in the last task.

2. Move the animation bar to **36** seconds on the Timeline.

3. In the Saved Viewpoints window, select **Front Entry**.

4. On the Animator toolbar, click (Capture Keyframe).

5. Repeat Steps 2 to 4 to create additional keyframes at the times and viewpoints listed below:
   - At **40** seconds, capture the **Turn1** viewpoint.
   - At **42** seconds, capture the **Turn2** viewpoint.

6. On the Animator toolbar, click (Stop), and then click (Play) to play the animation from the beginning. Note how the animation moves through each of the viewpoints that you selected.

8.2 Animating Objects

Touring a model is a great way to gain stakeholder buy-in, and being able to demonstrate how things move and work in the model helps stakeholders further understand how everything functions together in the project. Objects can be animated using a variety of tools found in the Animator toolbar:

- (**Translate Animation Set**): Provides a gizmo tool to modify the position of geometry objects.

- (**Rotate Animation Set**): Provides a gizmo tool to rotate geometry objects.

- (**Scale Animation Set**): Provides a gizmo tool to resize geometry objects.

- (**Change Color of Animation Set**): Displays the color palette in the Manual Entry bar, enabling you to modify the color of geometry objects.

- (**Change Transparency of Animation Set**): Displays the transparency slider in the Manual Entry bar, enabling you to modify the transparency of geometry objects.

Note that Capture Keyframe also adds viewpoints to the camera.

- (**Capture Keyframe**): Adds the current objects' position to an animation set.

- (**Toggle snapping**): Toggles snap on and off, enabling you to control whether you snap to other animation sets (translate, rotate, or scale).

How To: Animate Objects

1. In the Sets window, create a selection set or save set that contains all of the objects that you want to move.
2. In the Animator window, create a scene and add any necessary cameras to it.
3. In the Sets window, select the selection set you created.
4. In the Animator window, in the Tree pane, right-click on the *Mobile Crane* scene and select either of the following options:

The advantage of using a search set is that it automatically updates if the source file changes.

   - **Add Animation Set>From current selection**
   - **Add Animation Set>From current search/selection**

5. Type a name for the Animation Set.
6. Move the animation bar to the location on the Timeline where you want the animation to start.

7. On the Animator toolbar, click ⬛ (Capture Keyframe). Note that this captures the current location, rotation, or scale of the animation set.
8. Move the animation bar to the location on the Timeline where you want the animation to end.

9. On the Animator toolbar, click ⬛ (Translate animation set), ⬛ (Rotate animation set), or ⬛ (Scale animation set).
10. Click and drag the center of the gizmo to move the origin point.
   • When Rotate is selected, this sets the pivot point for all of the selected objects.
   • When Scale or Move are selected, you must hold <Ctrl> as you drag the gizmo to change the center of translation.
11. Use the appropriate gizmo shown in Figure 8–9 to move, rotate, or scale the selection set, as required.
   • Red makes changes along the X axis or in the X plane.
   • Blue makes changes along the Y axis or in the Y plane.
   • Green makes changes along the Z axis or in the Z plane.

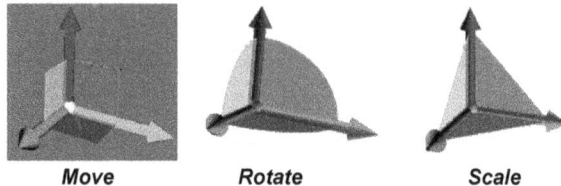

Move   Rotate   Scale

Figure 8–9

12. On the Animator toolbar, click ⬛ (Capture Keyframe). This captures the new location of the animation set.

Hint: Translation Errors

When a non-Autodesk file is appended in the Autodesk Navisworks software, a translation error might occur. A warning of the error does not display, but the error causes the X, Y, or Z axis to be incorrect.

If an error occurs, when you try to transpose objects along one gizmo axis (e.g., X axis), the objects instead move along a different axis (e.g., Y axis), as shown in Figure 8–10. This is a known issue, and has no resolution at the time of publication of this learning guide.

As the error cannot be fixed, instead simply select another axis on the gizmo to translate the objects until you find the axis that causes the objects to move in the desired direction.

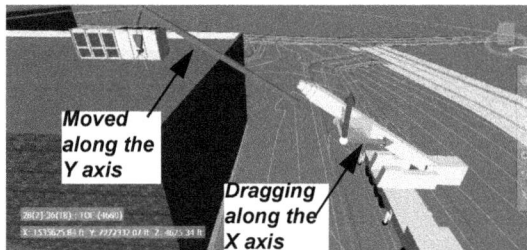

Figure 8–10

Practice 8b

Create a Complex Animation

Practice Objective

- Animate objects and note how they move in the model.

In this practice, you will animate the crane and note how it moves in the model, as shown in Figure 8–11.

Figure 8–11

Estimated time for completion: 15 minutes

Task 1 - Add views to the animation.

1. In the *Animator* practice files folder, open **NewElementarySchool-Crane.nwf**.

2. In the Animator window, uncheck the **Active** option next to **Overview**, thus making it inactive.

3. In the Saved Viewpoints window, click **Overview**.

4. In the Animator window>Tree pane, click ⊕ (Add Scene).

5. Click on the scene name and type **Mobile Crane** for the name.

6. Ensure that the animation bar is at zero on the Timeline.

7. Right-click on *Mobile Crane* and select **Add Camera>Blank Camera**. For the Camera name, accept the default name of **Camera**.

8. On the Animator toolbar, click 🔲 (Capture Keyframe). A black diamond displays in the Timeline at zero to indicate the start of the keyframe.

If the Animator window is not displayed, on the Home tab>Tools panel,

click ⌖ (Animator) to open it. Then, pin it open to make it easier to access.

Interpolate should be on by default. This is just a verification step.

9. Right-click on the keyframe and ensure that **Interpolate** is checked.

10. Move the animation bar to **4** seconds on the Timeline.

11. Pan and Orbit the model so that the Crane is displayed similar to the view shown in Figure 8–12.

Figure 8–12

12. On the Animator toolbar, click ⬛ (Capture Keyframe).

13. On the Animator toolbar, click ⬛ (Stop), and then click ▷ (Play) to play the animation from the beginning

---

Task 2 - Add a transition animation.

---

*If the Sets window is not displayed, on the View tab>Workspace panel, expand **Windows** and select **Sets**.*

1. Open the Sets window and pin it open to make it easy to access.

2. In the Sets window, select **Crane**. Note that the entire crane is selected in the model.

3. In the Animator window, in the Tree pane, right-click on the *Mobile Crane* scene and select **Add Animation Set>From current selection**.

4. Type **Crane** for the Animation Set name.

5. Move the animation bar to **4** seconds on the Timeline.

6. On the Animator toolbar, click ⬛ (Capture Keyframe).

7. Move the animation bar to **8** seconds on the Timeline.

8. On the Animator toolbar, click ⬛ (Translate animation set).

9. Use the Z axis (green arrow) on the Translate Gizmo to move the crane forward, similar to what is shown in Figure 8–13.

Figure 8–13

10. On the Animator toolbar, click [icon] (Capture Keyframe).

11. On the Animator toolbar, click [icon] (Stop), and then click

    [icon] (Play) to play the animation from the beginning

Task 3 - Add rotation animations.

1. In the Sets window, select **Crane Rise**.

2. In the Animator window, in the Tree pane, right-click on the **Mobile Crane** scene and select **Add Animation Set>From current selection**.

3. Type **Rise** for the animation name.

4. Move the animation bar to **8** seconds on the Timeline.

5. On the Animator toolbar, click [icon] (Capture Keyframe).

6. Move the animation bar to **12** seconds on the Timeline.

7. On the Animator toolbar, click [icon] (Rotate animation set).

8. On the Animator toolbar, click [icon] (Toggle snapping).

9. Click and drag the center of the rotation gizmo to the center of the hinge pin shown in Figure 8–14. Orbit and zoom the scene as required to display the pin better. With snapping toggled on, you should be able to snap to the center of the circle.

    *   Note: If you hold <Ctrl> when moving the gizmo, only the gizmo moves and not the selected objects.

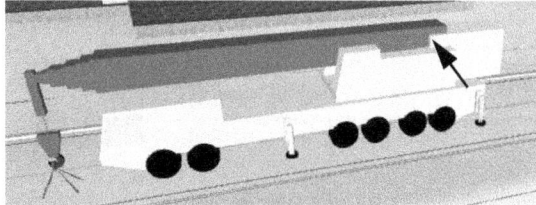

Figure 8–14

10. Use the X axis (red) plane of the gizmo to rotate the jib **30 degrees** around the X axis, as shown in Figure 8–15.

Figure 8–15

11. On the Animator toolbar, click ⬚ (Capture Keyframe). This captures the new rotation of the animation set.

12. In the Sets window, select **Hook and Cable**.

13. In the Animator window, in the Tree pane, right-click on the **Mobile Crane** scene and select **Add Animation Set>From current selection**.

14. Type **Gravity** for the animation name.

15. Move the animation bar to **8** seconds on the Timeline.

16. On the Animator toolbar, click ⬚ (Capture Keyframe).

17. Move the animation bar to **12** seconds on the Timeline.

18. On the Animator toolbar, click ⬚ (Rotate animation set).

19. Click and drag the center of the rotation gizmo to the top of the cable, as shown in Figure 8–16

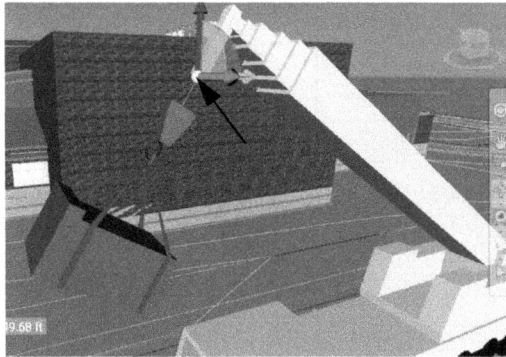

Figure 8–16

20. Use the X axis (red) plane of the gizmo to rotate the cable **30 degrees** around the X axis so that it is perpendicular to the ground as if gravity is pulling on it, as shown in Figure 8–17.

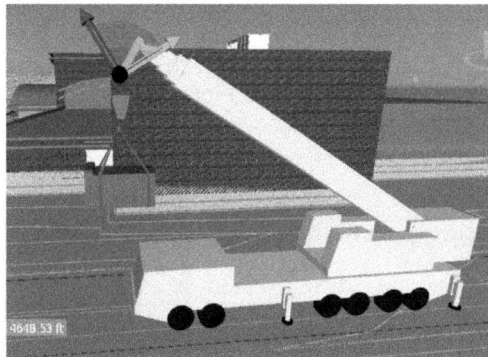

Figure 8–17

21. On the Animator toolbar, click ⬚ (Capture Keyframe).

22. In the Sets window, select **Crane Rotate**.

23. In the Animator window, in the Tree pane, right-click on the **Mobile Crane** scene and select **Add Animation Set>From current selection**.

24. Type **Rotate** for the animation name.

25. Move the animation bar to **12** seconds on the Timeline.

26. On the Animator toolbar, click ⬚ (Capture Keyframe).

27. Move the animation bar to **16** seconds on the Timeline.

28. On the Animator toolbar, click ⬚ (Rotate animation set).

29. Click and drag the center of the rotation gizmo to the center of the truck below the Jib, as shown in Figure 8–18

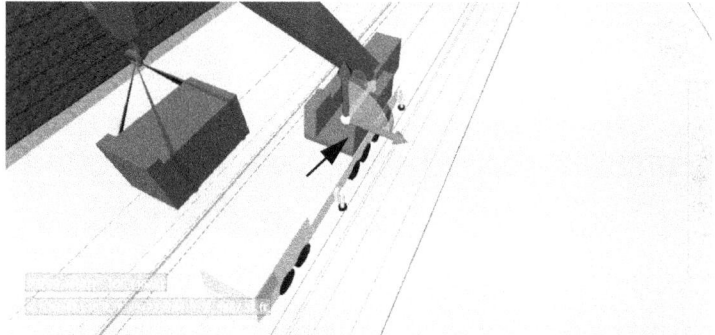

Figure 8–18

30. Use the Y axis (blue) plane of the gizmo to rotate the jib **90 degrees** around the Y axis so that it is pointing at the building and the X axis lines up with the truck, as shown in Figure 8–19.

Figure 8–19

31. On the Animator toolbar, click ⬚ (Capture Keyframe).

32. On the Animator toolbar, click ⬚ (Stop) then click ▷ (Play) to play the animation from the beginning.

Task 4 - Extend the Jib.

1. In the Sets window, select **Crane Jib Ext 4**.

2. In the Animator window, in the Tree pane, right-click on the **Mobile Crane** scene and select **Add Animation Set>From current selection**.

3. Type **Etx-1** for the Animation Set name.

4. Move the animation bar to **16** seconds on the Timeline.

5. On the Animator toolbar, click ⬚ (Capture Keyframe).

6. Move the animation bar to **20** seconds on the Timeline.

7. On the Animator toolbar, click ⬚ (Translate animation set).

8. Use the X axis (red arrow) and Y axis (blue arrow) on the gizmo to extend the jib the full length of the smallest extension, similar to what is shown in Figure 8–20.

It might be necessary to orbit the model after each move to ensure that the jib moves in the correct direction.

Figure 8–20

9. On the Animator toolbar, click ⬚ (Capture Keyframe).

10. On the Animator toolbar, click ⬚ (Stop), and then click ▷ (Play) to play the animation from the beginning.

11. Save the file.

Chapter Review Questions

1. In the Animator toolbar, what happens when you click

   (Capture Keyframe)? (Select all that apply)

   a. Captures a snapshot of the currently appended files.

   b. Captures a snapshot of the current viewpoint.

   c. Captures a snapshot of the current object positions.

   d. Captures key elements for later use.

2. What does the **Ping Pong (P.P.)** option do?

   a. Causes an animation to play in reverse when it reaches the end.

   b. Causes an animations to randomly shuffle in the Timeline.

   c. Causes an animation to replay once when it reaches the end.

   d. Causes an animation to replay continuously when it reaches the end.

3. Using the Timeline, how do you change the length of time an animation plays?

   a. Select the animation set, right-click and select **Set Duration**.

   b. Select the animation set and type a duration in the *Time Position* field.

   c. Select the animation set then drag the animator bar in the Timeline to set the length.

   d. Drag the diamonds in the Timeline to lengthen or shorten the duration.

4. How many cameras can you have in a scene?

   a. 1

   b. 2

   c. 3

   d. Infinite

5. How can you move the point of translation when moving, rotating, or scaling an animation set?

   a. The point of translation cannot be changed.

   b. In the *Item Tools* tab>Transform panel, click **Move**.

   c. In the *Item Tools* tab>Look At panel, click **Focus on Item**.

   d. Hold <Ctrl> as you drag the center point of the gizmo.

Command Summary

Button	Command	Location
	Add Scene	• **Window:** Animator
	Animator	• **Ribbon:** *Home* tab>Tools panel
	Capture Keyframe	• **Window:** Animator
	Change Color of Animation Set	• **Window:** Animator
	Change Transparency of Animation Set	• **Window:** Animator
	Delete	• **Window:** Animator
	Move Down	• **Window:** Animator
	Move Up	• **Window:** Animator
	Pause	• **Window:** Animator
	Play	• **Window:** Animator
	Reverse Play	• **Window:** Animator
	Rewind	• **Window:** Animator
	Rotate Animation Set	• **Window:** Animator
	Scale Animation Set	• **Window:** Animator
Orbit ˅	**Scene Picker**	• **Window:** Animator
	Step Back	• **Window:** Animator
	Step Forward	• **Window:** Animator

	Stop	• **Window:** Animator
0:36.25	Time Postion	• **Window:** Animator
	To End	• **Window:** Animator
	Toggle Snapping	• **Window:** Animator
	Translate Animation Set	• **Window:** Animator
	Zoom In	• **Window:** Animator
	Zoom Out	• **Window:** Animator

Construct: Project Scheduling

The next step in the BIM workflow is to construct the project. Creating a 4D simulation connects a 3D model to a construction schedule, which gives it that fourth dimension. This helps users better understand errors in the schedule or safety issues that need to be addressed.

In this chapter, you learn how to create and import a Gantt chart. Then, you connect model elements to the Gantt chart to create a construction simulation.

Learning Objectives in this Chapter

- Create a construction timeline.
- Import a construction timeline created in an external project management application.
- Run a time-based clash test.

BIM Workflow: Construct

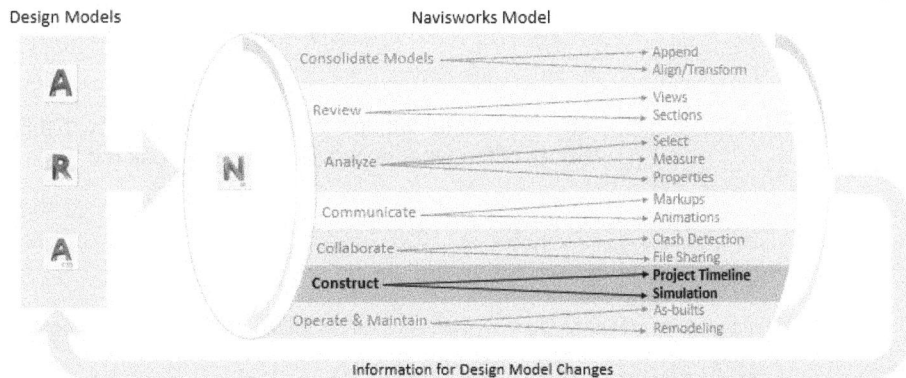

9.1 Introduction to TimeLiner

4D models visually communicate the relationships between model elements and the construction schedule. This can help stakeholders better understand any issues that might arise during the construction phase. The TimeLiner window (shown in Figure 9–1) is used to connect tasks in the Gantt chart with elements in the model to simulate construction.

You can create a Gantt chart in the Autodesk® Navisworks® software in two ways:

- Create a new chart from scratch.

- Import an existing chart from a project management software application.

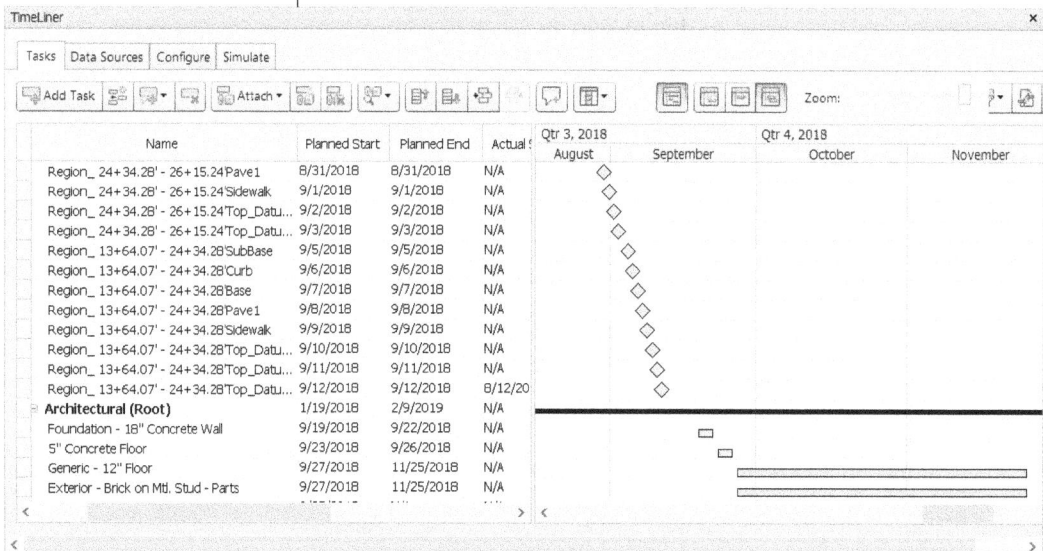

Figure 9–1

The TimeLiner window has four tabs, as shown in Figure 9–1. Most of the work is completed in the *Task* tab.

Tasks Tab

The *Tasks* tab contains a list of all of the active tasks in the left pane, and a Gantt chart in the right pane. Several columns are available in the task list pane that include information about each task. The columns can be reordered as required by dragging the column heading to a new location. The following information can be found in each column:

- **Active:** Displays a checkmark if the task is active and included in the simulation.

- **Status:** Displays two bars, as shown in Figure 9–2. The top bar represents the planned dates, while the bottom bar represents the actual dates. When the planned and actual dates match, the bars display in green. When they do not match, they display in red. If the date field is empty, the bar displays as clear.

Figure 9–2

- **Name:** Displays the task name.

- **Planned Start/End Dates:** Displays the planned start and end dates of the task.

- **Actual Start/End Dates:** Displays the actual start and end dates of the task.

- **Task Type:** Displays the types of tasks that can be assigned, which determine the objects' appearance. The task types are set up in the *Configure* tab.

- **Attached:** Lists the objects attached to the task from the model.

- **Total Cost:** Displays a monetary ($) amount connected to the task.

Data Sources Tab

The *Data Sources* tab is used to connect to external project management software. There are multiple project management databases that can be connected, as shown in Figure 9–3. A database can be connected for each discipline or each model attached to the project, if required.

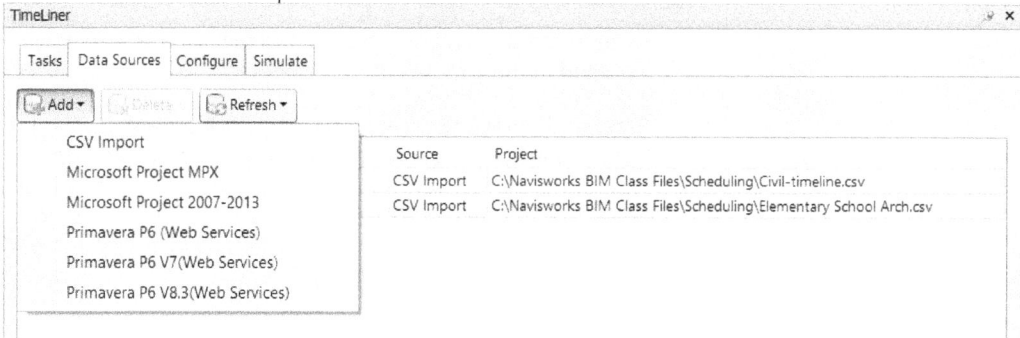

Figure 9–3

Configure Tab

The *Configure* tab enables you to set how you want objects to display at key times during a simulation. By default, there are three options, as shown in Figure 9–4:

- Construct

- Demolish

- Temporary

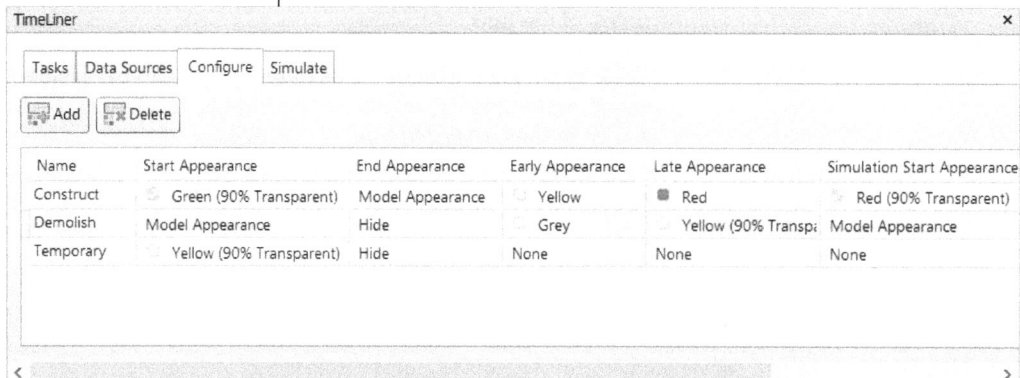

Figure 9–4

Simulate Tab

The *Simulate* tab enables you to play, stop, and go to any point in the simulation. Similar to the *Tasks* tab, it contains two panes: the task list is on the left, and the Gantt chart is on the right, as shown in Figure 9–5.

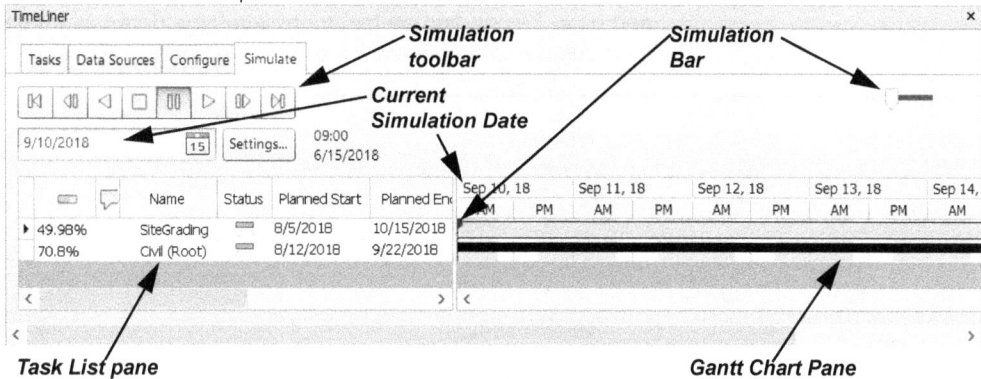

Figure 9–5

Task List Pane

The columns in the task list pane include information about each task. The columns can be reordered as required by dragging the column heading to a new location. The following information is found in each column:

- **(Simulation Progress):** Displays a percentage for how much of a specific task is complete in the simulation.

- **(Comments):** Lists the number of comments applied to a specific task.

- **Name:** Displays the task name.

- **Planned Start/End Dates:** Displays the planned start and end dates of the task.

- **Actual Start/End Dates:** Displays the actual start and end dates of the task.

- **Total Cost:** Displays a monetary ($) amount connected to the task.

- **Task Type:** Displays the task type that is assigned, which determines the objects' appearance.

Gantt Chart Pane

In the Gantt Chart pane, columns list dates, while bars show each task's duration in the schedule. The beginning of the bar is located at the start date, and the end of the bar is located at the end date. Depending on the zoom level, the dates might display as months and days, months and weeks, or quarters and months, as shown in Figure 9–6.

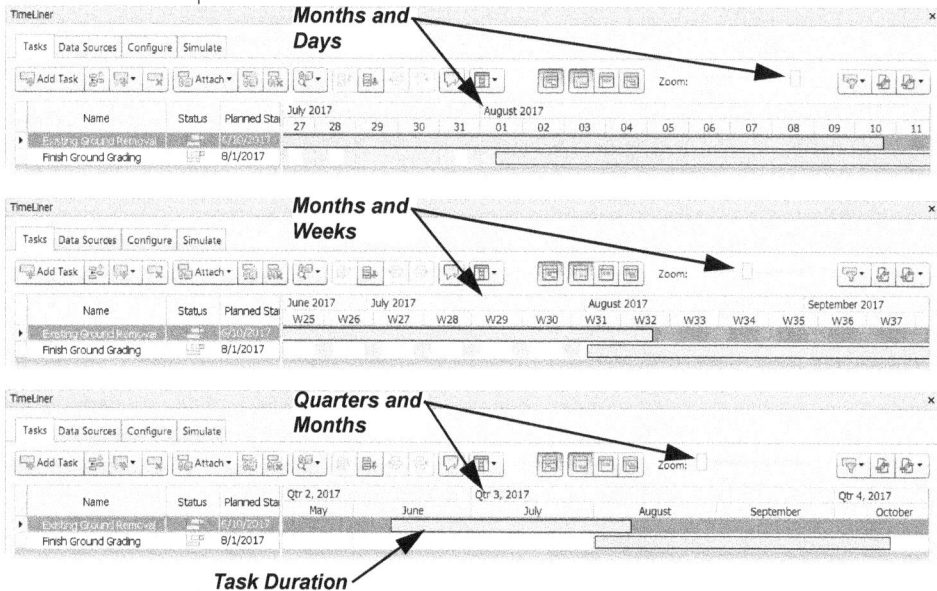

Figure 9–6

9.2 Manually Creating a Construction Simulation

Creating a construction simulation requires preparation. The models have to be created, and then merged together. Then the task list and Gantt chart must be created. Finally, the tasks must be connected to the task list.

General Steps

Use the following general steps to create a construction simulation:

1. Prepare the models.
2. Create save sets and search sets.
3. Add tasks to the Gantt chart.
4. Configure how objects display during the simulation.
5. Link the simulation to any previously-created animations.
6. Play the simulation.
7. Make any required changes.

Step 1 - Prepare the models.

In the Autodesk® Revit® software and the AutoCAD® Civil 3D® software, multiple parts form one object in the model. For example, Figure 9–7 shows the parts that form a wall, while Figure 9–8 shows the parts that form a corridor model.

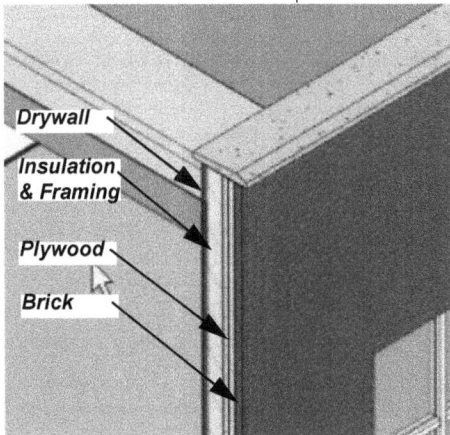

Drywall
Insulation & Framing
Plywood
Brick

Figure 9–7

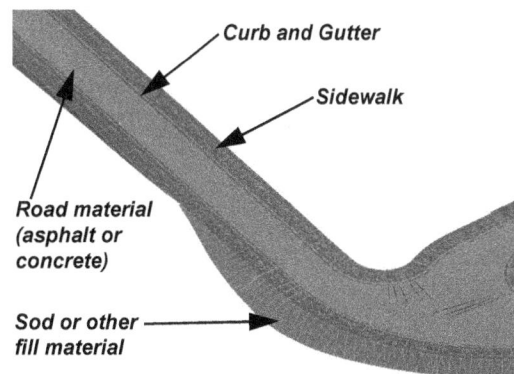

Curb and Gutter
Sidewalk
Road material (asphalt or concrete)
Sod or other fill material

Figure 9–8

During construction, an entire road would not be built at once. First, grading would set the datum elevation, then the sub-base and base would be laid down. Next would come the sidewalks, curb, and gutter. Finally, the asphalt or concrete would be poured for the wearing course of the road.

When creating a construction animation using TimeLiner, you can create a simulation to match a real construction schedule. In order to do this, you must separate objects into parts in the AutoCAD Civil 3D software and the Autodesk Revit software before importing the model into the Autodesk Navisworks software.

For more information on separating objects, see *Appendix A: Coordination Tools*.

Step 2 - Create save sets and search sets.

Saved sets and search sets make connecting objects to the construction schedule much easier. You should use saved searches whenever possible to ensure that the sets are updated when new models are appended in the Autodesk Navisworks software.

For more information on creating save sets and search sets, see *Chapter 4: Analyze Models*

Step 3 - Add tasks to the Gantt chart.

To manually create tasks in the Autodesk Navisworks software, you must be on the *Tasks* tab of the TimeLiner window. Using this method, each task is created one line item at a time.

- Start and end dates must be manually input for each line item.

- You cannot set the end date in reference to the start date (i.e., the number of days to complete).

- You cannot set the start of the next task according to the end of a previous task.

How To: Manually Add Tasks to the Construction Simulation

1. In the TimeLiner window>*Tasks* tab, click 🔤 (Add Task).
2. In the task's data fields, set the following:
   - *Name:* Type a name.
   - *Planned Start Date:* Set the date (MM/DD/YYYY format).
   - *Planned End Date:* Set the date (MM/DD/YYYY format).
   - *Actual Start Date:* Set the date (MM/DD/YYYY format).
   - *Actual End Date:* Set the date (MM/DD/YYYY format).
   - *Task Type:* Expand the list and select a task type. Task types are defined in the *Configuration* tab.
   - *Attached:* There are several options for attaching objects. Right-click on the field and select one of the following, as shown in Figure 9–9.

It is highly recommended to use search sets whenever possible to ensure that new items connect to the construction schedule.

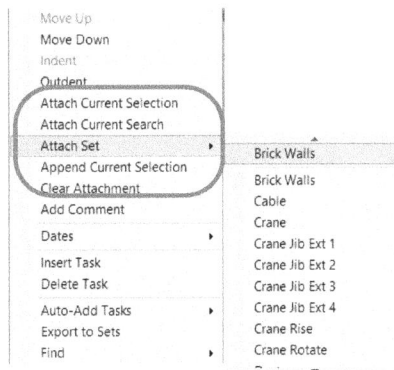

Figure 9–9

Step 4 - Configure how objects display during the simulation.

The *Configure* tab enables you to set how you want objects to display at key times during the simulation.

- You can remove options by clicking ⬚ Delete (Delete), which deletes the selected row.
- You can create additional options by clicking ⬚ Add (Add), which creates a new row. You can then use the down-arrows in each column to select how you want objects to display.
- Additional appearance definitions can be created by clicking **Appearance Definitions**.

How To: Create a New Appearance Definition

1. In the TimeLiner>*Configure* tab, click **Appearance Definitions**.
2. In the Appearance Definitions dialog box, click **Add**. A new row is added at the bottom of the list.
3. Select the new row and then click on the **Name** field to change the name.
4. Double-click on the color field to select a color from the Color palette. Click **OK**.
5. Slide the *Transparency slider* to set the opacity, as shown in Figure 9–10.

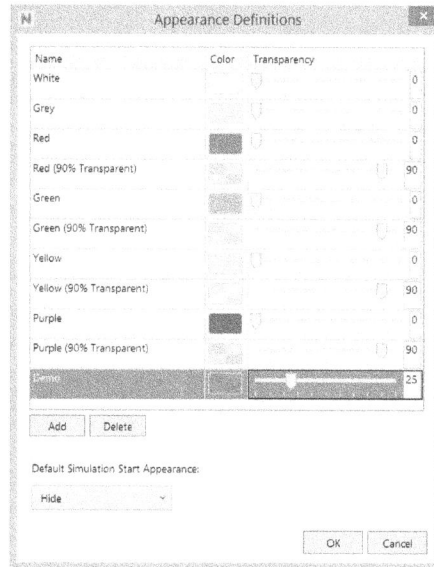

Figure 9–10

6. Expand the Default Simulation Start Appearance drop-down list and select the appearance you plan to use most often at the start of the simulation.
7. Click **OK**.

> # Step 5 - Link the simulation to any previously-created animations.

Simulations can be linked to any previously-created animations to demonstrate how everything moves around the site as construction proceeds.

Step 6 - Play the simulation.

Tools at the top of the *Simulate* tab enable you to navigate the simulation. The tools are as follows:

- ◁ **(Rewind):** Moves the Simulation bar to the beginning and changes the Scene view to match.

- ◁◁ **(Step Back):** Rewinds the simulation a frame at a time.

- ◁ **(Reverse Play):** Plays the simulation in reverse.

- ‖ **(Pause):** Pauses the simulation, enabling you to resume play from the same spot by clicking Play.

- ▢ **(Stop):** Stops the simulation, moves the Simulation bar to the beginning, and changes the Scene view to match.

- ▷ **(Play):** Starts the simulation from the current position of the Simulation bar.

- ▷▷ **(Step Forward):** Moves forwards a frame at a time.

- ▷▷ **(Forward):** Fast forwards the simulation to the end.

Step 7 - Make any required changes.

It is easier to make construction timeline adjustments before scheduling all of the sub-contractors due to busy project schedules. Being able to watch the construction virtually before breaking ground helps you predict any issues that might occur during the construction phase. Once an issue is uncovered, you can go back to the TimeLiner>*Tasks* tab to make any required changes to the construction timeline.

Practice 9a

Manually Create a Construction Simulation

Practice Objectives

- Consolidate models from multiple software sources.
- Align the models with each other.

Estimated time for completion: 25 minutes

In this practice you will manually add tasks to the TimeLiner window and attach them to objects in the model, as shown in Figure 9–11.

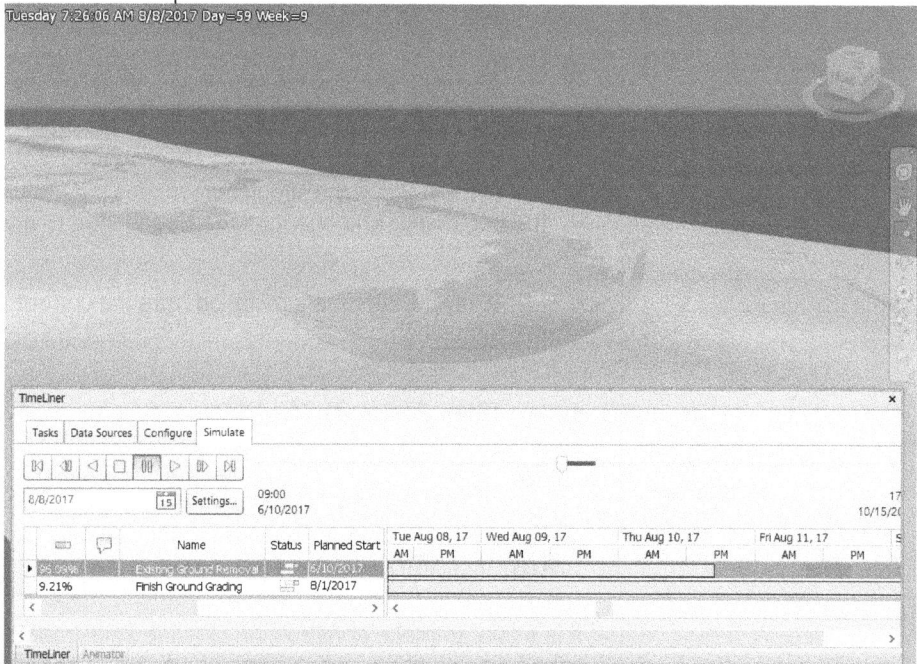

Figure 9–11

Task 1 - Append the parts models.

For TimeLiner to work properly, the original files must be correctly organized and objects should be separated into parts. In *Appendix A: Coordination Tools*, you will learn how to set up the Autodesk Revit file and the AutoCAD Civil 3D corridor model for use in TimeLiner. In this task, you will attach new models that have already been separated into parts for the simulation.

1. In the *Scheduling* practice files folder, open **NewElementarySchool-Prep.nwf**.

2. In the *Home* Tab>Project panel, click (Append).

3. In the Append dialog box, expand the *Files of type* drop-down list and select **Autodesk DWG/DXF (*.dwg, *.dxf)**.

4. Navigate to the *Scheduling* practice files folder, select **CorridorSolids.dwg**, and then click **Open**.

5. In the Selection Tree window, right-click on **CorridorSolids.dwg** and select **Units and Transform**.

6. In the Units and Transform dialog box, set the Origin values as: *X:* **0**, *Y:* **0**, *Z:* **0.15**.
   - Note: You are only doing this transformation for visual purposes. The finished ground surface included the corridor model, which ends up hiding the corridor. Therefore, you are raising the corridor to ensure that the corridor model is not hidden by the surface during the simulation.

7. In the *Home* Tab>Project panel, click (Append).

8. In the Append dialog box, expand the *Files of type* drop-down list and select **Revit (*.rvt, *.rfa, *.rte)**.

9. Navigate to the *Scheduling* practice files folder, select **Elementary-School-Architectural TimeLiner.rvt**, and then click **Open**.

Task 2 - Set up the file. (optional)

To make the connection between parts in the model and the Gantt chart, it is important to set up the file with saved sets and saved searches. In this task, you create saved sets for the Autodesk Revit model parts.

1. Continue working in the same file as the previous task.

This task can be skipped if you are short on time. If skipped, ensure that you open the indicated file in the next task so that the TimeLiner will work properly.

2. In the Selection Tree, expand **Elementary-School-Architectural TimeLiner.rvt>First Floor>Doors** and select the following, as shown in Figure 9–12:
   - Double Door
   - Single
   - Double

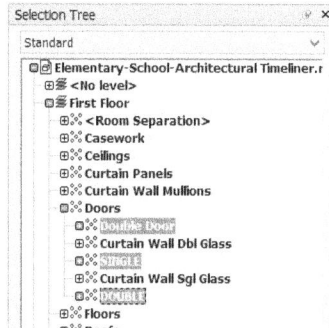

Figure 9–12

3. In the *Home* tab>Select & Search panel, click [icon] (Save Selection). Type **1st Floor Doors** for the name.

4. Expand **Elementary-School-Architectural TimeLiner.rvt> First Floor>Walls>Basic** and select the following, as shown in Figure 9–13.
   - Interior 6" Metal Stud
   - Interior 4" Metal Stud
   - Interior - 4 1/4" Chase Partition
   - Interior 4" Metal Stud - Chase

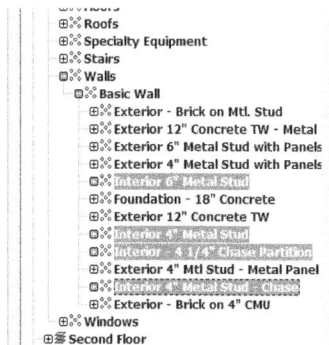

Figure 9–13

5. Save the selection as **1st Floor Interior Walls**.

6. Expand **Elementary-School-Architectural TimeLiner.rvt> First Floor** and select **Windows**, as shown in Figure 9–14.

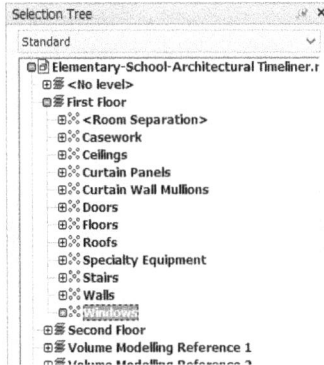

Figure 9–14

7. Save the selection as **1st Floor Windows**.

8. Expand **Elementary-School-Architectural TimeLiner.rvt> Second Floor>Doors** and select **SINGLE**, as shown in Figure 9–15.

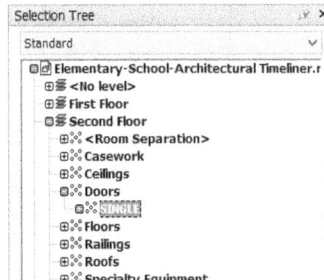

Figure 9–15

9. Save the selection as **2nd Floor Doors**.

10. Expand **Elementary-School-Architectural TimeLiner.rvt> Second Floor>Walls>Basic Wall** and select the following, as shown in Figure 9–16.
    - Interior 6" Metal Stud
    - Interior 4" Metal Stud

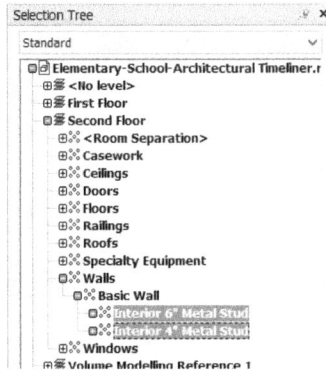

Figure 9–16

11. Save the selection as **2nd Floor Interior Walls**.

12. Expand **Elementary-School-Architectural TimeLiner.rvt> Second Floor** and select **Windows**, as shown in Figure 9–17.

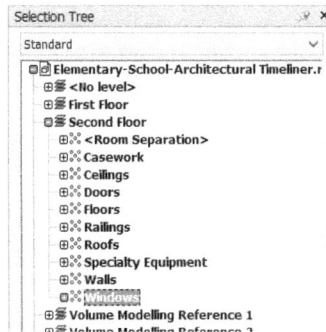

Figure 9–17

13. Save the selection as **2nd Floor Windows**.

14. Expand **Elementary-School-Architectural TimeLiner.rvt> <No level>** and select the following, as shown in Figure 9–18.
   - Curtain Panels
   - Curtain Wall Mullions

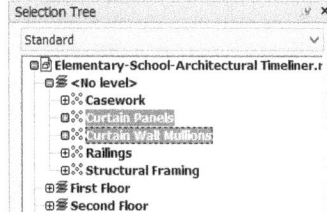

Figure 9–18

15. Save the selection as **Curtain Panels and Mullions**.

16. Expand **Elementary-School-Architectural TimeLiner.rvt> First Floor>** and select the following, as shown in Figure 9–19.
   - Curtain Panels
   - Curtain Wall Mullions
   - Doors>Curtain Wall Dbl Glass
   - Doors>Curtain Wall Sgl Glass

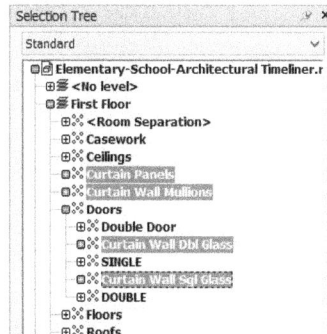

Figure 9–19

17. Save the selection as **Curtain Walls**.

18. Expand **Elementary-School-Architectural TimeLiner.rvt** and select the following, as shown in Figure 9–20.

- First Floor>Roofs
- Second Floor>Roofs

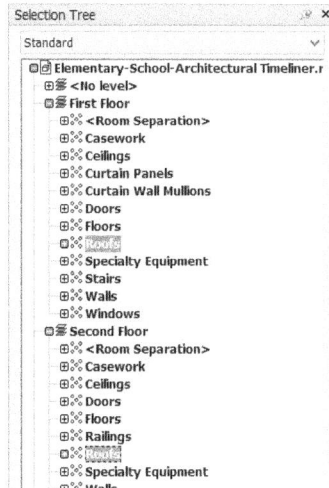

Figure 9–20

19. Save the selection as **Roofs 1 and 2**.

20. Expand **Elementary-School-Architectural TimeLiner.rvt> Volume Modeling Reference 1** and select **Roofs**, as shown in Figure 9–21.

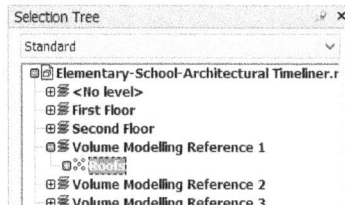

Figure 9–21

21. Save the selection as **Roofs Reference 2**.

22. Expand **Elementary-School-Architectural TimeLiner.rvt> Volume Modeling Reference 3** and select **Roofs**, as shown in Figure 9–22.

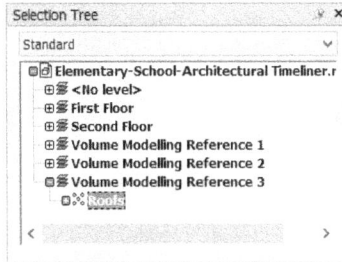

Figure 9–22

23. Save the selection as **Roofs Reference 3**.

24. Expand **Elementary-School-Architectural TimeLiner.rvt>Second Floor>Floors>Floor** and select **Concrete on Metal Desk**, as shown in Figure 9–23.

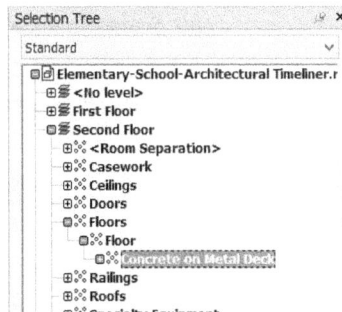

Figure 9–23

25. Save the selection as **Concrete on Metal Deck - 2nd Floor**.

26. Expand **Elementary-School-Architectural TimeLiner.rvt> First Floor>Floors>Floor** and select **Generic - 12"**, as shown in Figure 9–24.

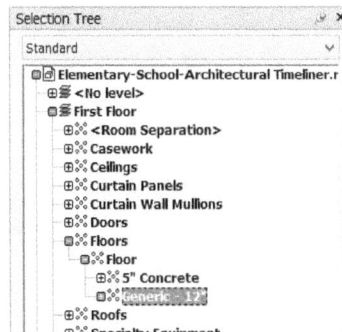

Figure 9–24

27. Save the selection as **Generic - 12" Floor**.

28. Expand **Elementary-School-Architectural TimeLiner.rvt> First Floor>Floors>Floor** and select **5" Concrete**, as shown in Figure 9–25.

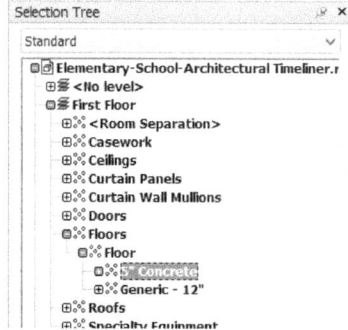

Figure 9–25

29. Save the selection as **5" Concrete Floor**.

30. Expand **Elementary-School-Architectural TimeLiner.rvt> First Floor>Walls>Basic Wall** and select **Foundation - 18" Concrete**, as shown in Figure 9–26.

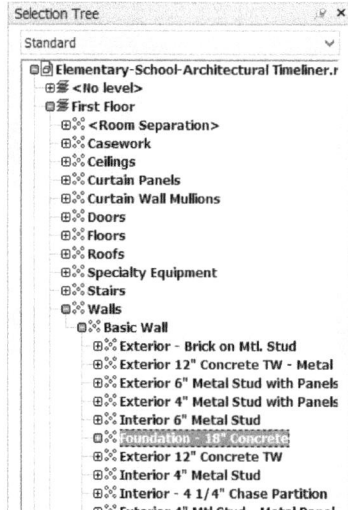

Figure 9–26

31. Save the selection as **Foundation - 18" Concrete Wall**.

32. Save the file.

Task 3 - Create tasks manually.

In this task, you will add the existing ground to finish ground grading to the Gantt chart using the task pane.

1. Continue working with the same file from the last task. If you skipped the last task then in the *Scheduling* practice files folder, open **NewElementarySchool-Manual.nwf**.

2. In the *Home* tab>Tools panel, click 🗓 (TimeLiner) to open the TimeLiner window.

3. In the TimeLiner window>*Tasks* tab, click 🔽 (Add Task).

4. In the task's data fields, set the following, as shown in Figure 9–27:
   - *Name:* **Existing Ground Removal**.
   - *Planned Start Date:* **6/10/2017**
   - *Planned End Date:* **8/10/2017**
   - *Actual Start Date:* **7/01/2017**
   - *Actual End Date:* **8/31/2017**
   - *Task Type:* **Demolish**

Figure 9–27

5. In the TimeLiner window>*Tasks* tab, click 🔽 (Add Task).

6. In the task's data fields, set the following:
   - *Name:* **Finish Ground Grading**.
   - *Planned Start Date:* **8/01/2017**
   - *Planned End Date:* **10/15/2017**
   - *Actual Start Date:* **9/10/2017**
   - *Actual End Date:* **11/21/2017**
   - *Task Type:* **Construct**

7. Save the file.

Task 4 - Connect objects in the model to tasks.

In order to review the grading change from the existing ground to the finish ground, you must attach the objects to the tasks. In this task you attach the existing ground to the first task and the proposed ground to the second task in TimeLiner.

1. Continue working with the same file from the last task.

*If you do not see this node, overwrite **Site Layout.dwg** with **SiteLayout-Edited.dwg** and then refresh the Autodesk Navisworks model.*

2. In the Selection Tree window, expand **Site Layout.dwg> C-TOPO-VIEW** and select **AIW_Existing_Ground**, as shown in Figure 9–28.

3. In the TimeLiner window, right-click on the **Existing Ground Removal** task in the **Attached** column and select **Attach Current Selection**, as shown in Figure 9–28.

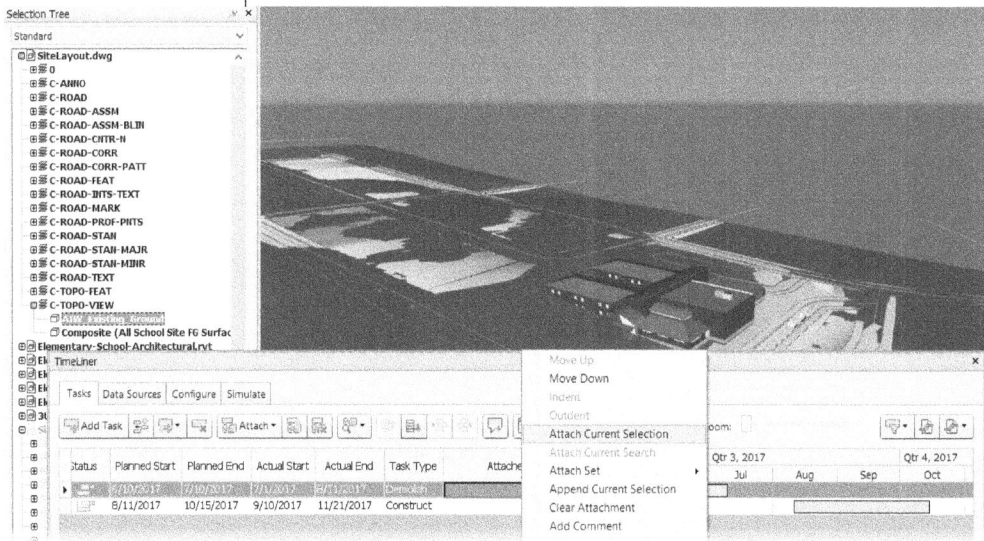

Figure 9–28

4. In the Selection Tree window, expand **Site Layout.dwg> C-TOPO-VIEW** and select **Composite (All School Site FG Surfaces)**.

5. In the TimeLiner window, right-click on the **Finish Ground Grading** task below the **Attached** column and select **Attach Current Selection**.

6. In the TimeLiner window, open the *Configure* tab.

7. Set the following parameters for the Appearance Definitions, as shown in Figure 9–29.

   Construct:

   - **Start Appearance:** Purple (90% Transparent)
   - **End Appearance:** Model Appearance
   - **Early Appearance:** Green (90% Transparent)
   - **Late Appearance:** Purple (90% Transparent)
   - **Simulation Start Appearance:** Hide

   Demolish:

   - **Start Appearance:** Model Appearance
   - **End Appearance:** Hide
   - **Early Appearance:** Green (90% Transparent)
   - **Late Appearance:** Red (90% Transparent)
   - **Simulation Start Appearance:** Model Appearance

   Temporary:

   - **Start Appearance:** Yellow (90% Transparent)
   - **End Appearance:** Hide
   - **Early Appearance:** None
   - **Late Appearance:** None
   - **Simulation Start Appearance:** None

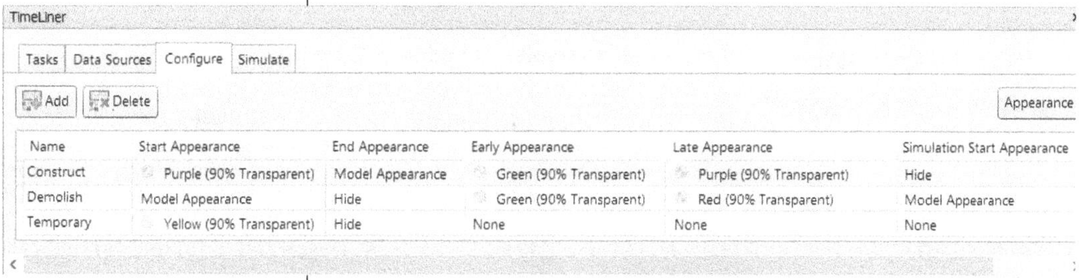

Name	Start Appearance	End Appearance	Early Appearance	Late Appearance	Simulation Start Appearance
Construct	Purple (90% Transparent)	Model Appearance	Green (90% Transparent)	Purple (90% Transparent)	Hide
Demolish	Model Appearance	Hide	Green (90% Transparent)	Red (90% Transparent)	Model Appearance
Temporary	Yellow (90% Transparent)	Hide	None	None	None

TimeLiner — Tasks | Data Sources | Configure | Simulate — Add | Delete — Appearance

Figure 9–29

8. In the TimeLiner window, open the *Simulate* tab.

9. Click ▷ (Play) to run the simulation.

10. Save the file.

9.3 Importing an External Task List

Most architecture, engineering, and construction firms use project management software to manage their project schedules. These programs make it easier to set dates based on the start or completion dates of an earlier task.

You can use TimeLiner to import project schedules from a variety of external data sources. Once imported, a task list can be created and automatically connected to model objects. The key to ensuring this information is correct is using saved sets and saved searches whose names match the task names in the project management database.

The following project management databases can be imported:

- CSV files
- Microsoft Project MPX
- Microsoft Project 2007-2013
- Primavera P6 (Web Services)
- Primavera P6 V7 (Web Services)
- Primavera P6 V8.3 (Web Services)

TimeLiner Rules

TimeLiner Rules assist in connecting tasks with items in the Scene view. There are three rules available, as shown in Figure 9–30. In all cases, the name cases must match.

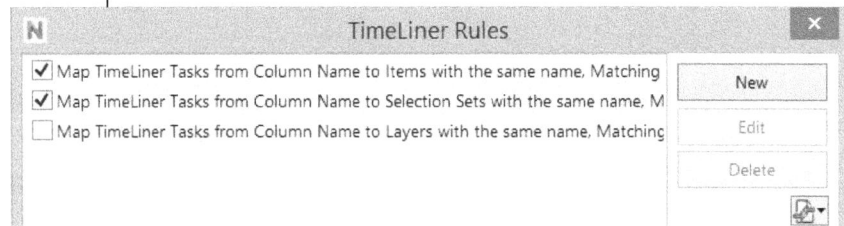

Figure 9–30

- Use the first rule when the item names in the Selection Tree match the task names in the project schedule.

- Use the second rule when the selection set names match the task names in the project schedule.

- Use the third rule when the layer names in the original file match the task names in the project schedule.

The first two rules are most often used with Autodesk Revit files, while the third rule is most often used to connect AutoCAD layers or AutoCAD Civil 3D corridor shapes.

How To: Import a Task List

1. In the TimeLiner>*Data Sources* tab, expand 🔲 (Add) and select the source database.
2. In the Open files dialog box, navigate to the file and select it.
3. Click **Open**.
4. In the Field Selector dialog box, map the TimeLiner column names to the external database fields, as shown in Figure 9–31.

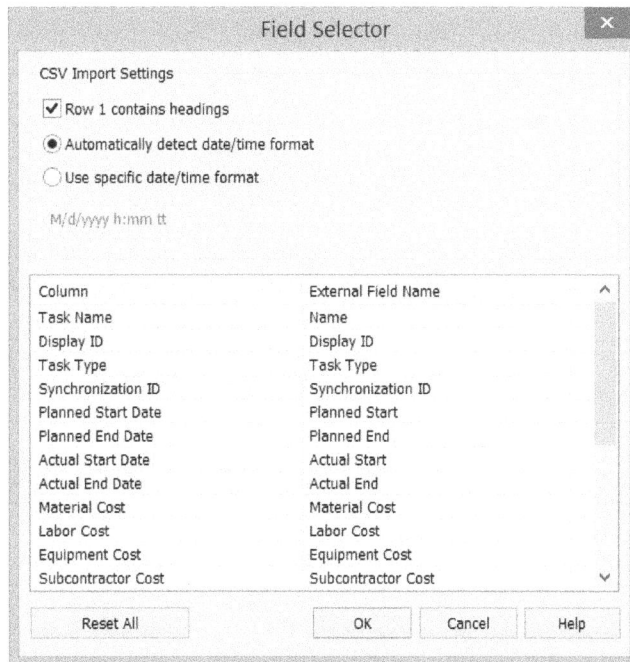

Figure 9–31

5. Click **OK**.
6. In the TimeLiner>*Data Sources* tab, right-click on the new data source and select **Rename**.
7. Type an appropriate name. The name you use displays in the Task pane.
8. In the TimeLiner>*Data Sources* tab, right-click on the new data source and select **Rebuild Task Hierarchy**.
9. If any fields are missing information, you might get an error message. Click **OK**.

10. In the TimeLiner>*Tasks* tab, click 🔲 (Auto-Attach Using Rules).

11. In the TimeLiner Rules dialog box, select the required rules and click **Apply Rules**, as shown in Figure 9–32.

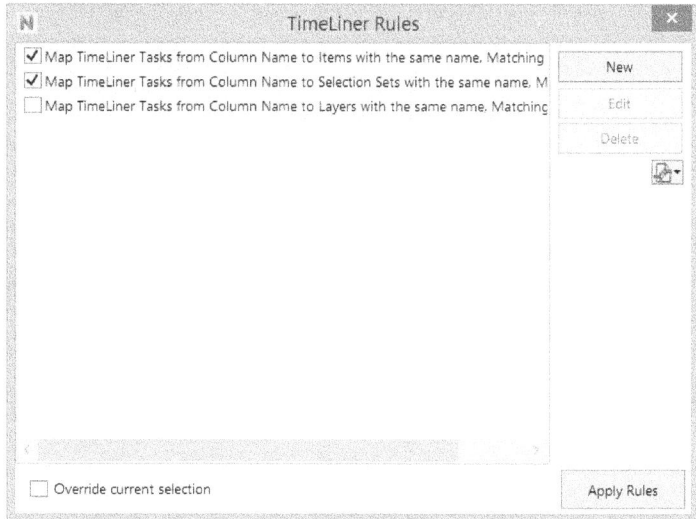

Figure 9–32

12. Ensure that all of the tasks have objects attached to them. If any are missing, manually attach the objects.

13. Play the simulation.

9.4 Combining TimeLiner and Animator

During a construction simulation, it can be helpful to view the model from multiple angles to understand how everything comes together. You can do this by setting up an animation first, and then connecting the animation to the project schedule.

Simulation Settings

The Simulation Settings enables you to connect an animation to the timeline and adjust a number of settings, as shown in Figure 9–33.

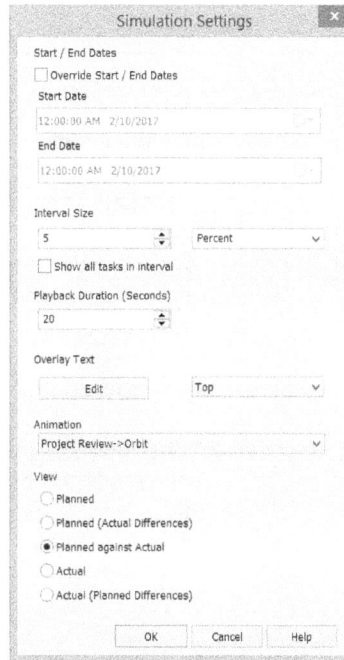

Figure 9–33

Start/End Dates

You can override the start and end dates for the animation . In doing so, this only changes what date the animation of the simulation starts. It does not automatically change the dates of the tasks according to the override start date. This means that if an override start date is selected that is the mid-point of the construction timeline, then half of the simulation shows as already being complete when you run the simulation.

Interval Size

The *Interval Size* determines how much of the Timeline plays at once. A numeric value, combined with one of the following, determine the interval:

- Percent
- Weeks
- Days
- Hours
- Minutes
- Seconds

Playback Duration (Seconds)

You can set the playback duration to control how long it takes to play the entire animation. The duration units are in seconds.

Overlay Text

Text can be added to the Scene view to communicate information about the simulation. The text can be placed at the top or the bottom of the Scene view.

Animation

The animation drop-down list provides a list of previously created animations. By default, it is set to **No Link**. TimeLiner only uses the camera viewpoints from the animation to tour the model while the TimeLiner simulation plays.

View

The dates that are used to animate the simulation are selected in the *View* area. You have the following options to chose from:

- Planned
- Planned (Actual Differences)
- Planned against Actual
- Actual
- Actual (Planned Differences)

How To: Add an Animation to TimeLiner

1. Create an animation with the required camera viewpoints. Note: Object animations are ignored unless they are added to the task list.
2. In the TimeLiner window>*Simulate* tab, click **Settings**.
3. In the Simulation Settings dialog box, expand the Animation drop-down list and select the animation with the required viewpoints, as shown in Figure 9–34.

Only animations that were previously created display in the list. You cannot create an animation at this point.

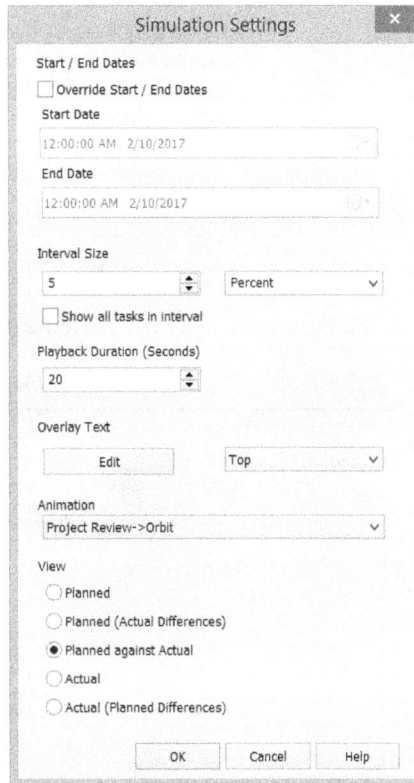

Figure 9–34

4. Click **OK**.

5. In the *Simulate* tab, click ▷ (Play) to run the simulation.

Practice 9b

Import an External Project Schedule

Practice Objectives

- Import an external project management database to populate the TimeLiner task list.
- Connect objects to tasks automatically using rules.

Estimated time for completion: 15 minutes

In this practice, you will connect an external project management database to automatically populate TimeLiner tasks. Then you will use rules to connect the tasks to the model automatically before running the simulation, as shown in Figure 9–35.

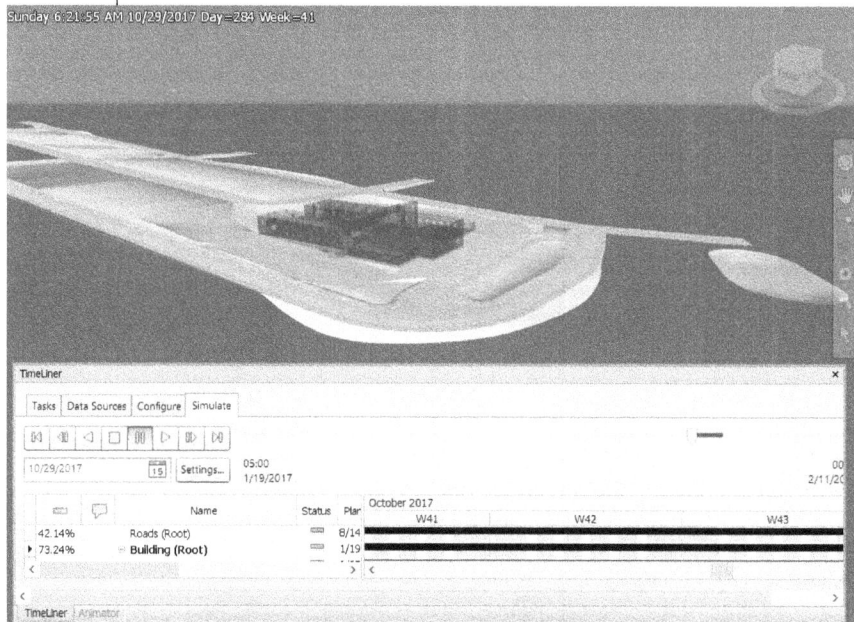

Figure 9–35

Task 1 - Connect the corridor schedule.

In this task, you will connect CSV file to import the tasks for the road construction schedule.

1. In the Quick Access toolbar, click 📂 (Open).

2. In the *Scheduling* practice files folder, open **NewElementarySchool-Import.nwf**.

3. In the TimeLiner>*Data Sources* tab, expand ⬚ (Add) and select **CSV Import**.

4. In the Open files dialog box, navigate to the *Scheduling* practice files folder and select **Civil-timeline.csv**.

5. Click **Open**.

6. In the Field Selector dialog box, map the TimeLiner column names to the external database fields, as shown in Figure 9–36.

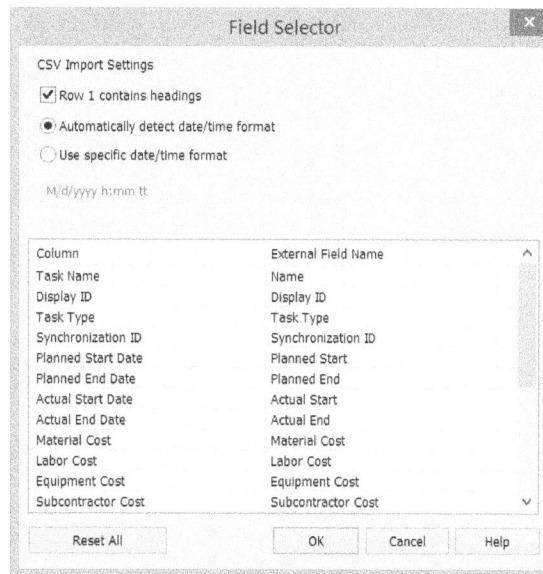

Field Selector		✕

CSV Import Settings

☑ Row 1 contains headings

◉ Automatically detect date/time format

◯ Use specific date/time format

M/d/yyyy h:mm tt

Column	External Field Name	⌃
Task Name	Name	
Display ID	Display ID	
Task Type	Task Type	
Synchronization ID	Synchronization ID	
Planned Start Date	Planned Start	
Planned End Date	Planned End	
Actual Start Date	Actual Start	
Actual End Date	Actual End	
Material Cost	Material Cost	
Labor Cost	Labor Cost	
Equipment Cost	Equipment Cost	
Subcontractor Cost	Subcontractor Cost	⌄

Reset All		OK	Cancel	Help

Figure 9–36

7. Click **OK**.

8. In the TimeLiner>*Data Sources* tab, right-click on the new data source and select **Rename**.

9. Type **Roads** for the name.

10. In the TimeLiner>*Data Sources* tab, right-click on the **Roads** data source and select **Rebuild Task Hierarchy**.

11. Note that some fields are missing information. Click **OK** in the Problems in Imported Data dialog box.

12. In the TimeLiner>*Tasks* tab, click 🔲 (Auto-Attach Using Rules).

13. In the TimeLiner Rules dialog box, ensure that only the last rule, **Map TimeLiner Tasks from Column Name to Layers with the same name, Matching case**, is selected. Click **Apply Rules**, as shown in Figure 9–37.

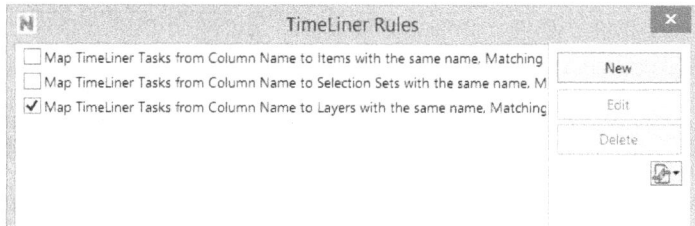

Figure 9–37

14. Close the TimeLiner Rules dialog box.

15. Ensure that all of the tasks have objects attached to them.

16. In the TimeLiner window, open the *Simulate* tab.

17. Click ▷ (Play) to run the simulation.

18. Save the file.

Task 2 - Connect the building schedule.

In this task, you will import the project schedule for the building components. Since not all of the object and set names match the task names, they do not connect automatically. Therefore, some tasks must be connected manually.

1. In the TimeLiner>*Data Sources* tab, expand 🔲 (Add) and select **CSV Import**.

2. In the Open files dialog box, navigate to the *Scheduling* practice files folder and select **Elementary School Arch.csv**.

3. Click **Open**.

4. In the Field Selector dialog box, map the TimeLiner column names to the external database fields shown in Figure 9–38, and then click **OK**.

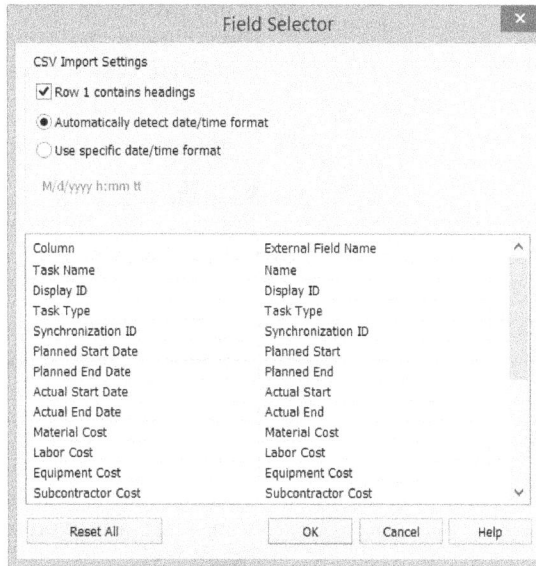

Figure 9–38

5. In the TimeLiner>*Data Sources* tab, right-click on the new data source and select **Rename**.

6. Type **Building** for the name.

7. In the TimeLiner>*Data Sources* tab, right-click on the Roads data source and select **Rebuild Task Hierarchy**.

8. Note that some of the fields are missing information. Click **OK** in the Problems in Imported Data dialog box.

9. In the TimeLiner>*Tasks* tab, click 🔲 (Auto-Attach Using Rules).

10. In the TimeLiner Rules dialog box, select the first two rules and click **Apply Rules**, as shown in Figure 9–39.

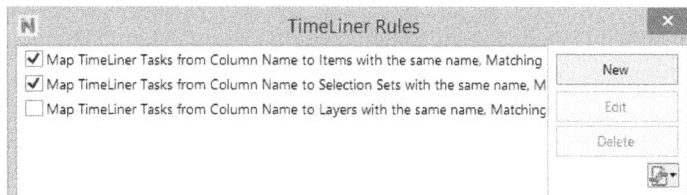

Figure 9–39

11. Review the tasks and note that not all of the tasks have objects attached to them.

12. In the Task pane, scroll down to *Masonry - Brick - Parts*.
Right-click on the **Attached** field and select **Attach
Set>Brick Walls** to connect the brick face to this task.

13. In the *Simulate* tab, click ▷ (Play) to run the simulation.

14. Save the file.

Task 3 - Orbit the model as you play the simulation.

In this task you connect an animation to the simulation to orbit
the model as the simulation plays.

1. In the TimeLiner window>*Simulate* tab, click **Settings**.

2. In the Simulation Settings dialog box, expand the Animation
drop-down list and select **Orbit>Overview**. Then, in the *View*
area, select **Planned against Actual**, as shown in
Figure 9–40.

Figure 9–40

3. Click **OK**.

4. In the *Simulate* tab, click ▷ (Play) to run the simulation.

9.5 Time-Based Clashes

One thing that can be very costly on a construction project is when things fit together on paper but do not fit together in the field. Construction simulations help you discover when a piece of equipment does not have the necessary room to maneuver on a job site. Combining TimeLiner, Animator, and Clash Detective, you can run a time based clash test, as shown in Figure 9–41.

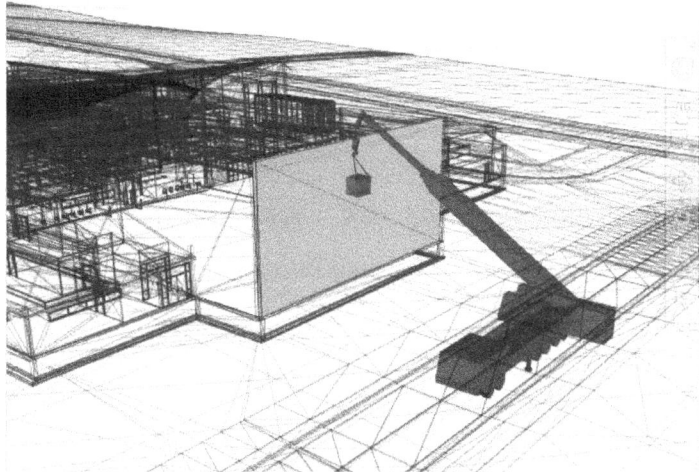

Figure 9–41

How To: Set up a Time Base Clash Test

1. In the Clash Detective window click 🔲 (Add Test). Rename the test as required.
2. In the Clash Detective window, open the *Select* tab.
3. In the *Selection A* area select the first item to compare.
4. In the *Selection B* area select the second item to compare.
5. In the *Settings* area, expand the Link drop-down list and select either an animation or TimeLiner.
6. Click **Run Test**.

> **Hint: TimeLiner Could Interfere**
>
> If you have recently run a TimeLiner simulation, the model might still be displaying the ending Scene view. This can interfere with the true results of a time-based clash test.
>
> If you suspect that clashes should have occurred, but the result showed zero clashes, then go into the TimeLiner window, activate the *Tasks* tab, and then re-run the clash test.

Practice 9c

Conduct a Time-Based Clash Test

Practice Objective

- Run a clash test.

Estimated time for completion: 5 minutes

In this practice you will use a combination of TimeLiner, Animator, and Clash Detective to create a time-based clash test, as shown in Figure 9–42.

Figure 9–42

Task 1 - Combine Clash Detective and Animator.

In this task you will run a clash detection with a link to an animation to ensure that the crane does not clash with the building.

1. In the *Scheduling* practice files folder, open **NewElementarySchool-Clash.nwf**.

2. In the Clash Detective window, open the *Select* tab.

If the Clash Detective window is not displayed, toggle it on in the Home tab>Tools panel.

3. In the Clash Detective window click (Add Test).

4. Select the name, then click on it and rename it to **Crane vs Building**.

5. In the *Selection A* pane select **Mobile Crane.skp**.

6. In the *Selection B* pane select **Elementary-School-Architectural.rvt**.

7. In the *Settings* area, expand the Link drop-down list and select **Mobile Crane** to link the crane animation to the test.

8. Click **Run Test**.

9. If you come up with **0** clashes, ensure that you make the *Tasks* tab active in the TimeLiner window. Then re-run the clash test. Figure 9–43 shows the results. Yours might be slightly different if you used an animation you created.

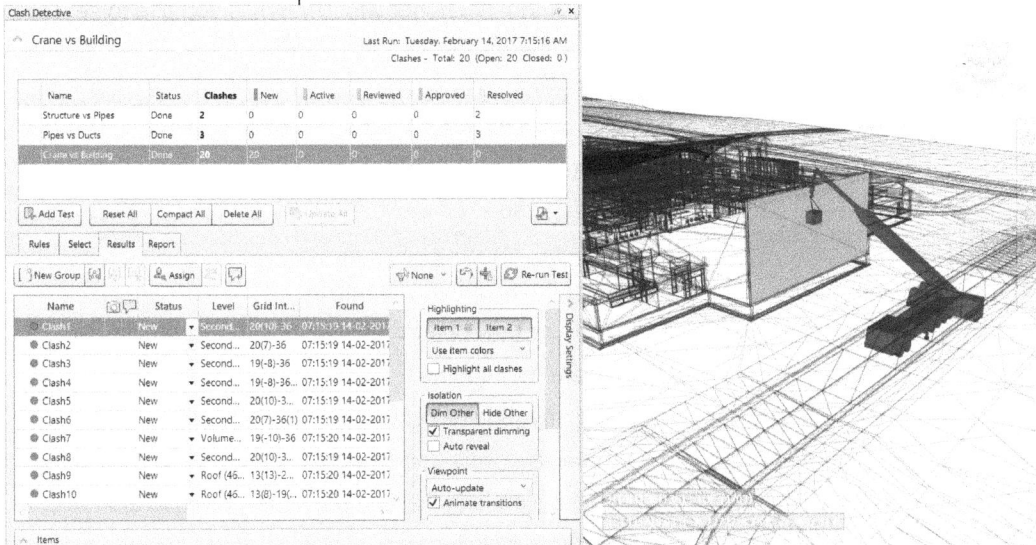

Figure 9–43

Chapter Review Questions

1. What tab in the TimeLiner window would you use to manually create a Gantt chart?

   a. *Tasks* tab

   b. *Data Sources* tab

   c. *Configure* tab

   d. *Simulate* tab

2. What tab in the TimeLiner window would you use to set up how items display during the simulation?

   a. *Tasks* tab

   b. *Data Sources* tab

   c. *Configure* tab

   d. *Simulate* tab

3. Put the following general steps in the correct order for creating a construction simulation:

   a. Configure how objects display during the simulation.

   b. Prepare the models.

   c. Make any required changes.

   d. Create save sets and search sets.

   e. Link the simulation to any previously-created animations.

   f. Play the simulation.

   g. Add tasks to the Gantt chart.

4. Which Rule would you most likely use to connect AutoCAD Civil 3D corridor shapes to the task list?

   a. Map TimeLiner Tasks from Column Name to Items with the same name, Matching case.

   b. Map TimeLiner Tasks from Column Name to Selection Sets with the same name, Matching case.

   c. Map TimeLiner Tasks from Column Name to Layers with the same name, Matching case.

5. Which window would you use to run a time based clash detection?

   a. Selection Tree

   b. Animator

   c. TimeLiner

   d. Clash Detective

Command Summary

Button	Command	Location
	Add Comment	• **Window:** TimeLiner>*Tasks* tab
	Add Configuration	• **Window:** TimeLiner>*Configure* tab
	Add Data Source	• **Window:** TimeLiner>*Data Sources* tab
	Add Task	• **Window:** TimeLiner>*Tasks* tab
	Attach	• **Window:** TimeLiner>*Tasks* tab
	Auto-Add Tasks	• **Window:** TimeLiner>*Tasks* tab
	Auto-Attach Using Rules	• **Window:** TimeLiner>*Tasks* tab
	Clear Attachment	• **Window:** TimeLiner>*Tasks* tab
	Columns	• **Window:** TimeLiner>*Tasks* tab
	Delete Configuration	• **Window:** TimeLiner>*Configure* tab
	Delete Data Source	• **Window:** TimeLiner>*Data Sources* tab
	Delete Task	• **Window:** TimeLiner>*Tasks* tab
	Export to Schedule	• **Window:** TimeLiner>*Tasks* tab
	Export to Sets	• **Window:** TimeLiner>*Tasks* tab
	Filter by Status	• **Window:** TimeLiner>*Tasks* tab
	Find Items	• **Window:** TimeLiner>*Tasks* tab
	Forward	• **Window:** TimeLiner>*Simulate* tab

	Indent	• **Window:** TimeLiner>*Tasks* tab
	Insert Task	• **Window:** TimeLiner>*Tasks* tab
	Move Down	• **Window:** TimeLiner>*Tasks* tab
	Move Up	• **Window:** TimeLiner>*Tasks* tab
	Outdent	• **Window:** TimeLiner>*Tasks* tab
	Pause	• **Window:** TimeLiner>*Simulate* tab
	Play	• **Window:** TimeLiner>*Simulate* tab
	Play Backwards	• **Window:** TimeLiner>*Simulate* tab
	Refresh Data Source	• **Window:** TimeLiner>*Data Sources* tab
	Rewind	• **Window:** TimeLiner>*Simulate* tab
	Show Actual Dates	• **Window:** TimeLiner>*Tasks* tab
	Show Planned Dates	• **Window:** TimeLiner>*Tasks* tab
	Show Planned vs Actual Dates	• **Window:** TimeLiner>*Tasks* tab
	Show/Hide Gantt Chart	• **Window:** TimeLiner>*Tasks* tab
	Step Back	• **Window:** TimeLiner>*Simulate* tab
	Step Forward	• **Window:** TimeLiner>*Simulate* tab
	Stop	• **Window:** TimeLiner>*Simulate* tab
	TimeLiner	• **Ribbon:** *Home* tab>Tools panel

Coordination Tools

When you are working in multiple software packages, it is often necessary to prepare your models before providing them to the BIM Coordinator. This chapter introduces some of the best practices for Autodesk® software users who plan to share their models in the Autodesk® Navisworks® software.

Learning Objectives in this Appendix

- Create views in the Autodesk® Revit® software.
- Add a real world coordinate to an Autodesk Revit model.
- Install the Autodesk® Civil 3D® Object Enabler.
- Share an Autodesk® InfraWorks® 360 model with the Autodesk Navisworks software.
- Prepare an AutoCAD Civil 3D corridor model for use in the Autodesk Navisworks TimeLiner.
- Prepare an Autodesk Revit model for use in the Autodesk Navisworks TimeLiner.

A.1 Creating a View in Autodesk Revit

When you append or open an Autodesk Revit model in the Autodesk Navisworks software, the display matches what was toggled on in the Autodesk Revit view when the model was saved. In order to ensure that unnecessary items (such as Masses) are not displayed, and that other necessary items (such as walls) are displayed in the Autodesk Navisworks software, you should create a view in the Autodesk Revit software.

There are a few key things to keep in mind when creating the view, which are:

- You must start with a 3D view.

- The view must have "Navis" in its name for the Autodesk Navisworks software to recognize it.

How To: Create a Revit View

1. In the Autodesk Revit software, set the view to a 3D view.
2. In the Project Browser, right-click on the view, expand *Duplicate View* and select **Duplicate**, as shown in Figure A–1.

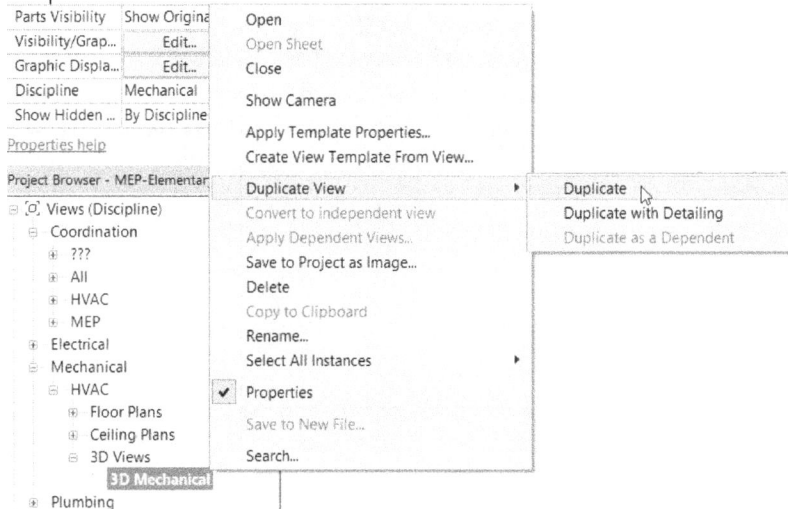

Figure A–1

3. In the Project Browser, right-click on the duplicated view and select **Rename**, as shown in Figure A–2.

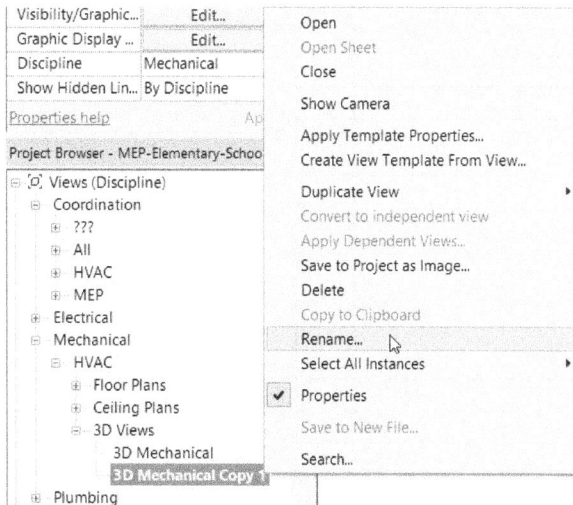

Figure A–2

4. In the Rename View dialog box, type **Navis** for the name and click **OK**. This step is important to ensure that the Autodesk Navisworks software recognizes the view.

5. In the Properties palette, next to *Visibility/Graphics Overrides*, click **Edit**, as shown in Figure A–3.

*Alternatively, you can type **VV**.*

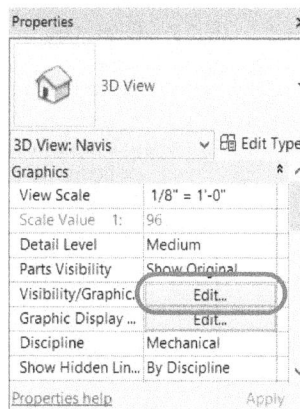

Figure A–3

Toggle off items such as masses, areas, and lighting. Toggling off lights ensures that there is no duplication from the electrical model.

6. In the Visual Graphics Override dialog box, in the *Model Categories* tab, clear the selection of any items that are not required, and select all of the items that need to be displayed in the Autodesk Navisworks software, as shown in Figure A–4.

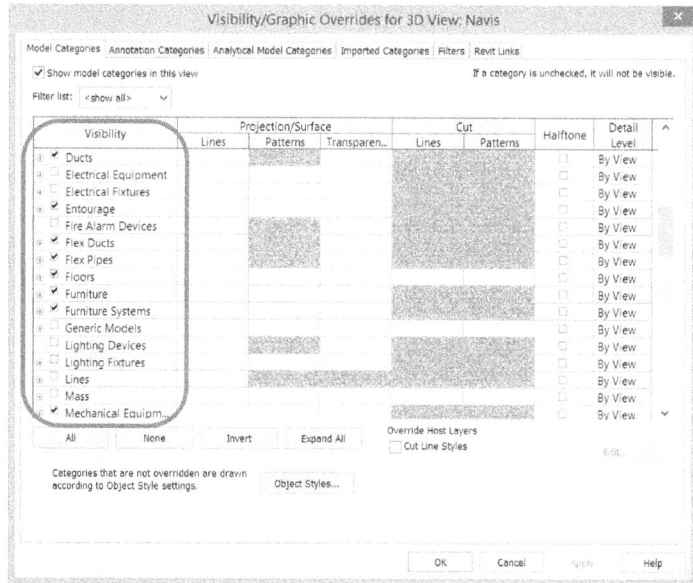

Figure A–4

7. Click **OK**.

8. Save the project and close the Autodesk Revit software.

9. In the Autodesk Navisworks software, ensure that you set the options as shown in Figure A–5 before appending the Autodesk Revit model to ensure that the view is recognized.

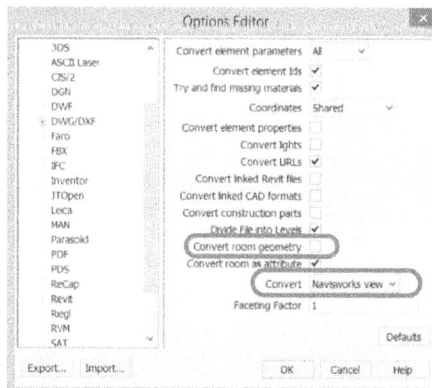

Figure A–5

A.2 Setting a Project Point in Autodesk Revit

Architectural models often have a base point of 0,0,0. However, when you import that model into the Autodesk Navisworks software and combine it with other files that use real world coordinates for their base point, the models do not line up. To fix this, you need to move and rotate the architectural model manually using the Units and Transformation dialog box in the Autodesk Navisworks software, as shown in Figure A–6.

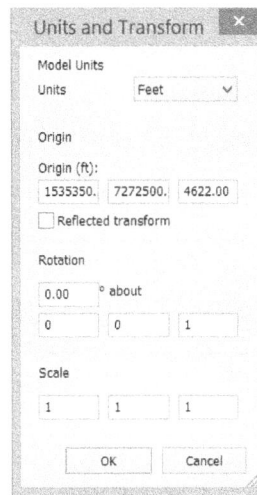

Figure A–6

The coordinates used for the transformation process is the centroid of the Autodesk Revit model. Because of this, figuring out the correct coordinates to enter can be challenging. Additionally, if there are multiple Autodesk Revit models, you will need to move and rotate each model individually.

In order to avoid this, Autodesk Revit users can include a project point in their model. The project point can be a point of their choosing. This makes it much easier to coordinate a building's location with other team members that are using different software.

Before you can set a project point, you must:

*   Communicate with the civil team members (engineers or surveyors) to know what coordinates to use.

*   Use a 3D view in the Autodesk Revit software to pick a point.

How To: Set a Revit Project Point

1. In the Autodesk Revit software, open the model that needs a project point.
2. Ensure that you are in a 3D view.
3. In the *Manage* tab>Project Location panel, expand the coordinates tool and click ⌞⁺¹'² (Specify Coordinates at Point).
4. In the Autodesk Revit model, click the point on the building where you want the reference point to sit. Ensure that you use the snap option appropriate for the selected point, as shown in Figure A–7.

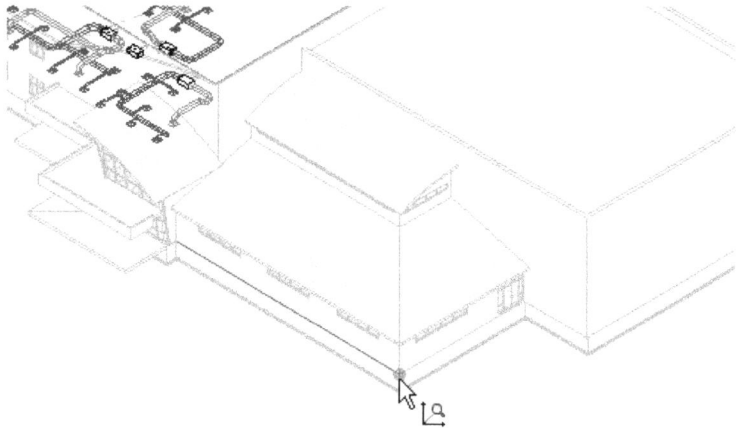

Figure A–7

5. In the Specify Shard Coordinates dialog box, type in the North/South, East/West, Elevation, and Rotation values, as shown in Figure A–8.

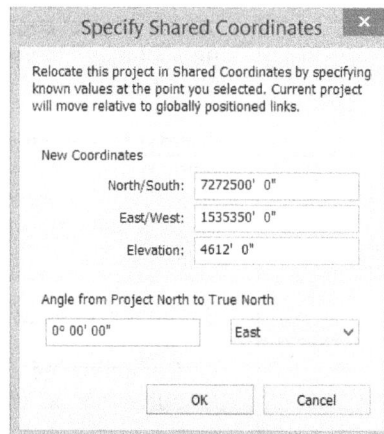

Figure A–8

A.3 AutoCAD Civil 3D Object Enabler

If you open or append an AutoCAD Civil 3D drawing in the Autodesk Navisworks software and boxes display where surfaces and roads should be (as shown in Figure A–9), then you need to install the AutoCAD Civil 3D Object Enabler. The Object Enabler ensures that objects that are created in the AutoCAD Civil 3D software can be used outside of the AutoCAD Civil 3D software.

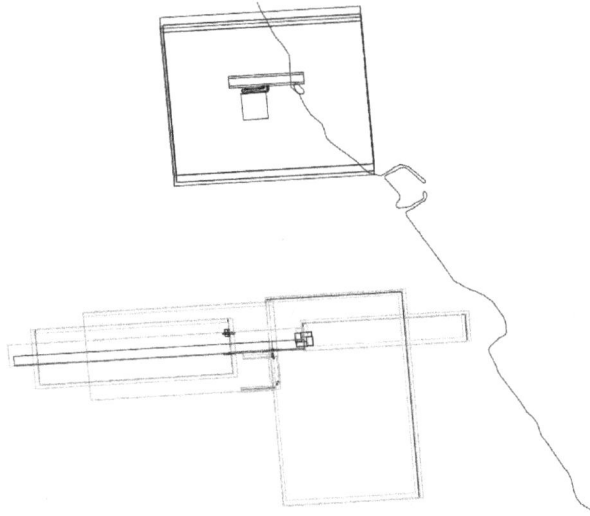

Figure A–9

An update for the object enabler is released with each new release of the AutoCAD Civil 3D software. The newest version is available for download from the Autodesk Knowledge Network (https://knowledge.autodesk.com) and can be easily found by searching for Civil Object Enabler each time you install new software.

There are usually two Object Enablers available: one for 32-bit operating systems, and one for 64-bit operating systems. Ensure that you download and install the correct .EVE file for your specific computer. For more information on the object enabler or how to install it, read the help document provided on the download page.

A.4 Creating an .FBX File in Autodesk InfraWorks 360

The best BIM workflows take full advantage of any software that adds value to the project. The photo realistic 3D models created in the Autodesk InfraWorks 360 software provide a way to display designs in context with their surrounding area. For infrastructure projects, the ideal workflow looks similar to the one outlined in Figure A–10. The software recommendations listed at the left of each phase provide the highest benefit to the project.

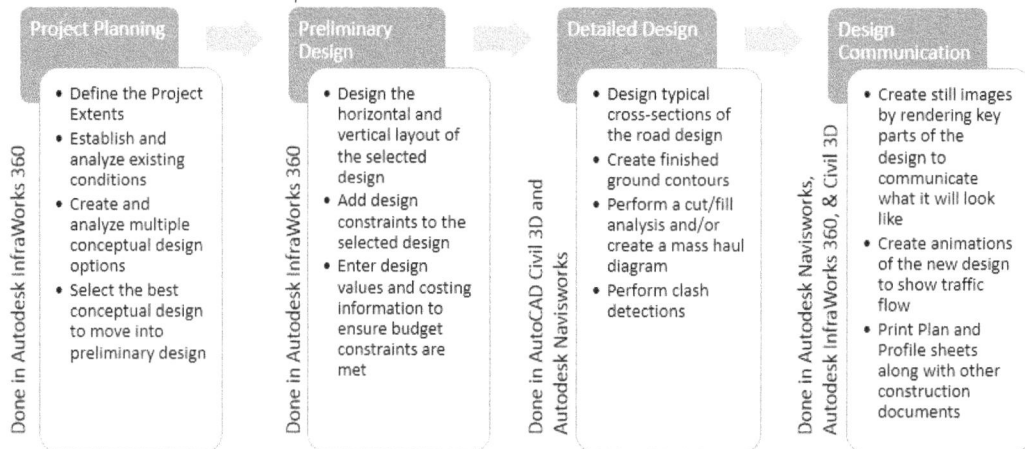

Project Planning

* Define the Project Extents
* Establish and analyze existing conditions
* Create and analyze multiple conceptual design options
* Select the best conceptual design to move into preliminary design

Done in Autodesk InfraWorks 360

Preliminary Design

* Design the horizontal and vertical layout of the selected design
* Add design constraints to the selected design
* Enter design values and costing information to ensure budget constraints are met

Done in Autodesk InfraWorks 360

Detailed Design

* Design typical cross-sections of the road design
* Create finished ground contours
* Perform a cut/fill analysis and/or create a mass haul diagram
* Perform clash detections

Done in AutoCAD Civil 3D and Autodesk Navisworks

Design Communication

* Create still images by rendering key parts of the design to communicate what it will look like
* Create animations of the new design to show traffic flow
* Print Plan and Profile sheets along with other construction documents

Done in Autodesk Navisworks, Autodesk InfraWorks 360, & Civil 3D

Figure A–10

If you follow this workflow, you can take advantage of using an early-stage Autodesk InfraWorks 360 model inside the Autodesk Navisworks software to uncover design problems and constructability issues more effectively. In the Autodesk InfraWorks 360 software, you can export the model as a single file or multiple files. By using multiple files, you can select specific features in the model to export.

How To: Export an Autodesk InfraWorks 360 Model to the Autodesk Navisworks Software

1. In the Autodesk InfraWorks 360 software, open the model you want to import into the Autodesk Navisworks software.

2. In the In Canvas Tools, click ![icon] (Settings and Utilities)> ![icon] (Export 3D Model).

3. In the Export to 3D Model File dialog box, do the following, as shown in Figure A–11:

- Define the area to export.
- Set the Target Coordinate System
- Determine if you want one file or several files.
- Click **Export**.

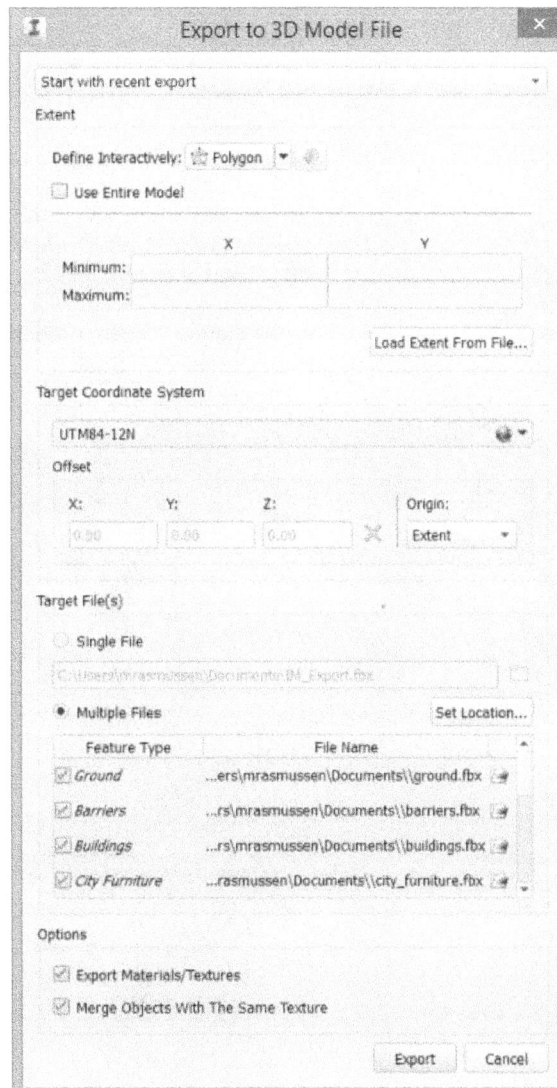

Figure A–11

4. In the Autodesk Navisworks software, you can open the .FBX file or append it to an existing Autodesk Navisworks model.

A.5 Preparing a Corridor Model for TimeLiner

In order to use the Autodesk Navisworks TimeLiner to display a simulation of a road being constructed, you must turn the corridor model into solid parts. This conversion is done in the AutoCAD Civil 3D software. By creating separate parts for each material (e.g, sub-base, base, sidewalk, etc.), you can animate the road being constructed one layer at a time, just like it would be during construction. It also enables you to break the road up into specific distances, since the contractor does not build the entire road at one time.

When converting a corridor to solids, it is important that the Layer Name Template match the item names in the Gantt chart, as shown in Figure A–12.

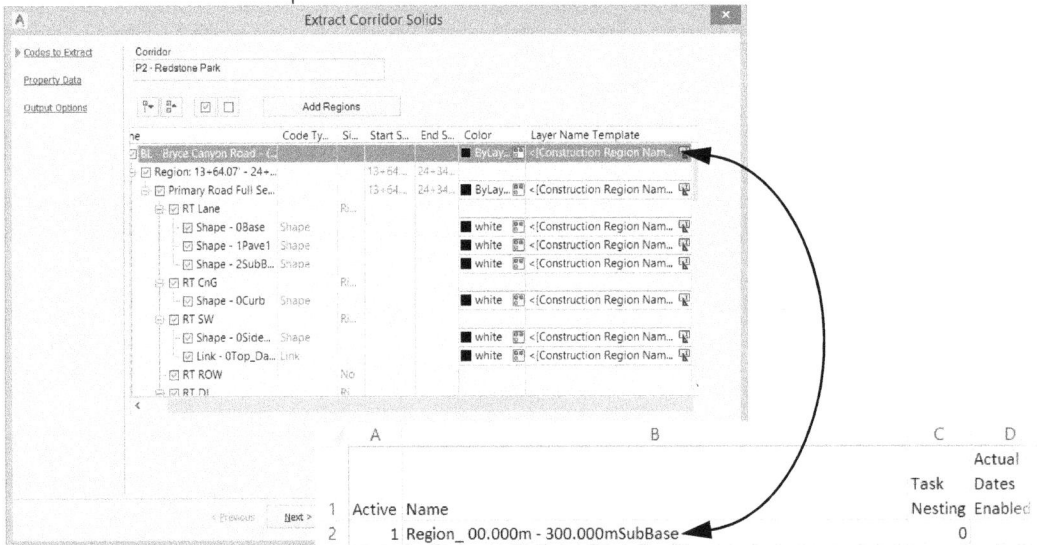

Figure A–12

How To: Extract Corridor Solids

1. In the AutoCAD Civil 3D software, select the corridor.
2. In the *Corridor* contextual tab>Corridor Tools panel, click

   (Extract Corridor Solids).
3. In the model, select only the regions for the area you want to extract. The options include:

   *Type **S**, **P**, or **A** in the command line to select the associated option.*

   - **Station Range (S):** Select a region first, and then you are prompted to specify the start station. You can use the cursor to select it, or you can type a start station in the command line. After setting the start station, you are prompted to set the end station.
   - **Within Polygon (P):** Enables you to select a previously-created polygon.
   - **All Regions (A):** Selects the entire corridor model.

4. In the Create Solids From Corridor dialog box, ensure that the Layer Name Template matches the item names in the Gantt chart. If you are using the Gantt chart (.CSV file) included in this learning guide, do the following to ensure the names match:

   - In the Name Template column, click (Modify Name Template) next to the Baseline, as shown in Figure A–13.

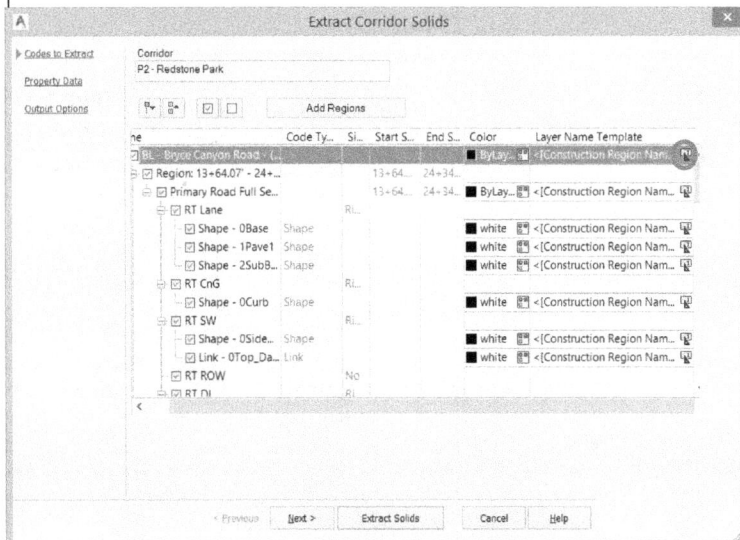

Figure A–13

Selecting the Name template for the Baseline ensures that all of the regions are updated to the new Name Template.

You must do this for each baseline listed in the Extract Corridor Solids dialog box.

- In the Name Template dialog box, do the following, as shown in Figure A–14:
  - Select **Construction Region Name** in the Property fields drop-down.
  - In the *Name* field, highlight everything and then click **Insert**.
  - In the Property fields drop-down list, select **Codes**.
  - In the *Name* field, place the cursor at the end, and click **Insert.**
- Click **OK**.

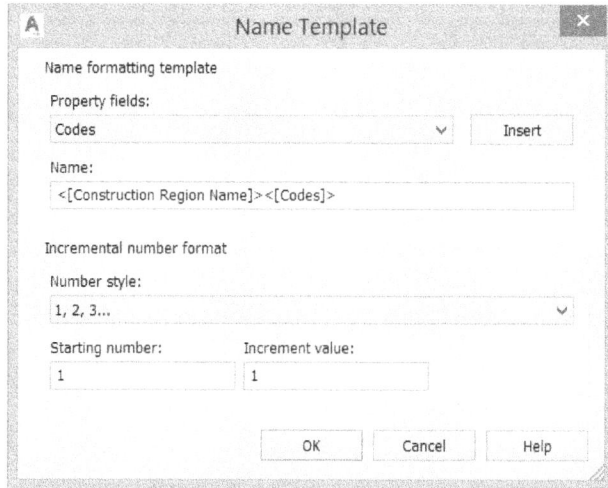

Figure A–14

5. In the Create Solids From Corridor dialog box, click **Next** twice.

6. In the Create Solids From Corridor dialog box>Output Options page (shown in Figure A–15), ensure that **AutoCAD 3D Solids (based on corridor sampling)** is selected. Then select where you would like the solids stored:

- Insert into current drawing
- Add to an existing drawing
- Add to a new drawing

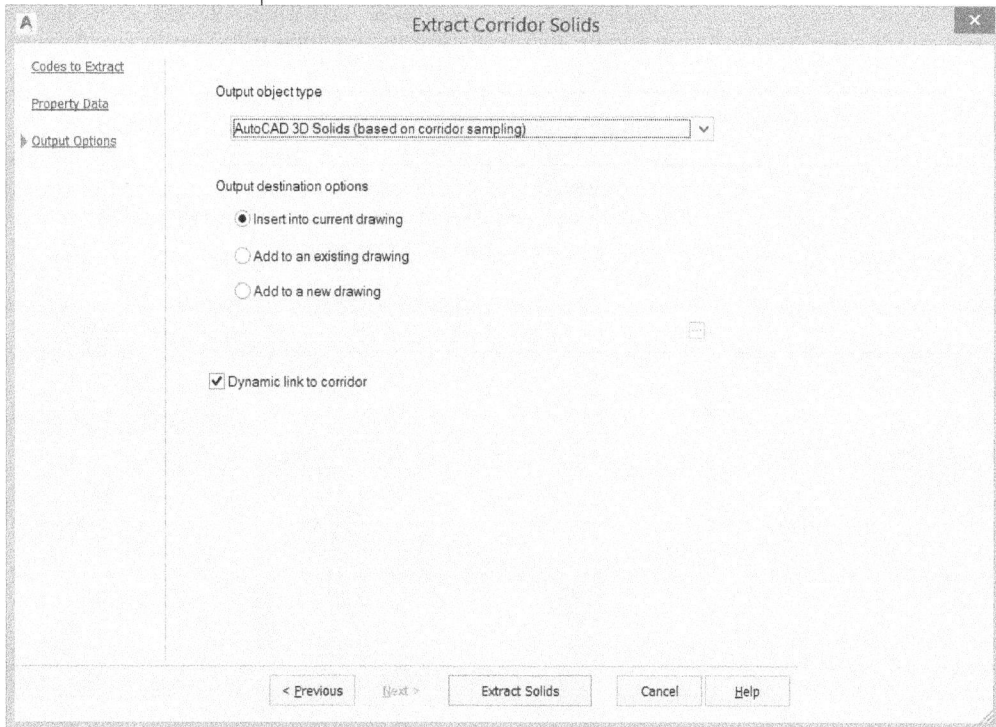

Figure A–15

7. Click **Extract Solids**.

A.6 Preparing an Autodesk Revit Model for TimeLiner

In the Autodesk Revit software, multiple parts form a single object. For example, Figure A–16 shows the parts that form a wall. However, during construction, a wall is built in parts, rather than as a single piece. Framing might be the first thing to go up, then plywood on the outside, insulation, drywall on the inside, windows, and finally the brick on the outer most part of the wall.

When creating a construction animation using TimeLiner, you want to simulate as closely as possible the construction schedule as laid out in the Gantt chart. In order to do this, you must separate all of the walls, ceilings, floors, etc. into parts in the Autodesk Revit software before importing the model into the Autodesk Navisworks software.

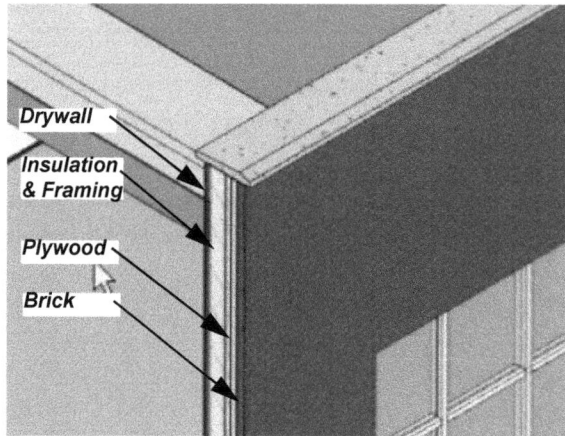

Figure A–16

How To: Separate Objects to Parts

Hint: It is helpful to use selection sets for this.

1. In the Autodesk Revit software, select the objects (all exterior walls, all interior walls, etc.) you want to separate to parts.
2. In the *Modify (Object)* contextual tab>Create panel, click ▢ (Create Parts).
3. Save the file.

Index

www.ingramcontent.com/pod-product-compliance
Lightning Source LLC
Chambersburg PA
CBHW080929220326
41598CB00034B/5731